SCOUSE POP

Popular Music History
Series Editor: Alyn Shipton, Royal Academy of Music, London, and City University, London.

This series publishes books that challenge established orthodoxies in popular music studies, examine the formation and dissolution of canons, interrogate histories of genres, focus on previously neglected forms, or engage in archaeologies of popular music.

Published

An Unholy Row: Jazz in Britain and its Audience, 1945–1960
Dave Gelly

Being Prez: The Life and Music of Lester Young
Dave Gelly

Bill Russell and the New Orleans Jazz Revival
Ray Smith and Mike Pointon

Chasin' the Bird: The Life and Legacy of Charlie Parker
Brian Priestley

Handful of Keys: Conversations with Thirty Jazz Pianists
Alyn Shipton

Jazz Me Blues: The Autobiography of Chris Barber
Chris Barber with Alyn Shipton

Jazz Visions: Lennie Tristano and His Legacy
Peter Ind

Lee Morgan: His Life, Music and Culture
Tom Perchard

Lionel Richie: Hello
Sharon Davis

Mosaics: The Life and Works of Graham Collier
Duncan Heining

Mr P.C.: The Life and Music of Paul Chambers
Rob Palmer

Out of the Long Dark: The Life of Ian Carr
Alyn Shipton

Rufus Wainwright
Katherine Williams

Soul Unsung: Reflections on the Band in Black Popular Music
Kevin Le Gendre

The Godfather of British Jazz: The Life and Music of Stan Tracey
Clark Tracey

The History of European Jazz: The Music, Musicians and Audience in Context
Edited by Francesco Martinelli

The Last Miles: The Music of Miles Davis, 1980–1991
George Cole

The Long Shadow of the Little Giant (second edition): The Life, Work and Legacy of Tubby Hayes
Simon Spillett

The Ultimate Guide to Great Reggae: The Complete Story of Reggae Told through its Greatest Songs, Famous and Forgotten
Michael Garnice

This is Hip: The Life of Mark Murphy
Peter Jones

Trad Dads, Dirty Boppers and Free Fusioneers: A History of British Jazz, 1960–1975
Duncan Heining

Scouse Pop

Paul Skillen

equinox

SHEFFIELD UK   BRISTOL CT

Published by Equinox Publishing Ltd.

UK: Office 415, The Workstation, 15 Paternoster Row, Sheffield, South Yorkshire S1 2BX
USA: ISD, 70 Enterprise Drive, Bristol, CT 06010

www.equinoxpub.com

First published 2018
First printing in paperback 2019

British Library Cataloguing-in-Publication Data
A catalogue record for this book is available from the British Library.
ISBN-13 978 1 78179 893 5 (paperback)
         978 1 78179 123 3 (hardback)
         978 1 78179 663 4 (e-PDF)

Library of Congress Cataloging-in-Publication Data
Names: Skillen, Paul, author.
Title: Scouse pop / Paul Skillen.
Description: Sheffield, UK ; Bristol, CT : Equinox Publishing, 2018. |
   Series: Popular music history | Includes bibliographical references and
   index.
Identifiers: LCCN 2018012275 (print) | LCCN 2018013065 (ebook) | ISBN
   9781781796634 (ePDF) | ISBN 9781781791233 (hb)
Subjects: LCSH: Popular music--England--Liverpool--1981-1990--History and
   criticism. | Popular music--England--Liverpool--1971-1980--History and
   criticism.
Classification: LCC ML3492.8.L58 (ebook) | LCC ML3492.8.L58 S55 2018 (print)
   | DDC 781.6409427/53--dc23
LC record available at https://lccn.loc.gov/2018012275

Typeset by Witchwood Production House Ltd

Contents

Foreword   vii

Preface   ix

Acknowledgements   xi

1   A Sense of Place   1

2   To Be Somebody: Ambition and the Desire to Be Different   29

3   Rainy-Day Music: Art Pop and the Scouse Romantic   95

4   Some Aspects of the Music Industry in Liverpool   111

5   The Audience Response   150

Appendix 1: List of interviews   170
Appendix 2: Scouse Pop *TV*   171
Notes   172
Bibliography   178
Index   182

Foreword

In the 1980s you could always rely on Liverpool for two things: bad news and good music.

These two commodities seemed to pour from the city with a mysterious and unstoppable force. The bad news was seldom of Liverpool's own making. Global economics were taking new and ominous turns: there was a vast experiment under way and the Mersey port was to play the part of an unwilling laboratory rat. But the good music was, somehow, quite essentially Scouse.

As a journalist I had the privilege of covering my home town's musical renaissance. This was a flowering of talent and success to match that Beatle-led frenzy of the early 1960s, when Merseybeat dominated pop charts everywhere. But now, in the age of Margaret Thatcher, my colleagues on the *NME* in London were perplexed. Where was the anger? Where was the rebellion? They asked me to explain why a city so hard pressed by youth unemployment, erupting in riots and seething with political turmoil, was so content with dream-like melodies and foppish bands with preposterously dippy names. Where were the anthems of protest, the thundering rhythms of rage?

These were valid questions for which I had no ready answer. A couple of years before, in 1976 and '77, punk rock had convulsed British music with records that voiced some unspoken sense that all the promise and optimism of the 1960s was illusory, and that bad times were just around the corner. Liverpool took note: when the Clash played at Eric's club it was for many a watershed moment.

But Liverpool goes its own way. It did not respond to punk with copycat Scouse Pistols or anything else. Instead, absorbing the punk principle that you can only be yourself, it embraced the new possibilities of independent music. From Echo and the Bunnymen to the Wild Swans, there arose records of stirring, high-flown romanticism, as yet too strange for major labels to process. If this generation's inspirations came from anywhere, it could have been from aromatic nights gazing out to sea. Liverpool tilts to the west, from a high sandstone ridge that completes its physical isolation from mainland England. On such nights you can lose yourself in a psychedelic Celtic sunset.

Historically, the city's musicians have not been especially interested in the latest craze. They are simultaneously rooted in the past and eager for new fusions. In the 1980s, while Duran Duran preened on MTV, Liverpool imaginations were fired by vintage Captain Beefheart LPs, or Arthur Lee's Love. Another London colleague came to visit and decided he was on some offshore colony, a musical Galápagos Island, where evolution had not stopped but simply headed in another direction. This was the local sensibility which had shaped my tastes, too. And in the next decade, when I had left the *NME* and could invent my own magazine, it led me to the concept of *MOJO*.

Now, thanks to Paul Skillen's assiduous research, we have the detailed portrait that this beguiling period of pop history deserves. In Liverpool there were those who became suddenly famous and those who remained steadily obscure. But all were all important to the story – stars were not the defining lights of this particular cosmos – and they are all represented here. Like any river, the Mersey has two banks, and its Wirral side repeatedly enriched the local music scene. Then there were the nominal outsiders, like Roger Eagle, Bill Drummond and Roger Hill, who arrived to find the Scouse outlook so congenial to their own. These too are not overlooked.

The more that Liverpool was written off, whether for being too stuck in Fab Four nostalgia or too bolshie to accommodate the new economic order, the more its young musicians responded with songs of emotional generosity and visionary breadth. I merely wrote about them, but they made the music, and I am proud that I knew them. And I am pleased that Skillen has documented what they did, in such eloquent detail.

Paul Du Noyer

Preface

Scouse Pop is a journey into the personalities and music of the successful pioneering Liverpool bands of the late 1970s and 1980s. It examines their motivations, their uniqueness and the routes to success that made them enduring musical innovators. The development of these suburban romantics from Liverpool represents a period of intense creativity which still resonates today. What made Liverpool unique was that its bands were all quite different from one another. Other cities around the world have risen to musical prominence at various points in their histories, but often with reference to a particular style. This was not the case in Liverpool. These bands regarded the idea of sounding like any of the city's other bands pointless. Their approach was one of avoiding replication but instead creating something credible and unique within the genre of high-quality pop music. The spirit of internal revolution at the heart of these bands retains a strong fascination for those interested in artistic creation and popular culture. Given the bleak and uninspiring context of unemployment, political turmoil and economic decline within which these bands emerged, one might reasonably wonder how it was that these young Scouse romantics achieved such worldwide success.

Scouse Pop explores this question in detail and examines the factors that facilitated the transformation of Liverpool teenage dreams into commercial and cultural impact.

During the late 1970s and early 1980s I regularly attended gigs around Merseyside as a contributor to the Liverpool fanzine *Merseysound*, edited by BBC Radio Merseyside's Roger Hill. I was able to witness many of the local bands rise from playing in small Liverpool venues to national and international success within a short space of time. Fascinated by the diversity and quality of the new generation of Liverpool bands, I offered my help to Dr Klaus Schwartze in reading over his comprehensive two-volume *The Scouse Phenomenon* – scrapbook-style publications featuring band "family trees", press cuttings and reviews. I was also involved in writing, performing and recording with Liverpool band This Final Frame, which released records in the UK, Europe and the Philippines.

Having developed many contacts since the late 1970s through my reporting, performing and recording, I find myself in a privileged position as regards access to primary sources, which reveal themselves in the many first-hand accounts you will encounter in this book. In fact, the responses I received and the eagerness to assist me in compiling the book – from bands, DJs, promoters, studio owners, labels and fans – have been overwhelming. Their contributions have provided material not just for this book but also for two television series – also called *Scouse Pop* – for the local Merseyside TV station Bay TV, in which my interviews with prominent figures of the 1980s scene were interspersed with live performances. Much of the latter is accessible via YouTube at the time of writing, and some of those interviews are quoted in the book.

Liverpool is full of characters, but this generation, which emerged at a such challenging time for the city, was in many ways a golden one, and this era a very special one in Liverpool's musical history.

Paul Skillen, July 2018

Acknowledgements

Scouse Pop as a concept was the idea of Mark Murphy who often has his best ideas over a pint of Peroni. Initially, Mark considered the book to be about "Those bands in Liverpool who are a little bit weird". As I began the research for the book, it became apparent that there was a reason for the weirdness, and *Scouse Pop* is about triumph over adversity, about character, spirit, creativity, resilience, collectivism and determination. The Scouse Pop generation that emerged out of 1980s Liverpool are unique. Liverpool is the only place in the world to have produced such a plethora of brilliant bands which have all been different from one another. The book has taken four years to write and without the unconditional support of the names listed below it could not have been written. I would like to give my sincere thanks to all those who have contributed, encouraged and supported my writing. It is your book as much as it is mine. I have merely captured your words and thoughts and tried to make some sense of it all.

Special thanks to: Karen Skillen, Hannah Skillen, Rachel Skillen, Mark Murphy, Alyn Shipton, Denise Hodgkinson, Neil Duffin, Chris Currie, Eddie Lundon, Gary Daly, Henry Priestman, Colin Vearncombe, Kerry Harvey-Piper, Andy McCluskey, John Gorman, Vintage Radio, Brian Nash, Ali Score, Frank Maudsley, Tommy Scott, Paul Hemmings, Mark Cowley, Mike Badger, Les Glover, Gary Lornie, Francesco Mellina, Dave Palmer, Jeremy Lewis, Geoff Davies, Paul Simpson, Hambi Haralambous, Noel Burke, Carl Henry, Colin Howe, Dave Balfe, Ian McNabb, John Weaver, Billy Butler, Roger Hill, Tony Snell, Spencer Leigh, Ken Testi, Garry Christian, Norman Jackson, Jayne Dodgson, Joe Musker, Rob Jones, Sam Jones, Terry Lennaine, Jerry Kelly, Mike Sutton, aLfie vera mella, Ana Nazario, Eugene Lino Tecson, Tim Peacock, John D. Hodgkinson, Mark Campbell, Andrea Bertolio, Lottie Holmes, Lindsay Barnes, Steve Meadows, Ian Banks, Paul Den Heyer, Dave Wood, Ged Ryan, Andy Jones, Pete Riley, Dave Jackson, James Lee, Sara Cohen, Mike Jones, Aine Mangalong, Sean Pugh, Simon Poole, Dave Williams, Gareth Noon,

David Elms, Gary Lornie, Tom Dootson, Kayleigh Heaps, Clare Chabeaux Tom Cox, Beth Falkingham, Lisa Simmons, Dean Bargh, Janet Joyce and all the staff at Equinox Publishing.

1 A Sense of Place

To offer a complete description of Liverpool as a place would be an onerous task, and there are many seminal works that already have attempted to define the city. Instead, this chapter describes a relatively short period in Liverpool's history. It is a snapshot focusing on certain aspects of Liverpool in the late 1970s and through the 1980s which aims to create a sense of place and provide some perspective for the emergence of a creative music scene.

It includes a personal anecdotal recollection of the changing economic landscape of 1970s Merseyside and how music connected with people's everyday lives. It also examines the attitude of certain key individuals in central and local government at the time. The reason for this political context is that Liverpool's treatment by central government played a large part in creating a perception of marginalization in the minds of young people. Some of these perceptions permeated the music produced by local bands. During the 1980s, Margaret Thatcher's Conservative government were careful to keep their negative opinions about the city private; however, following the 2011 release of documentation under the parliamentary thirty-year rule, it appears that the conspiracy theorists of the day were not entirely unjustified in their cynicism about a number of Thatcher's key ministers and their attitudes towards Merseyside.

This chapter also contains a brief overview of caricatures presented in popular television culture which fuelled common stereotypes and misunderstandings about the character of Liverpudlians. It presents a small selection of popular 1980s television programmes that portrayed Liverpool, but only in brief for illustrative purposes. The backdrop of the physical geography is also included and offered as a metaphor for the isolation sensed by those in Liverpool. The resurgence of the music scene serves as a testimony to the culture, belief and creativity which was evident in abundance among young musicians in Liverpool. The chapter finishes with the notion of a "sense of place" in terms of the mind-set of where Merseysiders saw themselves at the time. Individuals emerging from Liverpool were the embodiment of a place, an attitude, and a generally negative view from certain outsiders about the city's character and its worth.

A sense of place

Consumer goods, noxious gas clouds, smelly school blazers
and a rendition of 'Chirpy Chirpy Cheep Cheep'.

As a schoolboy in the early 1970s I would travel by bus from Woodchurch council estate outside Birkenhead to my secondary school in Rock Ferry. In retrospect, a journey on the 70A bus to Birkenhead central station was a lesson in social history. Relatively few residents on the estate had cars at that time; consequently the 8 am bus was always replete with workers who supplied the labour for Merseyside's many factories and industries – among them Kelvinator, Lever Brothers, Vauxhall, Cadbury, Squibbs and Birkenhead's big employer Cammell Laird.

If you were unfortunate enough to miss out on a downstairs seat, you would suffer the evil nicotine cloud on the top deck which meant that your school uniform stank for the rest of the day. When it rained, the mixture of damp air and tobacco fumes would test the survival of the finest pairs of lungs. A pit canary would have died within a few seconds of exposure to the top deck of the 70A bus. Despite the uncomfortable leatherette seats, steamed-up windows and overcrowding, the passengers remained cheerful and upbeat. Many were embarking on another day of difficult and repetitive tasks. An unusual feature of the journey was that, quite spontaneously, different sections of the bus would break into song. The impromptu set list depended on who had decided to start the singing and what was the latest song to dominate the charts. One morning a more confident member of the "factory girls' choir" had smiled at me and encouraged me to join in with a performance of 1970s band Middle of the Road's 'Chirpy Chirpy Cheep Cheep'.

Red-faced, I obliged.

Occasionally a selection of Beatles classics was rendered by would-be Lennons and McCartneys attempting to harmonize to 'Hey Jude' and 'All You Need Is Love'. People appeared to be happier in those days and the singing was a manifestation of their cheerful spirit. Paul Du Noyer acknowledges the peculiar British propensity to sing, citing a variety of settings, including charabancs to Blackpool. He qualifies this notion further by claiming that Scousers carried on singing long after the rest of the country had lost the habit (Du Noyer 2002: 3).

The post-war slum clearance in Birkenhead had taken some of the population from the terraced houses built for the shipyard workers into new houses with bathrooms and gardens. The 1960s had brought with it a consumer boom and now working-class people aspired to own some of the items being produced in the very factories where they worked. The consumer boom had resulted in the relative security of almost full employment. People on the estate were not rich; they were just less poor than they used to be.

The unlikely choral arrangement provided by the factory workers went on for a few years in the early 1970s until the number of workers travelling to work each morning began to dwindle. The days of factory workers singing on the bus were coming to an end as the industries that employed them started to close down. Some of the closures were the combined result of outsourcing to cheaper overseas factories and a downturn in consumer demand. By the time I had finished high school in 1978, the workers were no longer singing on the bus. In fact, there were very few workers on the bus at all. Boland (2008: 357) comments: "The global economic restructuring of the 1970s and 1980s dealt a huge blow to the Merseyside economy and Liverpool's in particular. Many firms either closed down or relocated." Murden summarizes the scale of the economic decline in the city from the late 1960s to the early 1980s:

> Between 1966 and 1977 no less than 350 factories in Liverpool closed or moved elsewhere, 40,000 jobs were lost and between 1971 and 1985 employment in the city fell by 33 per cent. Between 1979 and 1981 the rate of job losses accelerated to a frightening level, employment in the city falling by a further 18 per cent. By early 1981, 20 per cent of the city's labour force were unemployed and it was reported that there were just 49 jobs on offer for the 13,505 youngsters registered unemployed (Murden 2006: 428).

The bus journey was symptomatic of a period of severe economic decline. Parkinson (1985) describes how Liverpool became a de-industrialized city and was left to cope with mass unemployment and the consequent social problems. The relocation of trade to southern ports with closer links to Europe also hastened the decline. Boland (2008: 357) argues that "Over time, Liverpool represented a microcosm of Britain's problems: economic decline, urban decay, mass unemployment, political militancy, social unrest and crime."

Government, media and television culture: misconceptions about Liverpool

Hard nuts to crack! Trying to make water flow uphill. Tarzan comes to Liverpool.

In the early 1980s the image of Liverpool and its inhabitants had deteriorated in the eyes of the national press. Scraton describes how representations in the press became increasingly more pejorative, damaging the perception of Liverpudlians nationally: "Liverpool people had a negative reputation, their natural and cultural inheritance being aggression and belligerence, but within the broad categorisation lay subcategories of greater lawlessness and violence" (Scraton 2007: 28). For some residents of Liverpool, these aspersions were accompanied by a sense of being marginalized by central government. Liverpool's reputation for political and industrial militancy was picked up on by certain sections of the press who were unsympathetic to the plight of the city. Liverpool was largely represented as a desperate place with high unemployment, high rates of crime, poor housing and few prospects.

The people of Liverpool became caricatured as individuals living on the edges of society trying to survive in the bleakest of economic climates. This popular myth seeped into the psyche of the British public and became entrenched. According to Avraham (2000), newspapers routinely ran sensationalist crime stories and, as a result, over time certain cities become tarnished with an image of lawlessness. Having analysed press articles about Liverpool since the 1980s, Garcia (2006) claims that such a fate befell Liverpool. The most common topic Garcia found in the articles was football, owing to the dominance of both Liverpool and Everton football clubs during the 1980s. Football aside, the most frequently recurring themes associated with Liverpool in the national press were crime, violence and drugs. Garcia is also inclined to believe that such articles contributed to negative perceptions of Liverpudlians. Olivier Sykes (2004) agrees with Garcia's assumption and labels these perceptions "word of mouth clichés" and "macro myths". Boland suggests that the national press portrayed Liverpudlians as "Humorous, argumentative, thieving, violent, lazy scroungers" (Boland 2008: 364). Finlo Roher, reporting for the BBC in 2002, claimed that the negative stereotypes of Liverpudlians were the creation of a London-centric media: "When newspapers need a feature on juvenile crime, poverty, drugs or the inefficient workings of the criminal justice system, the lazy journalist looks no further than Liverpool" (Roher 2002).

There was little in the way of resources, jobs, prospects or even hope in Liverpool at that time. When the population of a city is subjected to extreme economic pressure, it should come as no surprise if the pressure is released in an incendiary manner, and Liverpudlian frustration exploded on the streets of Toxteth in July 1981 (Sinclair 2014). The reaction of the local press to the Toxteth riots is exemplified in a one-word front-page headline in the *Liverpool Echo* which read simply "Devastated". The newspaper's 6 July 1981 edition was dominated by reports of the city's turmoil with accompanying commentaries entitled "Night of a city's heart attack" and "Why did this ever happen?"

Disturbing scenes of violence enacted by both black and white youths against the police, with CS gas being used against the rioters, projected the city into the national and international news spotlight (Boland 2008: 359). In the aftermath of the riots, the city was in both a reflective and desperate mood and there was a feeling of abject ruin, both physical and emotional (Scraton 2007: 25–30).

That the youth of the city found their situation difficult and their future uncertain is a consequence of both the national and local political situation in the 1980s. This chapter includes a brief examination of the forces at work in the city at that time, of how young people in the city were treated, and how this context fomented certain attitudes in local youth culture.

Between 1979 and 1983 Liverpool's council consisted of a ruling Liberal and Conservative coalition led by Trevor Jones. This was balanced by a Labour opposition. Following the riots in 1981, however, the Trotskyist Militant faction started to gain greater support in the District Labour Party (Frost and North 2013). Militant's influence here grew as a direct result of the general perception that Thatcher's Conservative government was indifferent to the plight of the city. Frost and North describe Militant as Marxist-inspired socialists within the Labour Party and suggest that Liverpool was particularly receptive to Militant's ideas because it had found itself "on the wrong side of all the changes in global trade" (Frost and North 2013: 57).

Thatcher's response to the Toxteth riots was to dispatch her Environment Secretary Michael Heseltine to Liverpool as "Minister for Merseyside" to lead a programme of urban regeneration. Heseltine stayed in Liverpool for two-and-a-half weeks on a fact-finding mission, and then challenged his prime minister by insisting on real powers and a £100 million budget to attempt to improve the city (Wainwright 2012). Wainwright quotes from Heseltine's autobiography, *Life in the Jungle*, in which the politician recalls his impressions on visiting Liverpool:

> Day after day we walked the streets of Liverpool in a hectic series of visits here and consultations there, we travelled hither and thither in a blaze of publicity. "Why do you waste your time there – with them?" I was asked again and again by Conservative sympathizers in the prosperous suburbs. "There are no votes for us." But within days a pattern clearly emerged. Put simply, this was a city without leadership. It was that void I hoped that I could fill. It was almost as though, subconsciously, people were waiting for it to happen. The apparent goodwill for a new direction was expressed on all sides (quoted in Wainwright 2012).

Heseltine formulated plans to improve Liverpool's prospects, despite the lack of enthusiasm from the Conservative supporters to whom he refers in the above extract. In retrospect, the more cynical voices in the city who opposed Thatcher's government have been proved correct in their assumption that there was little appetite from some key cabinet members to help Liverpool. In a BBC news article about the release of government files in 2011 under the thirty-year rule, Chancellor Sir Geoffrey Howe urged Thatcher not to spend public money on Merseyside, cautioning his prime minister:

We do not want to find ourselves concentrating all the limited cash that may have to be made available into Liverpool and having nothing left for possibly more promising areas such as the West Midlands or, even, the North East. It would be even more regrettable if some of the brighter ideas for renewing economic activity were to be sown only on relatively stony ground on the banks of the Mersey. I cannot help feeling that the option of managed decline is one which we should not forget altogether. We must not expend all our limited resources in trying to make water flow uphill.

Thatcher rebuked Howe and warned him that "This is not a term for use, even privately, It is much too negative." John Hoskyns, head of Thatcher's No. 10 policy unit, agreed with Howe and wrote:

The automatic assumption within Whitehall and in the country will be that such a minister, if he is to be seen taking action, which is, after all, his political raison d'être, must be seen to spend money. This money is likely to be money wasted. Neither the chosen minister nor Whitehall as a whole will have much idea of how to tackle the real problem-solving task, as distinct from the (important) political gesture (BBC 2011).

Notwithstanding these declarations of opposition to greater funding for Liverpool from within the Conservative ranks, Heseltine went ahead with his rejuvenation plans for Liverpool, starting with the regeneration of the Albert Dock and the redevelopment of the International Garden Festival site. Projects initiated by Heseltine met with mixed success, although the publicity he generated put Liverpool in the national spotlight in the early 1980s (Frost and North 2013).

However, after the Toxteth riots, the city was in a desperate financial situation for the following two years. Liberal MP for Mossley Hill David Alton outlined the lack of opportunity for Liverpool youth in his motion in the House of Commons on 4 July 1983:

Imagine life in a city where one in five people are on the dole, where half the people in some districts are without a job and where young people face a lifetime without employment. Imagine life in an area where the major employer – such as United Biscuits – suddenly decides to pull the rug from under the feet of its 2,000 employees. What prospects do those people have of finding another job? At their local Old Swan employment office 15,610 people are shown to be without work and a miserable 130 jobs available. At the Toxteth office 9,405 people are jobless with only 110 vacancies. At Garston 9,148 people are without work with only 103 vacancies. At Everton

3,795 people are unemployed and only 32 jobs are available (Alton 1983).

Although free at the time, higher education accounted for less than 10% of the 18-to-24-year-old population in England in 1981 (Bolton 2012). For comparison, 48% of the same age group applied for higher education in England in 2016 (Universities UK 2016). As mentioned, high numbers of young people were trying to find training or employment. Apprenticeships were scarcer owing to the closure of many local firms. David Alton also covered this in his House of Commons motion:

> Liverpool has been losing jobs hand over fist, at the rate of as many as 10,000 a year recently. A host of firms have shed jobs or left Liverpool and its hinterland. The litany of names includes Kraft, Bowyers, Lyon's Maid, Plessey, the Harrison Line, Barker and Dobson, Tate and Lyle, Courtaulds, Kellogg's, Peyton Calvert and, more recently, Binns, United Biscuits, Schweppes and the Liverpool Central Oil Company (Alton 1983).

The Youth Training Scheme (YTS) conceived in 1981 by the Conservative government was intended to provide young people with opportunities to gain training in a variety of jobs. The training place was guaranteed and paid slightly more than unemployment benefit, with YTS rates being between £23.50 and £27.50 a week. Organizations accredited to accept YTS recruits benefited from low-cost youth labour but were required to provide 13 weeks of training. At the end of the training, participants were awarded a certificate. However, Main and Shelley (1990) report that around 58% of employers were unable to offer YTS recruits a job at the end of their training. Although YTS provided work experience, in Liverpool there were relatively few real job prospects, as made clear in David Alton's statistics quoted above, and a high proportion of young people were engaged in neither education, training nor employment.

Liverpool was not unique in experiencing hard times: Tyneside, South Wales and Northern Ireland, for example, also had high unemployment levels. However, as adult unemployment in Liverpool rose to over 20% there was a feeling that the city was experiencing a decline on an alarming scale. This was summed up by David Alton:

> Liverpool has a deepening sense of dismay and unparalleled despondency. For generations now, there has been a feeling of insecurity in the city. All live with a question mark over their head. Will they be next? Since 1971 unemployment has risen by a staggering 200 per cent and the lives of citizens have been destroyed and their family lives decimated. One by one whole

families succumb to the creeping plague of unemployment. Abraham Lincoln said that a nation cannot survive half slave and half free. In the north of England, in Liverpool, life is different from parts of the leafy suburbs of the southeast where unemployment is only 4 per cent or 5 per cent. Liverpool people are becoming the slaves of the employment exchange. This is a different world – another nation – and its case is rarely listened to in the House. If it goes on much longer, the area will become the Siberia of Western Europe (Alton 1983).

This sense of marginalization and being disenfranchised by central government left the youth of the city feeling disregarded. It was as though they were not part of their own country. Peter Hooton, former youth worker and singer in Liverpool pop group the Farm, summed up the feelings of many young people at the time:

When Thatcher was in power, we felt that she looked at Liverpool and thought: "Well, they're not really English, are they?" Liverpool has always seen itself as separate from the rest of the country. As a city, it has more in common with Belfast and Glasgow than it does with London. There was the big influx of Irish and, because it's a port, it's always been international. We look to America and Ireland – to New York and Dublin – more than we look to London (Peter Hooton, quoted in Grady 2014).

Whilst "Minister for Merseyside" Michael Heseltine was busy with the early regeneration projects, the local Labour Party was creating its own agenda by gradually adopting the policies of the socialist Militant Tendency group. By the time of the 1983 council elections, the District Labour Party had assembled a raft of Militant-style policies set out its local manifesto. It was socialist by design and proved popular across the city, resulting in a Labour victory in the local elections and a Labour council being formed (Frost and North 2013). Prominent Militant protagonists Derek Hatton and Tony Mulhearn began to exert pressure on the local party in order to see their agenda come to fruition. However, as Crick (1986) observes, only sixteen of the elected local councillors were actually supporters of Militant. Although the local Labour Party had disparate views among its members, the Militant supporters, such as Hatton, Byrne and Mulhearn, seemed to have the loudest voices. Despite internal disagreements, Labour took control of the city council and elected non-Militant John Hamilton as leader. Owing to the strong Militant presence on the council, Derek Hatton was elected as his deputy (Crick 1986).

The new council immediately cancelled the 1,200 redundancies planned by the previous administration, council rents were frozen, and an ambitious house-building programme was initiated. Regrettably, the council did not have adequate funds to complete its projects. The council protested that one of Labour's election pledges had been to campaign for more money from central government, so Hatton approached the government for additional funds (Sinclair 2014).

There was some support for Liverpool in certain sections of the press. The *Liverpool Echo*'s "Save our City" campaign of 1984 claimed that the level of deprivation in Liverpool was due to the failure of national government to invest in houses, jobs and infrastructure. National opinion polls in May 1984 revealed that 70% of Liverpool voters questioned thought that Liverpool was not getting a fair deal from the government.

Parkinson (1985) suggests that Liverpool's problems were not all a result of the council's political stance and that central government should shoulder some of the responsibility to help the city despite the Conservative government's programme of cuts. Prime Minister Margaret Thatcher was so concerned that Liverpool was about to go bankrupt that at a meeting of the cabinet in 1983 she considered appointing commissioners to run the city. Optimism was a difficult concept to promote at a time when investment was so scarce, but Thatcher was never going to communicate a message of despair about Liverpool because her neoliberal agenda ran on a positive doctrine of enterprise, business and an entrepreneurial attitude (Sinclair 2014).

With an improved Labour vote in the May 1984 council elections, Minister for the Environment Patrick Jenkin came under increased pressure to address Liverpool's issues as the city's financial crisis deepened. During May and June 1984 Jenkin assembled a "Task Force" of local officials and civil servants to examine the city's finances (Frost and North 2013). Having examined the books, the Task Force concluded that the budget could not be balanced without greater funding. This prompted the *Liverpool Echo* headline of 11 June 1984, "Whitehall whizz kids stumped".

Following the examination of the council's finances, Labour councillors Hamilton, Hatton, Byrne and Mulhearn were called to a meeting in London in June 1984. The meeting was to hear whether additional funds were to be made available to the city in order to finance their housing projects and protect local council jobs. With the city on the brink of financial collapse, Jenkin awarded the city an extra £20m (Frost and North 2013). The Labour council celebrated this increased funding in a manner that implied they had gained a political victory over the Conservative government. Some councillors and their supporters were heard singing "Here we go, Here we go, Here we go" in a triumphant manner copied from a chant sung at Hatton's beloved Everton football club (Frost and North 2013).

The national press were not impressed by the actions of the council and claimed that the government had been held to ransom. *The Times* (11 July 1984) ran the headline "Danegeld in Liverpool to buy off Militant" and the *Daily Express* (10 July 1984) opined that the increased funding for Liverpool was "A shoddy and cowardly deal". Neither did the national press reports enhance Patrick Jenkin's standing in the Conservative Party. But Liverpool's finances had been given a stay of execution until the next round of government spending the following year.

The next major development in the political struggle surrounding Liverpool's finances happened on 7 June 1985 when Patrick Jenkin visited the city to see for himself the state of some of the poor housing stock. As reported in the *Daily Post* (8 June 1985), under the heading "Jenkins [*sic*] visits Liverpool slums", the minister was reported to remark that these dwellings were "very grim indeed", adding "I have seen families living in conditions the like I have never seen before. They are grim indeed and beggar description." Jenkin even intimated the possibility of more sustained funding for Liverpool in the future. Parkinson (1985: 121) quotes Jenkin as saying " I will do my very best to ensure that allocation to Liverpool under the Housing Improvement Programme and the Urban Improvement Programme, taken together, will enable the council to make positive progress in dealing with the city's severe needs."

Local councillor in charge of housing Tony Byrne took the comments by Jenkin as an indication of continued support. However, Byrne later accused the government of reneging on Jenkin's promise when the Merseyside Task Force contested the idea that any promise had been made in terms of further funding for housing in Liverpool (Frost and North 2013). The council ploy to defy government financial restraints for a second year running had backfired, and action by the district auditor was narrowly averted when the council took out loans to cover their over-budget spending. The council then chose what can be assumed to be a negotiating tactic of issuing redundancy notices to every single council employee (Crick 1986). This became the pivotal point at which the Labour council's attempt to defy government policy began to unravel.

In the Labour Party nationally, leader Michael Foot had presided over a crushing defeat in 1983, with Neil Kinnock subsequently elected to take his place. Labour had a diminished presence in the House of Commons with Kinnock wielding less influence over the government than his predecessor. Kinnock was also implacably opposed to the Militant movement and its actions in Liverpool. He saw Militant as a key factor in making Labour unelectable and refused to support the council in their dispute with the government (Sinclair 2014). In 1985, at the Labour Party conference in Bournemouth, Kinnock used his party leader's speech to criticize Militant for "The grotesque chaos of a Labour council hiring taxis to scuttle round a city handing out notices to its own workers".

The brief and turbulent reign of the Militant-influenced Labour council was not universally supported in Liverpool. Some residents objected to the council's confrontational approach to central government. In October 1985 thousands of Liverpudlians attended a "Liverpool against Militant" demonstration at the Pier Head (Frost and North 2013), an event that even spawned a single entitled 'Liverpool against Militant.'[1]

Stephen Fay in *The Spectator* (13 July 1985), in an article entitled "Militant versus the people", claimed that there was widespread opposition in Liverpool to some of the council's tactics and opposition too to some of its cooperative housing policies. Fay cites Militant's treatment of the Eldonian Community Association. The Eldonians, led by Tony McGann, were involved in a cooperative housing scheme to rehouse 145 families in Liverpool, a scheme that was to be controlled by the tenants with the support of the government-funded English Industrial Estates. Following Labour's victory in the 1983 council elections, Militant declared that they would keep the Eldonian plans but that the development would be council housing and not cooperative housing and therefore out of tenants' control. Tony McGann described the decision as devastating. According to Fay, this led to a political battle between Liverpool council and local residents, exposing Militant's uncompromising and ideological stance ruling out a pragmatic and organic approach to Liverpool's housing problem (Fay 1985).

In June 1986, deputy leader of Liverpool council Derek Hatton was expelled from the Labour Party following a disciplinary hearing. The remaining 47 Labour councillors were charged £106,000 by the district auditor which, despite an appeal, led to the demise of the Labour council; it lost overall control of the city in the 1987 election (Sinclair 2014).

The 1980s were a difficult time for Liverpudlians. The city had endured high unemployment, lack of investment, poor housing and civil unrest. It was also a political battleground (Sinclair 2014). Within this troubled environment, young people in the city got on with their lives as best they could, and many turned to music as an outlet for their frustration and disillusion. Regardless of the negativity surrounding the city, the music scene remained vibrant. It was one way in which young people could express their talent. Hardship had bred creativity, determination and difference and it this became most apparent in the city's pop music. As Du Noyer pointed out: "Yet amid the fragmentation, the 1980s would still be an heroic decade for Liverpool music, whatever the city's fortunes in other respects" (Du Noyer 2002: 167). The author supports this notion by stating that in January 1984 there were as many Liverpool bands in the top 20 of the UK national chart as there were in the heyday of the Merseybeat era in January 1964 (Du Noyer 2002: 167).

Many parts of Liverpool have undergone a dramatic transformation since the 1980s and the past thirty years have witnessed a slow and steady revival of the city's fortunes, in many ways as a result of the arts and cultural industries. The mixture of art and commerce has been successful in attracting capital development in recent years. The Tate Modern Art Gallery at the Albert Dock, the Echo Arena, the redevelopment of Liverpool Central Library and the rebuilding of the Everyman Theatre are just some of the notable contributions in the arts sector to the city's resurgence. A recognition of Liverpool's importance as a vibrant cultural centre with a long history of innovation and creativity came in 2008 when Liverpool became European Capital of Culture (Sykes, O. *et al.* 2013).

Parts of Liverpool's city centre would no longer be recognizable to a visitor from the 1980s. Recent regeneration has transformed Liverpool back into a vibrant port. Investment from European funds and some regional development activity has helped stimulate its economy and encouraged private investment from companies such as Peel Holdings and Grosvenor Estates. The Strand has new modern additions to its iconic Three Graces, and the Albert Dock has become a tourist hub. The Echo Arena allows the bigger acts in entertainment and sport to visit the city, and the growth of clubs, restaurants, bars and entertainment venues has encouraged a different view of Liverpool to emerge.

The growth of the higher-education sector has also breathed new life into the some of the more neglected parts of the city, with new courses and new student accommodation. The new Liverpool Institute of Performing Arts has attracted many talented musicians and dancers from across the world. And this has encouraged even more talent to develop and perform at local music venues.

Popular TV culture

Tarmac gangs, permed hair and shellsuits, pottery hens, and Margaret Thatcher's toilet.

The impression of Liverpool fostered by popular television culture in the 1980s was arguably built on common misconceptions and stereotypes. Despite the vague strands of reality behind these caricatures, they were more about parody and fallacy. In mainstream TV programmes such as BBC TV's *Bread*, *Harry Enfield* and *Boys from the Blackstuff*, as well as ITV's *Spitting Image*, Liverpool was portrayed as a city containing aggressive and often feckless men and brash, downtrodden women. Children were often ill educated, out of control and engaged in petty crime, car theft and fraud. People from outside the area considered it madness to leave your car unattended within a five-mile radius of the city. According to Jones and Wilks-Heeg, "Liverpool became virtually synonymous with urban social problems in the news media, feature films and television drama and a destination for those seeking out urban blight (Jones and Wilks-Heeg 2004: 344).

Misconceptions about Liverpool and its people subsequently took on a life of their own and popular television supported them. Already with a reputation for being poor, rough around the edges and in decline, the city had its negative stereotypes reinforced by certain popular television programmes; and, as these stereotypes were persistently repeated, they became ingrained in the nation's psyche. One example was the satirical puppet show *Spitting Image*, which ran from 1984 to 1996. In Series 3 Episode 3, Margaret Thatcher and her cabinet were depicted as being seated in front of a map of the United Kingdom. Thatcher's puppet compared all the regions to parts of her own house. Liverpool was her lavatory. The cabinet then sang an impromptu chorus of 'You'll Never Walk Alone'.[2]

It was the less favourable aspects of the city that were routinely depicted in popular TV culture. Alan Bleasdale's *Boys from the Blackstuff* broadcast on the BBC in 1982 portrayed the poverty and loss of dignity that many experienced when searching for work. Carla Lane's comedy series *Bread*, broadcast on the BBC in 1986, derived much of its humour from the way Liverpudlians would involve themselves in underhand activities in order to get by. Harry Enfield's comic characters "The Scousers", broadcast on his eponymous show on the BBC from 1990, took the stereotype a stage further by exaggerating the hairstyles, fashion and clichéd mannerisms to make Liverpudlians look ridiculous.

One exception to the relentless negativity was Channel 4's television soap opera *Brookside*, which ran from 1982 to 2003. There were indeed references to austerity, politics and crime, but the programme was more concerned with the personal lives of its characters. Some residents of the eponymous close were aspirational middle-class families, such as the Grants, who had left their council estate for a four-bedroom detached private house. Some characters were experiencing hard times, such as the Collins family, but this was as much a personal journey of a family in social decline as it was a contemporary political statement.

Boys from the Blackstuff

Alan Bleasdale's *Boys from the Blackstuff* was a seminal TV drama, set in Liverpool in the early 1980s. According to Boland (2008), the popularity of the series had a huge impact on Britain and its perceptions of Liverpool. The series told the stories of five unemployed tarmac labourers as they attempted to find work. The central characters were depicted as struggling to survive and trying to come to terms with the insecurity of life on the dole. It captured the mood of anger in economically depressed areas of the UK as unemployment began to rise. The series integrated stories of struggle with lighter elements of surreal sardonic humour, and the sheer desperation of the characters found resonance in communities around the country. The series won a BAFTA award for best drama series of 1982, and Bernard Hill's character Yosser Hughes introduced the phrases "Gizza job" and "I can do that" into the national vocabulary. Boland comments:

> The most memorable character, Yosser Hughes, was mentally disturbed by unemployment and his inability to provide for his young children. His oft repeated plea to employers to get work

– "Gizza job" – quickly became a comedic but pejorative external reference to place (Liverpool) and people (Scousers) (Boland 2008, 357).

The catchphrases even spawned a craze of comedy T-shirts emblazoned with Yosser's desperate pleas for work. One could argue that these shirts were offensive in their trivializing attitude towards the serious plight of a population ravaged by unemployment. It was hardly a laughing matter for those affected. Julie Walters also had a key role in the drama as Angie, and delivered some of the series's most emotive lines, echoing the feelings of many Liverpudlians at the time about the indignity and insecurity of life on the dole: "It's not funny, it's not friggin' funny. I've had enough of that 'if you don't laugh you'll cry'. I've heard it for years. This stupid soddin' city's full of it . . . Why don't you fight back, you bastard? Fight back."[3]

Her outburst summed up the frustration, disappointment, the broken promises, and the bleak outlook. Many appreciated *Boys from the Blackstuff* as gritty, realistic drama (Lewis 2016), and it did indeed reflect reality for some. However, critics of the series such as Alwyn Turner argued that it was not a true picture of life in Merseyside. According to Turner, *Boys from the Blackstuff* is:

> A series of melodramatic vignettes in which madness, mayhem and death can be directly attributed to a dole officer trying to check up on whether people are breaking the law. And your natural inclination to sympathy is cynically exploited: in this version of society, those who work for the Department of Employment are comparable to the Gestapo, and those who don't pay tax are heroic resistance fighters trying to reclaim some sense of dignity to all our lives (Turner n.d.).

Steve Redhead, author of football culture book *Sing When You're Winning* (1987), claims that the negative image portrayed of Liverpool by the characters in *Boys from the Blackstuff* was seized upon by football fans in other parts of the country to taunt Liverpool FC supporters. So opposition fans used to taunt Liverpool supporters with a new version of 'You'll Never Walk Alone':

> Sign on, sign on,
> With hope in your heart,
> And you'll never work again,
> You'll never work again

Redhead (1987) suggests that Liverpudlians' acceptance of their fate, their pessimistic outlook and their self-pity contributed to the bleak caricature bestowed on them by the rest of the country.

However, many Liverpudlians were resilient. The unemployment crisis in Liverpool simply meant that many people left the city for work elsewhere; they did not sit around feeling sorry for themselves. During the 1980s the Monday-morning train service from Liverpool Lime Street station to London was nicknamed "The Tebbit Express" after Conservative Secretary for State for Employment Norman Tebbit. Tebbit had made a speech to the Conservative Party conference in Blackpool in 1981 in which he had said: "I grew up in the thirties with an unemployed father. He didn't riot: he got on his bike and looked for work and he kept looking until he found it." This train service took Liverpudlians to other areas of the country where there was employment. To some extent, the "ordinary people" Bleasdale attempted to depict had much more energy and positivity than the memorable characters of his TV series.

Nonetheless, some of these expatriates to more prosperous regions of the UK found themselves convicted of claiming unemployment benefit while working in the service sector. Du Noyer claims that:

> In 1987 there were 5000 Liverpudlians in Bournemouth of whom the police alleged 2000 were engaged in crime. Some had casual work in hotels but still signed on for the dole. Feared and loathed by locals, they colonised their own pubs and clubs (Du Noyer 2001: 160).

This outbreak of Liverpudlian migrant workers engaged in benefit fraud unfortunately did nothing to dispel perceptions that Scousers were underhand people and not to be trusted.

Bread

One of the most popular sitcoms of the 1980s was *Bread*, written by Carla Lane and set in Liverpool. The series featured a supposedly typical Liverpool family attempting to make a living during harsh economic times – a Catholic extended family from the Dingle area of Liverpool a few miles outside the city centre. The head of the family was strong matriarch Nellie Boswell. She had an estranged and feckless husband called Freddie who had left her for his "bit on the side", Lilo Lil. There were five children: Joey, Jack, Adrian, Aveline and Billy, who all lived at home. The boys were wheelers and dealers and the daughter was pretty and vacuous. The successful soap had a simple formula: how a Liverpool family survived in Thatcher's Britain. The children contributed money to the household budget in the form of hard cash deposited regularly into an ornamental pottery hen. The money was generated largely through benefit fraud and the sale of stolen goods. The series played to and reinforced the characterization of Liverpudlians as amusing lovable rogues.

When *Bread* was first screened in May 1986, it was roundly condemned by the critics. According a TV review in *The Times* (16 May 1986), *Bread* "Reinforces the cultural stereotype of the inhabitants of that self-destructive city as a bunch of spongers abusing the welfare state". A further article in *The Times* predicts "little of a future" for the show: "Carla Lane bastes an ordinary sitcom with a watery sauce of Catholicism and social concern . . . The poverty rings hollow too" (Shakespeare 1986). The *Weekly News* (3 December 1988) ran an interview with actor Peter Howitt who played Joey. Howitt was keen to distance himself from his Liverpudlian screen character who earned money while claiming social security benefit. Joey was the epitome of cool in his leather jacket and Jaguar car, and regularly produced money to provide for household upkeep although its provenance was always a mystery. Howitt stated: "I never wear black leather gear like Joey Boswell. I will help promote the programme by doing personal appearances but Joey and I are light years apart."

In a thirty-year retrospective article for BBC News, Bronwyn Jones (2016) remarked that *Bread* did nothing to improve the image of Liverpool in the 1980s and only served to reinforce unfair stereotypes which were prevalent at the time: "Bread presented the city in the national imagination as home to workshy, benefit-cheating dossers." Rohrer (2002) also argues that damaging perceptions of Liverpool had been exacerbated by sitcoms such as *Bread*: "Some people still see as fact the fictional city evoked in the 1980s sitcom Bread, a place of work-shy, dole-cheating chancers who love their mum."

Even the *Liverpool Echo*'s former TV editor Peter Grant agrees that *Bread* "didn't do the city any great favours". Grant claimed that the characters were "cartoon-esque" and could have worked just as well "without that backdrop of being scroungers" (quoted in Jones 2016). Grant urged the public not to take the depictions of Scousers too seriously because the main purpose of the show was comedy. Other areas of the country might have been more offended had they borne the brunt of this subcultural stereotyping, but most Liverpudlians appeared simply bemused by the series and thought of it as a parody, not something reflecting the reality of how the vast majority of the city's inhabitants dealt with the harsh economic climate and lack of prospects (Belchem 2006b).

The Scousers

Harry Enfield's "The Scousers" depicted Liverpudlian men as quarrelsome with an ability to start an argument in an empty house. Their permed hair and moustaches drew inspiration from the Liverpool FC coiffures of the 1980s, especially that of Graeme Souness, and from the Terry Sullivan character from the Channel 4 soap *Brookside*. Their catchphrase "Calm down! Calm down!" became synonymous with an idea that Liverpudlians were constantly in the middle of a fight. The pair, Barry and Terry, wore nylon shellsuits and trainers and were always arguing and squaring up to each other in a comical karate stance before eventually being persuaded to "calm down". *The Independent's* Jayne Merrick (2012), self-identifying as a Liverpudlian, says, "Not for us British reserve" and claims this ability to tap into one's emotions may be part of Liverpool's Irish Catholic heritage, or a determination by Liverpudlians to set themselves apart from the rest of the country. Enfield's caricatures once again reinforced a perception of feckless men and common women in a domestic scenario forever on the brink of erupting into conflict.

One episode of *Harry Enfield's Television Programme* featured the "Scousers' Wedding". In this sketch, the groom and his best man were drunk, the bride was pregnant, the best man's speech was inappropriate, the bride walked out and the reception ended in a fight. It seemed like every seaside postcard wedding cliché had been applied with the sole aim of mocking Scousers. Enfield's show enjoyed excellent ratings and "The Scousers" appeared in every series.

The notion of lazy, untrustworthy Liverpudlians has continued in popular television media into the present day with television characters such as Jim Royle and Twiggy from BBC TV's *The Royle Family*, and *Coronation Street* villain Pat Phelan. Belchem (2006b) suggests that popular media and popular perception has punished Liverpool for its "self-defeating otherness".

A sense of place: the geography and the music

Looking out to sea. Nothing to do in Liverpool.

Liverpool's very geography speaks to the city's marginalized youth of the 1980s. It curls around the north-west coastline shunning the rest of England and looking out towards the Irish Sea, describing an isolation that was genuinely felt. Liverpool, as we have seen, was arguably not a top priority of central government, and without the investment and jobs to halt the city's decline, the youth of the city turned their back on the country and got on with their lives, detached from what was happening in the rest of England.

Liverpool's geography and long history as a port permitted a culture of travel, escape and opportunity to prevail even in the most austere of times. The tangible geographical escape route was reflected in an escapist mind-set, with young musicians dreaming of more enriching life experiences beyond the social and economic shackles of their surroundings. These internal revolutions in the minds of the new breed of Scouse Romantic musicians gave them passage from the reality of their surroundings to somewhere more exciting, passionate and understanding.

The concept of a "Scouse Romantic" pop musician dates back to the 1960s, evident in the many Merseybeat bands whose songs had escapist themes. Billy Kinsley believed that every man should have a dream, the Beatles romanticized parts of the city such as Penny Lane and Strawberry Fields, while Gerry Marsden transformed the ferry crossing between Liverpool and Birkenhead into something more than a regular commute. However, the 1980s Scouse Romantic spirit differed from that of the escapist 1960s Merseybeat bands in one salient aspect. For many, the 1960s represented a decade of social change, hope and optimism, whereas by the early 1980s the hope had been replaced by cutbacks, decline and despair.

In the years after the Second World War, British social history was still fashioned by rationing and austerity. However, by the start of the 1960s, government commitments to health and education had ushered in an era of optimism for the baby-boomer generation (Muncie 2000). In some parts of the country there was full employment and, as mentioned in the opening to this chapter, Liverpool had its fair share of employers. New social housing estates were being built and there was a consumer boom for labour-saving appliances. The 1960s can be characterized as a decade of reform and progress. Young people anticipating better times ahead no longer conformed to older generations' expectations and teenage rock 'n' roll rebellion was born (Muncie 2000).

However, by the start of the 1980s Liverpool was mocked and pitied: a grim tourist attraction for anyone who wanted to see what decline and lack of prospects looked like. It became the subject for a song by Katrina and the Waves – 'Going Down to Liverpool' – which was later covered by the Bangles and became a minor hit ('I'm going down to Liverpool to do nothing / All the days of my life'). A sense of otherness prevailed. A *Daily Mirror* article of 11 October 1982 advised Liverpudlians to "Build a fence around Liverpool and charge an entrance admission. The city is a 'showcase of everything that has gone wrong in all of Britain's major cities'." In Du Noyer's words, Liverpool had gone from "Beat city" to "Beaten city" in just over a decade (Du Noyer 2002: 160).

Brief context of a post-Beatles lull

More car parks. Eddie Amoo and Billy Kinsley enjoy 1970s success. Art pop arrives too soon. The punk ethos lives on. Ken Testi "grows his own". Local bands dance in the rubble.

As part of the post-war rock 'n' roll rebellion, Merseybeat bands emerged and found success on national and international stages in the 1960s. However, by the early 1970s the Merseybeat scene had subsided along with its energy and enthusiasm. The music scene in post-Beatles Liverpool was quiet and empty. Grass-roots musical innovation in the city had stagnated. The early 1970s in Liverpool were characterized by a lack of venues, a lack of direction and a lack of creative energy. Many of the city's well-known venues were gone. The famous Cavern club in Mathew Street was closed in 1973 during the construction of the Merseyrail underground loop and became a car park. The Iron Door club in Temple Street, which had hosted local bands such as Rory Storm and the Hurricanes, Billy J. Kramer and the Coasters, and the Undertakers, had also become a car park. The Tower Ballroom in New Brighton was destroyed by fire in 1969 but fortunately the views it offered across the River Mersey ensured that it would not become yet another car park and it is now the site of River View Park housing estate.

There were still venues around the city in which local bands could perform, such as The Masonic in Berry Street, Whispers in Bold Street and Pickwick's in Fraser Street, but nothing to make up anything like the dynamic music scene that had prevailed just over a decade earlier. Ken Testi, co-founder of Eric's club in Mathew Street, sums up the musical malaise of the mid-1970s:

> When Roger and I thought about starting a club in Liverpool, there were not that many venues in Liverpool for young people. The Beatles thing was over and there was not that much in the way of music coming out of Liverpool . . . Liverpool had plenty of young people wanting to be in bands but there was not much out there for them and there was no real sense of direction.[4]

Popular music in the 1960s was marked by periods of dominance by different styles: rock 'n' roll, psychedelic music and Motown. In mid-1970s Britain, glam rock, progressive rock and reggae became dominant, none of which particularly flourished in Liverpool. The changing trends left some of the local musicians from the 1960s out of fashion, so they sought out the venues and audiences that would still be receptive to their style of music. In this vein, local bands such as Faron's Flamingos and the Chants continued to perform on the social club circuit around the UK and at specialist music events at home and abroad.

Liverpool bands did make occasional assaults on the charts during the 1970s, however, most notable among which being the Real Thing and Liverpool Express. These bands demonstrated that Liverpool still had a capacity to produce high-quality songs with wide appeal, courtesy of exceptional songwriters like Bill Kinsley and Eddie Amoo. Kinsley and Amoo had their roots in the 1960s scene but were able to evolve and adapt to musical changes in the following decade. Eddie Amoo, singer with the Real Thing, started his career in the 1960s with doo-wop band the Chants, whose first gig was at The Cavern club in 1962 where they performed four songs *a capella* halfway through a Beatles gig. The Beatles had asked the Chants to audition at The Cavern and were so impressed that they invited them to perform during one of their own packed-out shows. In 1975, after thirteen years with the Chants, Eddie joined the Real Thing and a more commercially successful period began. Chart success came with 'You to Me Are Everything' and the Real Thing became an established mainstream soul band. Their success continued in the 1980s with their chart hit 'Can You Feel the Force?' (Cooper, K. 2015).

Billy Kinsley of Liverpool Express had a long songwriting pedigree dating back to his days with the Merseybeats and the Merseys. Liverpool Express enjoyed national and international success in the 1970s with the hit singles 'You Are My Love', 'Every Man Must Have a Dream' and 'Dreamin''. Billy's writing had evolved from straightforward 1960s rock 'n' roll to a more subtle and refined brand of music, deeper, more emotional and mature. The quality of their songs enabled them to score hit records that stood out from the trends of the day. Beverly Paterson from *Something Else!* describes their "best of" album as follows:

> Liverpool Express wires their tight and catchy material with layers of luscious harmonies, condensed hooks and neat and organized structures. State of the art production charges the thoughtfully-written and performed songs with a spotlessly-scrubbed sheen, but the energy and approach remains squarely on the organic side of the coin . . . Romantic lyrics, impassioned vocals, a clingy tempo and nice melodies will always stay in style (Paterson 2013).

The success of Liverpool Express and the Real Thing was followed in the mid-seventies by Elvis Costello with his own unique brand of reggae-inflected New Wave pub-rock. He was interesting and different but, although his accent was distinctly Liverpudlian, he emerged out of the London pub-rock scene rather than Merseyside. Elvis was soon acknowledged as an innovative singer-songwriter. Nick Kent said of his debut album *My Aim Is True*: "Forget all those Springsteen comparisons – the latter'll die before he ever writes anything half as good as this. Forget the Van Morrison schtick too. They're worlds apart and Elvis is currently worlds better."[5]

Deaf School

The Real Thing, Liverpool Express and Elvis Costello gave Liverpool some recognition on the national pop scene. Yet there was another band that may not have been as commercially successful as these three but was equally important.

Deaf School were formed in Liverpool College of Art in 1973. Their music was diverse and ranged from pop-rock to cabaret. The line-up fluctuated and some gigs had as many as thirteen people performing at once. Core members of the band had pop pseudonyms: singer Anne Martin was "Betty Bright", Steve Allen on vocals was "Enrico Cadillac", John Wood on keyboards was "The Right Reverend Max Ripple" and Clive Langer was "Cliff Hanger". Their strange names accompanied their unconventional appearance, with stage make-up and theatrical costume (Du Noyer 2013). Their endearing appeal was their uniqueness, and their eclectic approach to composing a set knew no boundaries – their unmistakable energy and originality differentiated them from the rest of the music scene both locally and nationally. Subsequent achievements by individual members are a testament to the prodigious talent within the group: Clive Langer became a successful record producer working with Madness, David Bowie, Morrissey and Dexy's Midnight Runners (he also co-wrote the classic song 'Shipbuilding' with Elvis Costello); Steve Allen joined Ian Broudie to form the Original Mirrors; and Anne Martin formed her own band Betty Bright and the Illuminations.

Their first album, *2nd Honeymoon*, spawned their famous single 'What a Way to End It All', which was frequently played as the last song at the end of musical events in Liverpool. The album set the tone for their future musical works, being hard to define with a range of musical styles all on the same record, from the rock-inspired 'Knock Knock Knocking' and 'Get Set Ready Go' to a Parisian-sounding ballad entitled 'Final Act'. Deaf School's music and live performances offered a sense of drama and enjoyment. According to Paul Du Noyer, "In the whole history of Liverpool music two bands matter most. One is the Beatles and the other is Deaf School" (quoted in Guy 2013).

Despite never having enjoyed success at a national level, their influence can be seen in the work of artists such as Madness and Dexy's Midnight Runners. Du Noyer expertly documented the band's influence and stature in his poignant book *Deaf School: The Non-stop Art Punk Rock Party* (2013). Why the band failed to become a household name was purely a matter of timing. They were the right band coming from a city with a great musical tradition but they emerged into a musical world at a time when the tectonic plates were shifting so rapidly that they were left stranded on the wrong side of transient musical fashion and direction. The punk rock revolution of the late 1970s changed trends in pop music and rendered some bands deeply unfashionable almost overnight. Deaf School were a casualty of this rapid change, but they remain a reference point for all that was to happen in Liverpool in the wake of the musical earthquake triggered by punk rock. They had established an art school ethos in the city and made the important statement that bands need not follow the latest musical direction. In fact, their bold musical manifesto encouraged others to be different and experimental, and their unpredictable behaviour and appearance became an inspiration to the Scouse Pop bands of the 1980s.

The punk rock ethos

Punk rock swept through Britain in the latter part of the 1970s, inspiring teenage rebellion and causing parental anxiety in a manner identified by Stanley Cohen in his seminal work *Folk Devils and Moral Panics* (1973), which was based on the media portrayal of the mods and rockers teenage groups in the 1960s. Supergroups consisting of guitar heroes with long hair, suede boots and flared jeans became outdated overnight. Sales of patchouli oil plummeted. In came spiky-haired rebels blurting out their raucous condemnation of their musical predecessors. Punk briefly took the music industry on a bewildering journey confronting the commercial orthodoxy of the big labels. This challenge to the establishment empowered youth culture and led to the explosion of a plethora of short-lived punk bands.

Adolescent punks were at once easily identifiable and a source of apprehension for their elders. But inevitably it was not long before it was being marketized by major record companies, transforming it into a commercialized parody of itself within a year. In Merseyside the punk movement never really manifested itself in an outbreak of new bands, unlike many other cities. There were a few notable exceptions such as Birkenhead's Instant Agony and Liverpool's Ponderosa Glee Boys. Nonetheless, its legacy was significant, evidenced by the mentality of the 1980s music scene with its DIY "have a go" culture, which punk had conceived. You needed more attitude than talent, more noise than melody and more rebellion than compliance. The "I don't care" attitude had permeated into the psyche and soul of teenagers spirit in the late 1970s.[6]

This brash teenage confidence built on rebellion had liberated many of the individuals playing in bands in Liverpool and the surrounding area. An era of looking different, singing a different tune and dancing to a different beat was in ferment in the city's suburbs. In the bedrooms of Kirkby, the basements of Kensington and the hired rehearsal spaces in Liverpool, something was happening under the radar which only needed a catalyst to trigger a reaction that would herald the dawn of a new chapter in the musical life of Liverpool.

Eric's as a catalyst

As the 1970s progressed, the post-Beatles lull was challenged by a more optimistic approach to music, thanks to exposure to a variety of influences and opportunities to perform. The focus of this resurgence began with the opening of Eric's club in Mathew Street in October 1976, situated opposite the car park that was the site of the original Cavern club. The idea for Eric's was conceived by Roger Eagle and Ken Testi, who were later joined by Pete Fulwell. Roger was a DJ, promoter and club manager; Ken was an early promoter of Queen and later the manager of Deaf School; and Pete managed bands such as Wah!, It's Immaterial and the Christians. He was also co-owner of local label Inevitable Records. Local, more alternative, teenagers were frequent attendees of Eric's to watch the new bands performing at the venue. Although the city was in the midst of hard times, there was an excitement and energy among the city's youth culture which was inspiring – and Eric's appeared to be the epicentre of this musical revolution (Sykes, W. 2012).

Eric's put on many unsigned bands that later became household names, among them the Police, the Cure, the Clash and U2. These bands, brought in from out of town, were often supplemented by new local bands as support acts. The latter were a manifestation of owner Ken Testi's "We will grow our own" philosophy in which he and co-owner Roger Eagle actively sought out teenagers interested in music to both attend the club and also form their own bands. Local bands such as Echo and the Bunnymen, the Teardrop Explodes, Orchestral Manoeuvres in the Dark and Wah! would regularly perform at Eric's, supporting bigger bands from outside the city. Bringing in a diverse range of bands from out of town had an impact on the embryonic local bands: firstly by raising the bar in terms of the standards of originality required to make an impact and excite audiences, and, secondly, it gave the local bands an opportunity to mix with innovative musicians and experience the diversity of styles that Roger and Ken's idiosyncratic venue was keen to promote (Sykes, W. 2012).

The Scouse phenomenon and what made 1980s Liverpool unique

In 1982, Inevitable Records boss Pete Fulwell hosted a radio documentary for BBC Radio 4 entitled *Dancing in the Rubble* (BBC 1982). In it he claimed that Liverpool had over 1,000 bands writing and performing their own material. Around the same time, German writer Dr Klaus Schwartze was compiling a definitive "family tree" of the members of many bands in his two-volume *The Scouse Phenomenon* (Schwartze 1985, 1987). These books identified thousands of musicians who played in a myriad of bands from Deaf School to Frankie Goes to Hollywood and beyond. It still serves as a valuable reference point, and was helpful in research for this book. As Schwartze's books testify, the Liverpool scene in its entirety is too big to allow a fully comprehensive account of the music in the city during the 1980s to be presented here. Chapter 2 will therefore focus on a selection of bands that made an impact on the national and international pop music scene.

Histories of popular culture in the UK often connect periods of innovation with particular regions. A genre of music emerges in a certain city and is then developed by a number of bands that seem to share a musical style. During the 1980s, Manchester, Sheffield, Glasgow and the Midlands all cultivated a cluster of bands with a strong stylistic resemblance to one another. In the early 1980s, the Midlands had the Specials, the Selecter and UB40, with a ska and reggae sound; Sheffield had the synth-pop of the Human League, Heaven 17 and (the more experimental) Cabaret Voltaire; and Glasgow was associated with the sound of jangly guitars playing upbeat pop songs with bands such as Orange Juice, Aztec Camera, Altered Images and Lloyd Cole and the

Commotions. And, in the late 1980s, Manchester had its indie dance-infused style ("Madchester") courtesy of the Inspiral Carpets, the Happy Mondays and the Stone Roses. This pattern of regional movements is replicated around the world, other examples being New Orleans jazz, Seattle grunge, Rio samba, Detroit Motown, Philadelphia soul and Jamaican reggae. Liverpool itself, in the 1960s, was associated with a post-war rock 'n' roll rebellion style of music ("Merseybeat"), and spawned over a dozen chart-topping bands playing in a rock 'n' roll style.

However, the salient point of this book is that Liverpool in the 1980s remains unique in comparison with other cities in that many of the successful bands that emerged from Liverpool deliberately went out of their way to differ from their local and national contemporaries. The 1960s produced a "Mersey sound", but the 1980s produced "Mersey sounds". This is fully explored in the next chapter which features interviews with members of fourteen successful bands who discuss their formation, their influences and their desire to be different.

Whether the bands featured in the next chapter expected to be successful is certainly debatable. Some aspired to be pop stars but many just wanted to make music. The choice of bizarre psychedelic names such as Echo and the Bunnymen, Orchestral Manoeuvres in the Dark (OMD) and Half Man Half Biscuit testifies to this. All the above were unconventional in comparison to their 1980s pop peers: OMD were using new instruments, Half Man Half Biscuit were exploring unconventional subject matter, and Echo and the Bunnymen were experimenting and blending various styles of pop music in an avant-garde manner. Commercially, it made little sense, but artistically, in Liverpool, it worked. Inevitable Records boss Jeremy Lewis said of the labels in Liverpool: "In Liverpool during the early 1980s, the modern major label ethos of 'What is everybody else doing? We'll do one of those' did not exist."[7]

There were certain, albeit limited, factors that allowed the bands to flourish and were conducive to artistic expression. Firstly, there was the mentality of Liverpool's marginalized youth and their desire to be different. Secondly, there was the support of local media which allowed alternative music to be played and written about. Thirdly, the local independent record labels, with their DIY "can do" ethos, enabled local bands to release records. And, finally, there were local venues where the bands could play live. The existence of these last three propitious elements was thanks to several individuals who recognized that something special was happening in Liverpool and who responded passionately to the music. These individuals were music lovers, record shop owners, venue owners, DJs and writers. They compensated for the limited resources in the city with commitment, enthusiasm and industry (Cohen 1991).

A sense of place: landscapes of the mind and Scouse resilience

China Crisis "living in hock". Models of resilience. It is cosier by the fire.

This chapter has thus far attempted to present a notion of identity and a sense of time and place. It will now endeavour to explain this sense of place in terms of the mind-set – the "Scouse attitude" – of the successful Liverpool band China Crisis. Aside from an abundance of talent and an abrasive attitude towards conformity, the concept of Scouse attitude can be understood as a spirit of resilience – a salient quality in explaining what energized the individuals discussed here, epitomized by China Crisis as well as those others who, like them, made it to become professional musicians. We can examine this further using Cooper's model of resilience (Cooper, Flint-Taylor and Pearn 2012). This has four distinct aspects: (1) Vision and purpose; (2) Adaptability; (3) Social support and seeking expertise; and (4) Confidence.

The first interview for this book was conducted with Gary Daly and Eddie Lundon of China Crisis. Gary (vocals) and Eddie (guitar) formed the band in 1979 in Kirkby on the outskirts of Liverpool. They were later joined by Dave Reilly on drums in 1981. China Crisis had five UK top 40 singles and three top 40 albums and enjoyed international success. On analysis, their road to success follows a textbook pattern, going from resilience to achievement, as predicted in Cooper's four dimensions of resilience. China Crisis can therefore serve as an example of this process.

Figure 1: On the set of the *Scouse Pop* TV programme, September 2016: (left to right) author Paul Skillen, China Crisis's Gary Daly and Eddie Lundon, and *Scouse Pop* TV producer Neil Duffin. Photograph by Tom Cox

The first element of resilience is *vision and purpose*. One could argue that early 1980s Merseyside was not the ideal time or place for two working-class lads from a social housing estate to seek international success. Lundon explains a situation that may be comparable to other bands at the time:

> What we did have was the songs. The songs gave us an opportunity to say what we wanted to say. It also gave us a purpose to record and perform. All of the early songs, like 'African and White' and 'Working with Fire and Steel' and that kind of thing did come from a political basis. There weren't that many job options in Kirkby at the time. We were going through the Thatcher thing, and Kirkby at the time was like a social experiment. New town set-up, industrial and everything, and then bust within a decade. Basically, the place was shutting down. So there weren't many alternatives. Unemployment was going up and we kind of locked ourselves away and got on with what we were doing . . . so we kind of isolated ourselves and got on with our own business.[8]

The notion of independently creating music despite adverse conditions is evident in Eddie's comments. The songs of China Crisis demonstrate their own particular view of the world. They became something the band could unite around and gave them a sense of purpose in trying to further develop their musical careers.

Following the first element of *vision and purpose*, the band demonstrated Cooper's second element, *adaptability*, by making the most out of the situation they found themselves in. An example of this adaptability is found in the next phase of the China Crisis story.

Owing to scarce resources, some musicians in Kirkby operated a loan arrangement with their instruments to allow them to make their early recordings: they would borrow other bands' equipment on an ad hoc basis and make their own instruments available to others whenever they were needed. Occasionally, similar-sounding tracks emerged because the instruments being used were the same. In order to differentiate themselves from the other bands sharing the same equipment, China Crisis would have to do something innovative. Much of the equipment they did actually own was purchased from catalogues so they could "play now and pay later":

> *Eddie:* Everything was on credit and we kind of lived in hock [laughs]. If we needed a drum machine, or a synth, we'd get them all on credit from the catalogue.

> *Gary:* . . . and we'd get people to sign HP forms for us and we'd pay it off to get amps or whatever we needed. But we also had a little

cooperative kind of thing in Kirkby, around 1980/81/82, where we swapped and shared equipment. Me and Ed had a portastudio, a guitar and a synth and someone else had mics and a mic stand and another synth. Then you'd have it for three to four days and then you'd have to pass it all along to someone else and they have it for so many days, so it went round like that. But the idea was, it was like the way we'd been brought up really, it was all a bit like *"you gotta share".* It's like having a ball for a game of footie: *"you gotta share".* We could've all sounded the same because we were all using each other's instruments . . . but we made sure that we didn't because we were always trying different ideas.[9]

Apart from scarcity of resources, the other major hurdle they faced was a lack of space in which to write or rehearse. The many council estates that had been built in the post-war period on the outskirts of Liverpool were designed with some notion of open spaces, but nonetheless had to conform to prescribed density targets. The rooms were small, and often families were too large for the allocated space. This led to Gary and Eddie making the maximum use of whatever space they could find and utilizing small items of musical equipment to their full advantage. It was a case of making a virtue out of a necessity, as Gary explains:

When you think about it, the reason why we ended up in the bedroom was because the portastudio was designed as such that you could plug it into your stereo. So where do you have your stereo? Well I had it in my bedroom with all my records. So that's where we made music. Ed and myself lived in average-sized houses, but there was eight in our three-bedroom house, and there were ten in Ed's. So if you think about, it there's no space to do anything anywhere. You don't get your own space if you're one of all those many kids. So we spend some days at Ed's, maybe a couple in ours, and then if Ed's mum and dad went out at the weekend we could drag musical equipment into the living room . . . It's a bit cosier by the fire![10]

Despite these difficulties, the teenage duo carried on regardless of what might appear prohibitive constraints.

The next element of Cooper's resilience model is one of *seeking social support and expertise* in order to make connections. In the case of China Crisis, it was the next logical step to take their demo tapes to the nearest recording studio, which was Amazon Recording Studios in Stopgate Lane just outside Kirkby. The studio was also home of Liverpool label Inevitable Records. Label co-founder Jeremy Lewis thereby became the next step in the process of making connections. Jeremy explains what he saw in the band:

They were just two kids who sent me a demo tape recorded on a portastudio. It wasn't punk. It wasn't rock. I was not sure it was reflective of the contemporary pop scene at the time. In fact, I was not sure what it was . . . but I liked it. That was enough for me. So having the studio set up, I thought it would be worth seeing what they could do in a professional recording studio.[11]

The fact that someone with recording expertise found the band interesting and wanted to record takes us to the fourth element of Cooper's model of resilience, which is *confidence*. Even though Gary and Eddie were not immediately successful, their perception of their own ability was bolstered by the interest and encouragement of a professional in the field. Their increased confidence encouraged them to continue with their original music. Following positive reviews of their first single 'African and White', China Crisis went on to record their successful debut album *Difficult Shapes and Passive Rhythms: Some People Think It's Fun to Entertain* (1982).

As an example of resilience, China Crisis demonstrate Cooper's model (Cooper, Flint-Taylor and Pearn 2012). The next chapter considers how other successful Liverpool bands also developed their musical creativity and demonstrated resilience in order to achieve international recognition.

2 To Be Somebody: Ambition and the Desire to Be Different

The context for difference

This chapter looks at some of the bands that enjoyed chart success during the late 1970s and '80s and aims to identify their artistic traits by means of conversations with band members and those close to the bands. The chapter does not claim to be a definitive account or an inclusive list of innovative bands but merely a viewpoint from some of the individuals who were present at the time and involved in music, creativity and youth culture. Some of these individuals were in the eye of the storm while others were more on the periphery. However, common themes emerge and testify to the Scouse resilience identified in the previous chapter. Also, identifying objective truth is a difficult task, as one band member will often have a view of his band's history that conflicts with that of other members of the same band. As such, it is acknowledged that this chapter presents only selective viewpoints.

Trying something new: In what ways were the Liverpool bands creative and different?

> 'Liverpool has always made me brave, choice-wise. It was never a city that criticized anyone for taking a chance.' *David Morrissey*[1]

In terms of creativity, the theory underpinning this book which was stated in Chapter 1 is that successful Liverpool bands in the 1980s were different from each other and did not attempt to follow the latest local or national pop music trends. None of the bands interviewed falls into the categories of punk, disco or New Romantic, which were popular trends at the time. Whether they could be truly considered unique is open to debate. The bands' styles are examined in terms of originality using a creativity map designed by Norman Jackson (2011), a writer on creativity. The bands featured are by no means an exhaustive list: many others demonstrated similar traits of innovation and difference.

Types of creativity

In his article "Developing personal creativity through lifewide education" (2011), Norman Jackson offers the following general definition of creativity: "Being inventive with someone else's ideas and involved with re-creation, re-construction, re-contextualization, re-definition by adapting things that have been done before and doing things that have been done before but differently". Jackson then breaks down the notion of creativity into four broad themes: (1) ways of thinking, (2) attitudes, (3) effects and (4) feelings.

The bands featured in this chapter have been grouped in order to exemplify these four particular strands of creativity. Their origins are discussed to offer context for their individuality, and interviews were conducted to explore their notions of creativity and difference.

Roger Hill speculates on difference in Liverpool bands

One of the most authoritative voices on Liverpool music is BBC Radio Merseyside broadcaster Roger Hill. He acknowledges that the bands of the Scouse Pop era (late 1970s and 1980s) differed from one another and that some were musical innovators: "There were some bands which were quite unique in their approach. These bands did influence future developments either by the way they looked or the way they sounded."[2] Roger recognized that something unique was happening in Liverpool and he would feature these innovative and unusual bands on his Radio Merseyside show.

He goes on to qualify the notion of uniqueness by arguing that, although there were some groundbreaking bands, not all were true innovators as they were drawing their music from a variety of well-established influences. Roger argues that uniqueness was often accompanied by a forcefulness of personality among the bands' members, driving them to success. These individuals tried to act differently, look different and sound different from national music trends. They also had personalities that were uniquely Liverpudlian. From this localized oddness came a sense of something fresh and exciting. Roger explains:

> It's a personal view, but if you take the core bands of Teardrops, Bunnymen, Jayne Casey, Dead or Alive and Wah!, what made them distinctive were the personalities involved. They were very much of Liverpool. The peculiar quirks of those individuals produced individual music which is *sui generis*: it does not follow form or fashion.[3]

Roger believes that the bond with Liverpool was empowering but also held them back from developing their music beyond the initial establishment of their sound:

> The environment at the time suited those individuals. They were always going to be in seminal bands or in the public eye. However, they were not driven by musical development *per se* or about what they could sound like next. If I think about bands such as Echo and the Bunnymen, they developed and got more grandiose but their musical style has not shifted much from their early days. I think that some bands were able to thrive in the micro-environment of Liverpool but they were also limited in Darwinian terms because they were anchored to the city and so did not progress much further in musical terms.[4]

His view is that the time and the place contributed to a difference in styles between the bands but that only a few of the bands were in fact unique.

1. New ways of thinking

Andy McCluskey's upside-down bass and the future of pop. Half Man Half Biscuit carried aloft through provincial towns. Tommy Scott gets cold feet with the Bride of Frankenstein. Why members of China Crisis do not wear frilly shirts.

Jackson's first strand of creativity, *ways of thinking*, involves having new ideas and an open mind to develop music that differs from the mainstream. The bands in this section were developing their art with energizing ideas, and adapted and refined genres rather than being revolutionary. In this respect they were connecting new approaches and new ways of engaging with pop music. The very nature of popular music is that it must be accessible and so the bands developed their strands of creativity within the parameters of the pop song.

This section will examine four seminal Scouse Pop bands who demonstrated originality and uniqueness setting them apart as innovators or musical auteurs: Orchestral Manoeuvres in the Dark (OMD), Half Man Half Biscuit, Space and China Crisis. Each created a style that was original at the time; and each was credible, creative and accessible.

OMD embraced new forms of instrumentation and were generally considered groundbreaking. They shaped the future and are in many ways a reference point for the subsequent development of popular music. Roger Hill acknowledges their innovativeness: "OMD were precursors of dance. They produced music based on synthetic beats. In 1980/81/82, they were predicting music which would happen in the '90s."[5] While comparisons with German synthesizer pioneers Kraftwerk will always be made, OMD took synthesizers into the world of pop music in a way that other bands did not. The mixture of conventional drums and bass with synthesizer overtones, the absence of guitars and the unconventional lyrics gave them a unique sound. This was complemented by strong melodies. The songs were memorable and instantly appealing in the true sense of pop.

Half Man Half Biscuit were never part of the Eric's scene and were fiercely Birkonian rather than Liverpudlian. Their strand of observational comedy contained acerbic lyrics combined with a wide variety of musical styles. They displayed the absurdities of modern life in a random and unique manner. One could argue that they have roots in the folk tradition, which can include songs about the vagaries of life. DJ Andy Kershaw described them on his BBC Radio 3 show as "The most complete and authentic British group since the Clash".[6] However, the variety of musical and lyrical references from punk to folk passing through rock and country make them bewildering to absorb. The sound of the music is amusing even before a word has been sung. According to Roger Hill:

> Half Man Half Biscuit are completely unique. Their songs are of themselves and have a distinct and amazing character and it is that which we must celebrate. [Founder and writer] Nigel Blackwell is not aloof from the music scene, he is extremely well informed. He comments on the music scene either in the content or the style of everything he does.[7]

Although Space achieved international success during the Britpop era of the mid-1990s, their musical origins are in the 1980s. Britpop itself was arguably the last great trend in British popular music and spawned many bands who acknowledged the prodigious British bands of the 1960s such as the Beatles, the Who and the Rolling Stones. While being associated with Britpop, the music Space produced bore little similarity to bands such as Blur, Oasis or Pulp. Their music was difficult to categorize; while some songs reflected the Britpop genre, most did not. Writer, producer and label manager Dave Balfe acknowledges his own part in the Britpop movement and argues that it was not a unique genre, being too closely aligned to previous styles: "The problem with Britpop, which I take some responsibility for, was that it legitimized the past and now a band is considered innovative if they are ripping off a band that hasn't been ripped off before."[8]

What made Space unique during the Britpop era was the sheer variety of styles they embraced, such as pop, rock and Latin American, while the lyrics covered a broad range of subjects including horror movies. In the words of Jennifer Blake:

> Space are from Liverpool, but any attempts to cast the band under the somewhat meaningless title of "Britpop" should be quickly

dismissed. Other than the fact that the members of Space are British and make superb pop music, they have little in common with bands like Blur and Oasis. In fact, they have little in common with any other band. Their quirky originality is what makes them so much fun to watch, leaving the audience not sure what to expect.[9]

The final band under discussion here is China Crisis. The duo from Kirkby did not emanate from the Eric's stable: they were never frequent visitors to the club and were detached from anything resembling an indie rock style apparent in the likes of Echo and the Bunnymen, Wah! or Dead or Alive. The band had a way of communicating with the listener through well-crafted melodies that create a particular feeling. As Roger Hill says, "China Crisis produced some music which was quintessentially Liverpudlian. They made music which was perennial, but was outside the core energies of rock 'n' roll. It is more of a mood which takes you over."[10]

The next section examines these four bands from their formation through to the development of their innovative musical style.

Orchestral Manoeuvres in the Dark

Figure 2: Orchestral Manoeuvres in the Dark in the early 1980s: (left to right) Andy McCluskey and Paul Humphreys. Photograph by David Elms, OMD Finatics

Orchestral Manoeuvres in the Dark (OMD) are an electronic pop group from Wirral, Merseyside. The core members are Andy McCluskey and Paul Humphreys. This duo has been accompanied by various band members over the years but their most famous line-up included Malcolm Holmes on drums and multi-instrumentalist Martin Cooper. The main innovations the band brought to pop music were the experimental use of synthesizers and digital technology; they also had unusual subject choices for popular music songs. The technology allowed OMD to experiment with new sounds while building on the format of the traditional pop song, with the synthesizer allowing them to create previously unattainable sound arrangements. Popular weekly *Sounds* described OMD as "unlimited in potential".[11]

To begin with, the synthesizers were supplemented by electronic rhythm machines and tape recordings, with their reel-to-reel tape recorder – named "Winston" after the main character in George Orwell's novel *1984* – a prominent feature in their early performances (West 1982). However, when OMD became a four-piece in 1980, conventional drums and bass were used for some recordings and live work. Early audiences of the band noticed that singer Andy McCluskey was playing his bass upside down. A right-handed player with a left-handed bass? Andy explains:

> I had not really been in bands until I was about fifteen. Then a friend of mine was in a band and played bass guitar. I thought that this was really cool. So I thought "I will play bass." However my friends already had a bass player so I thought "DRUMS!" Everyone wants to play drums so I fancied being a drummer but I couldn't afford a drum kit. I then thought that I could be a guitarist. I practised for a few weeks and found that it hurt my fingers. So I thought that's no good and I succumbed to being a bass player. I remember on my sixteenth birthday I asked everyone to give me money instead of a present. I had the grand total of 27 quid. I got the train from Meols Station [in Wirral] and went to Park Selling Service, a second-hand shop in Birkenhead. The only bass in my price range (I mean the cheapest one) was a left-handed bass and that was 32 quid. So I went back on the train to Meols and asked my dad to lend me a fiver. I promised to walk the dogs or do the dishes for another month in order to pay him back – and I also asked for my train fare back to Birkenhead. So I ended up with a left-handed bass. I didn't even know that you could change the strings around so I ended up playing it upside down. Even now when I can afford a right-handed bass, I need to have the strings upside down. It is good fun when you hand it to another bass player.[12]

Andy had dabbled in a few local bands in the mid to late 1970s such as Equinox, Pegasus, Hitler's Underpantz, the Id and Dalek I Love You. These bands were generally more conventional in their instrumentation using guitars, drums and bass. During the mid-1970s progressive rock was a predominant influence in Britain. Andy recalls his conversion to electronic-based music:

In 1975 I heard Kraftwerk on the radio. I started going over to Probe Records shop in Liverpool and looking around the German import section. I only had an old record player, but Paul, the electronics genius, managed to cannibalize two old record players and make a stereo. I started going to Paul's house to listen to this German electronic music. Our mates who were into Genesis and Yes said "Why are you listening to this electronic crap?"[13]

Despite the more conventional influences on Andy's earlier bands, he grew increasingly more interested in electronic music. While Andy was involved in the various bands that preceded OMD, he also maintained an experimental electronic side project called VCL X1 with his schoolfriend Paul Humphreys, who acted as a roadie for Pegasus (West 1982). After a short stint with Dalek I Love You in 1978, Andy decided to make VCL X1 his priority and the band was renamed Orchestral Manoeuvres in the Dark. The name was taken from a list of song lyrics which Andy had scribbled on his bedroom wall and was chosen because the duo did not want to be mistaken for a punk band. OMD compiled a set and started to perform as a duo. Their first gig was at Eric's in October 1978 (West 1982).

Following a few local gigs, they sent a demo tape to *Granada Reports* journalist Tony Wilson to see if he could arrange a slot for them on a Granada TV programme. Wilson originally disliked their music, but, luckily for OMD, Wilson's wife loved it and insisted that their demo tape continued to be played on Tony's car stereo. Wilson turned OMD down for a TV appearance but invited them to make a record on his new Factory label and was subsequently to describe their sound and approach as "the future of pop".[14]

Much to the annoyance of the band, an inevitable reaction was heard from the more conservative voices in music at the time who claimed that the new technology was doing all the work for the band, and that electronic bands were not "real musicians". In response to this, McCluskey politely suggests, "Well you try and do it then!" (West 1982).

Nonetheless, the originality of the band in their instrumentation and lyrical content was setting them apart from the more derivative music in the charts. As Andy explains:

It goes back to wanting to do something differently as a teenager. When we were young, as well as playing different music, we avoided clichéd lyrics. So we would write songs about things which we thought were interesting. We were writing songs about aeroplanes, telephone boxes and oil refineries. If it was a song about a relationship, we would try to make it sound more oblique and I refused to use the word "love" until the third album.[15]

Figure 3: Andy McCluskey in 1985. Photograph by David Elms, OMD Finatics

The rambling thoughts of the adolescent McCluskey were physically inscribed on his bedroom wall in Meols, a suburb of Wirral, where he would jot down ideas and eventually use some of them in OMD songs. Here Andy discusses his sources of inspiration and the unusual subject matter of his lyrics (literally off the wall, in this case):

> At times I became an anorak and went around art galleries, collected postcards and read books. So lyrics for 'Enola Gay', 'Joan of Arc' and 'Tesla Girls' came from that type of source. Without sounding too deep, there are lyrics that also come from somewhere in me. When you listen to a piece of music you have produced and are genuinely excited by it, then you realize that you have done something new and fresh, you feel inspired – you are consciously trying to get yourself into a strange altered state where something is going to come out of you from *I don't know where* and it is those moments which are the eureka moments. You can beat yourself up for weeks and months and nothing comes out – and then out of the blue comes an original idea.[16]

OMD were atypical in the early 1980s when guitar-based bands dominated the pop charts. They were neither manufactured nor image-conscious, as their early television appearances testify. In their first appearance on BBC's flagship TV show *Top of the Pops* in 1980, when their third single 'Messages' had entered the charts, they dressed in plain shirts, with Andy wearing a slim tie.

They mimed badly. They were statuesque, anchored to their keyboards and used a minimal drum kit. Their reel-to-reel tape machine, Winston, twirled around in the background providing the only movement on stage. This was an anti-performance: no jumping around excitely, no over-expressive lead singer – just a straightforward delivery and a song without a refrain.[17]

One could take the view that OMD were using unconventional techniques and taking an anti-fashion stance to court attention. However, it is undeniable that their use of new technology was innovative, and furthermore that they produced great tunes. As BBC broadcaster Spencer Leigh comments:

> You do have the bands like OMD who at the time said "we shun guitars" which was quite a radical thing to do. You talk to Andy McCluskey now and he says he loves guitars. At the time they were making out that they didn't and they were radically different because of this. It was a different sound in the way the synthesizers were being used. In the 1980s when bands were using synthesizers, people thought it was a bit of a gimmick, a bit of a cheap way to do things and much better to have the actual instruments. However, the synth bands in the 1980s did contribute something very valid and I would much rather have, say, OMD to Gary Numan who seems to be lacking in melody whereas Andy McCluskey and Paul Humphreys certainly had melody.[18]

OMD remain one of the seminal bands to emerge from Liverpool during the 1980s. Despite various splits and reformations over the past four decades, they continue to perform to sell-out arenas to the present day. They have produced thirteen albums to date and sold millions of records worldwide. Their legacy is appraised by John Doran, editor of online publication *The Quietus*, who describes them as "One of the best bands ever" and regards them as the only Liverpool band to "live up to the monolithic standards of productivity and creativity set in place by the Beatles" (Doran 2008). Three years later, Doran went on to explain why he rates OMD so highly:

> One group more than any other managed to successfully combine yearning, lovelorn, romantic content within a futuristic, "European", supposedly "cold" form was Liverpool's Orchestral Manoeuvres In The Dark . . . They seem less like a geographical anomaly and more like another big-hearted Liverpool group with an ear for a timeless melody (Doran 2011).

Figure 4: Half Man Half Biscuit in 1986: (left to right) Neil Crossley and Nigel Blackwell. Photograph by Geoff Davies, digitalised by Dave Williams

Another Merseyside band unique in its way of thinking was Half Man Half Biscuit. Like OMD, they came from Wirral, but their music bore no similarity. Along with the two long-standing members of the band, Nigel Blackwell (vocals and guitar) and Neil Crossley (bass), Half Man Half Biscuit's original line-up included Simon Blackwell on lead guitar and Paul Wright on drums. Both musicians had previously played with Birkenhead band Attempted Moustache.

Their earlier material was guitar-based rock verging on punk, whereas the music that followed often defies categorization. The distinctive feature of Half Man Half Biscuit is their unique brand of observational comedy, with raucous music serving as the backdrop to brilliantly witty lyrics. Their perceptive and acerbic views of contemporary society is characterized by a seemingly random choice of subject matter. Some tracks start with one subject and finish on another. A *Liverpool Echo* pop special described them as: "Not so much of a band but a way of life . . . Nobody has ever looked in the mirror of life the way they did . . . Half Man Half Biscuit had a sense of humour as dry as a drought."[19] There is no recognizable pattern to their songs and the lyrics and subject matter can be heard nowhere else. The music often parodies popular music genres while their lyrics lampoon popular culture. The *Liverpool Echo* said of their songs 'The Len Ganley Stance' and 'Dickie

Davies Eyes': "Who else would write a song that was homage to a snooker referee or Dickie Davies?"[20]

The band's manager Geoff Davies describes his initial impressions of the band:

> Nigel and Neil came into Probe Records and left us with their demo tape. I had learnt not to listen to tapes in front of the bands, so I said to them, *"I am not listening to that now!"* Later on I looked at the titles of the songs and I thought if the music is as good as the titles then I'm interested. Annie and I listened to the tape in the car on the way home from work and the first track was 'God Gave us Life'. I listened to the lyrics which were: "God gave us life, so that we could take sweets off strange men in big cars and get driven to the woods to stroke non-existent puppies but he also gave us Una Stubbs, Little and Large Keith Harris . . ." and the list went on and on. I said to Annie, "Did I hear that right?" and Annie said, "Yes." I replied, "Fuckin' hell, isn't that wonderful!" By the time I had listened to the second track I thought I have got to do something with this band. So when they came back to the shop a few days later I said, "It is just great. I want to do an album with you." There was nothing like it. The lyrics were great, there were some great tunes. It was just smashing really: you had just not heard anything like it![21]

The sheer absurdity of the lyrics and unorthodox musical style appealed to Geoff and he agreed to manage and record the band for release on his own Probe Plus label. Although the band has never signed a formal contract with Probe Plus, they began to sell thousands of albums. Their approach both in content and marketing defies convention. One might assume that their strange observational ramblings on random topics would not be saleable. Geoff Davies disagrees:

> I have always been a believer in the idea that no man is an island – so if I like it then someone else is bound to like it too! It may be half a dozen individuals or it may be thousands of people. But I thought that they were great and I could not imagine anyone else thinking otherwise. I got involved with the band because I personally liked it.[22]

Half Man Half Biscuit indeed stirred the consciousness of many, and their appeal was far more widespread than Geoff Davies could have envisaged. Their unique brand of music did prove saleable and their debut album *Back in the DHSS* topped the indie charts and reached number 60 in the national UK album chart. 'The Trumpton Riots' was released as their first single and topped the British independent chart in 1986. This led to an appearance at the Glastonbury Festival the same year.

The band's success defies explanation in terms of conventional approaches to music promotion: the music and lyrics were not mainstream and could not be played on daytime radio. They were difficult to promote to a pop market. They had no obvious image. The lyrics were obscure and contained swearing. And they had no obvious appeal to one particular demographic. No obvious marketing strategy suggested itself. But it was their very bizarreness that was their most effective asset. According to Roger Holland (2006), "HMHB are very English, very angry, very literate, very funny and, above all else, very different."

Their rise to independent chart popularity was propelled by Radio 1 DJ John Peel who played them regularly and recorded twelve sessions with them on his nightly Radio 1 show. He famously commented: "In a decently ordered society, members of Half Man Half Biscuit would be routinely carried shoulder high through the streets of every city they visited."[23]

The appearance of Half Man Half Biscuit on BBC's *The Old Grey Whistle Test* on 6 May 1986 to perform 'The Trumpton Riots' showed how the band were misperceived. In an act of literal-mindedness, the show's producers placed a cutout of the Trumpton fire brigade (from the children's TV show) in their fire engine in front of the band.[24] The establishment (in this case the BBC)'s inability to "get" the band was almost the point: Half Man Half Biscuit cut across the tedious fakery of mainstream culture and spoke the language of ordinary, bored, bright but cynical young people. On the show, as was their habit, the Biscuits did not smile. They were a band who played comic songs, not a band of comics. There were no zany performances, just a sneering delivery of ridiculously funny material.[25]

Despite their lack of image and media-friendliness, Half Man Half Biscuit were becoming increasingly popular nationally, with television, chart placings and tours now a reality. However, Nigel Blackwell, the anti-rock star, refused to be drawn into the clichéd lifestyle and in 1986 the band split up. The reason as quoted by Probe Records was "musical similarities".

Their insistence on shunning publicity was most famously manifested in their refusal to appear on Channel 4's music programme *The Tube*. The reason given was that it coincided with a regular Friday night football fixture at Prenton Park, home of Nigel Blackwell's beloved Tranmere Rovers. Even an offer to transport the band by helicopter to the match after their appearance was refused.

To the delight of their devoted fans, the band reformed in 1990 replacing Simon Blackwell on lead guitar and Paul Wright on drums with Ken Hancock and Carl Henry respectively. They announced their return on the John Peel show. The Biscuits have never looked back and have continued to go from strength to strength. Their approach remains unconventional: they continue to play to large audiences with little in the way of organized publicity, these events being sporadic but attended by fiercely loyal supporters – grown men pogo-dance near the stage as though they were seventeen again. Many now bring their children, although the material is far from family-friendly.

The band produce an album every couple of years which always makes the national independent charts. In order to maintain a regular output, the band rehearses to a workmanlike schedule, which equates to a routine Monday-night session in their secret hideout in Birkenhead. A strict rule is that they will not rehearse on a Bank Holiday Monday because bank holidays should be observed by all workers. The band fiercely protects its anonymity and only rarely gives interviews. Posed photographs of Nigel Blackwell are seldom to be seen in the press. One could take the view that Nigel's approach is revealed in his classic track 'Look Dad No Tunes': "My life is comfortable, but I don't want that image for my band. / Inside I am reasonable but I'll make out they just don't understand."[26]

Nigel's predictable refusal to be interviewed for this book only adds to the enigma that is Half Man Half Biscuit. They are a band that people talk about and often quote, but they themselves do all their own talking in their songs. Some of their songs make little sense but nonetheless strike a chord. Some are dark, but still funny, despite the subject matter. Some are obscure and hard to understand, but still cherished.

Nigel Blackwell is often assumed to be the sole author, but there are also tracks by Neil Crossley. And there are accomplished musical contributions from Carl Henry and Ken Hancock. How the songs emerge remains a mystery, however: their creative process is not as predictable as their rehearsal schedule might suggest. According to drummer Carl Henry: "I think that Nigel is of the opinion that songs just happen and it is impossible to put it into words."[27]

Half Man Half Biscuit have demonstrated new approaches to pop songs bringing in parodies of celebrities and obscure historical characters. As a testament to their enduring popularity, the market for retro Dukla Prague football shirts and Joy Division oven gloves has remained buoyant.[28]

Space

Space is a band from Liverpool formed in 1983, the three original members being Tommy Scott on vocals, bass and guitar, Jamie Murphy on guitar, and Andy Parle on drums. Keyboard player Franny Griffiths joined the band the following year. Space frontman Tommy Scott was brought up in Stockbridge Village on the outskirts of Liverpool where he allegedly drew inspiration for his iconic hit single 'My Beautiful Neighbourhood'. He began in bands such as Hello Sunset and the Australians following an involvement in the North Liverpool Musicians Resource Centre scheme in the 1980s, which was run to help unemployed young people in Liverpool train to become musicians.

(This same scheme brought together other notable Liverpool bands Cast and the La's.)

Figure 5: Tommy Scott (centre) of Space, pictured with the author (right) and producer Neil Duffin, on the set of the *Scouse Pop* TV programme in August 2016. Photograph by Tom Dootson

As mentioned earlier, Space achieved their success in the mid-1990s. Although often associated with the Britpop movement, Space was not typical of those bands. Their unique sound and style was an eclectic mix of whatever seemed to be running through Tommy Scott's mind at the time. Influences are as diverse as post-punk, ska, techno, hip-hop and vintage film scores, with each member of the group having a different taste in music. The lyrics often contain dark humour and deal with unpalatable subjects, such as serial killers ('My Beautiful Neighbourhood'), mental illness ('Dark Clouds') and social outcasts ('I'm Unlike Any Lifeform You've Ever Met').

In an interview with Stuart Maconie, Tommy divulged some of the unlikely influences on his songwriting, which often had little to do with music at all: "I'm into films and telly. The songs I write depends on what film I'm into at the time. Some days I'm Noël Coward, some days I think I'm Quentin Tarantino, some days it's Speedy Gonzales."[29]

The songs Space produce are unique and each album contains a multitude of themes; there can be a mixture of styles within just one song. As such, each track has to be taken individually on its own merits: the listener is not sure what is coming next. For many Space fans, this is the endearing quality that drew them to the band. According to Tommy:

> I used to be called wacky. I used to hate it – but now I just don't care. We were once described as "queasy listening". It is because I just do not want to stick to one genre of music. I am into everything so why can't it just all go into one song? Why would you want to do just country or rock? Why can't you just do what you want?[30]

Tommy's musical logic challenges convention in an industry that likes to categorize artists into marketable genres. Tommy explains the songwriting process:

> I basically write the song and put in a few bits and bobs and then I take it to the lads. I never tell anyone what to do. They all put their own stuff on it. That is good too. Franny puts on his '80s influence and techno stuff, Jamie also put his influence on it (he thought he was in Led Zeppelin) and I put in all my influences from horror movies.
>
> Different musicians alter the dynamics of the band and having played with different people it changes all the time. When we reformed, we listened back to the *Spiders* album: it seemed so slow – it was more like trip-hop, so when we got Phil and Alan in, they were more into punk stuff. They gave the music a raw edge and we sounded a bit more rocked-up when we played it live.[31]

At times, Space's music is utterly confusing yet enjoyable. The *NME*'s review of their 1996 *Spiders* album went: "Ultimately, we have to be thankful for who we are about to receive because Space are worthy of a superlative that is all too rare in new British pop right now. No not 'novelty' just 'unique'."[32] A sardonic humour permeates the music, and very little can be taken at face value. There is a sense of an in-joke being referenced which you are not quite sure about. The cartoon atmosphere within their music has huge appeal. Their audience seem to understand and revel in the madness, with gigs being lively events, the audiences straining at the leash to get out of their seats and have a good time.

There is humour, art, emotion and romance in their music, but presented from such an oblique angle in a way that is rarely seen in other bands. This strangeness makes them stand out. Tommy claims that this uniqueness is organic and was never manufactured:

> I didn't go out of my way to write odd music: it just happened – it's the way I write. We just didn't want to be like every other band. We went into a practice room with a song; we then recorded it and

released it. We didn't know what would happen after that. There was no plan; it was just natural. If Space had been contrived, it would have been rubbish.[33]

There was a distinctive Scouse swagger about the band and a bemusing perspective on life. Aaron Cooper (2015) wrote:

> The most popular single from [the] album . . . would probably be 'Female of the Species'. Like most of the album, it straddles the fine line between being genius and utterly annoying. In early 1997 there was nothing like it on pop radio, with it's [sic] over the top, cheeky lyrics about falling in love with a female super villain, teamed with it's [sic] smooth 1960s jazz with generic late 1990s production. After all these years, I still can't tell if they were serious or trying to make the weirdest pop music ever recorded.

Tommy acknowledges some of his musical influences but they do not appear to be the main driving force behind his ideas. He cites the originality of local Liverpool bands the Teardrop Explodes, Echo and the Bunnymen and OMD as inspiration and also cites personal favourites Spizzenergi who were role models in using a broad palette: "The Liverpool '80s scene is the best for me because the bands were different. You would have Teardrops and the Bunnymen then OMD. They were all different and Liverpool was like that in the '80s."[34]

A unique-sounding band from a city with a musical heritage, they walked a fine line between accessibility and originality. Surprisingly, Space's appeal translated to other parts of the world, bringing them international success. Tommy offers an explanation of how Space became a successful export to the United States: "America was the home of 'quirk' anyway – they've got bands like Devo and Beck – so they liked us. It was a great feeling to go there and see a crowd queueing around the block to see us play."[35]

The appeal of the band's music persuaded the hit British TV drama of the 1990s *Cold Feet* to adopt 'Female of the Species' as its theme tune. The series centred on three couples and their tangled relationships in a comic and melancholy drama which appealed to a prime mass audience slot at 9 pm on ITV. 'Female of the Species' has a Latin-flavoured beat and crooned vocals laced with a seductive sense of fun. It was also used behind the credits on the 1997 film *Austin Powers: International Man of Mystery*. Tommy has latterly explained that the song is in fact about the bride of Frankenstein, with the title being lifted from Rudyard Kipling's 1911 poem 'The Female of the Species'. Tommy has an amusing take on the popularity of the song and its association with the TV series:

My wife had bought me tickets to see Tom Jones. I was surprised when he came on stage and sang 'Female of the Species'. All the housewives got up and started dancing and singing away to my song. I was sat there quietly in the audience watching all of this going on and they didn't have a clue who I was! I think the TV series made the song better known than the band.[36]

China Crisis

Figure 6: China Crisis. Eddie Lundon with Gary Daly in the background, Cavern Club, 2012. Photograph by Gareth Noon

This notion of inventing a genre using new ways of thinking was also employed by Kirkby band China Crisis. Chapter 1 has outlined their initial attempts to develop a career in music and how their unique sound was drawn from their experimental early days trying out new ideas despite limited access to space and funds. Gary Daly explains their mind-set in their early days:

> Kirkby in the '80s was a bit like today, it was all Job Creation but no real jobs for young people, so you had to take work experience. But the difference was that you weren't quite so hounded about your dole like you are today, so it was enough if you were living at home to sort of pay a little bit of your dole for your keep and it would see you through. With the small amount of money we had left we got the synths and the bass guitar from Mum's catalogue. We certainly weren't New Romantics, all frilly shirts and that sort of thing. That was a cardinal sin. That was London. We were Liverpool . . .[37]

China Crisis attracted the attention of a local record company quite early on in their careers when a demo tape was passed to Inevitable Records boss Jeremy Lewis via a New Romantic band from Wirral called Through a Glass Darkly. China Crisis's first release on Inevitable was 'African and White', an unusual track with hypnotic rhythms which were half human, half drum machine. The compelling rhythm was influenced by the third member of the band, Dave Reilly, a talented teenager engaging with a new style of drumming. At the forefront of a new breed of drummers eschewing the old rock clichés, he seemed to have an inbuilt metronome and no great ego about whether he or the drum machine was most prominent in the track; he expanded the range of rhythms that could be used through a clever combination of real and synthetic sounds. 'African and White' oozed emotion with a relaxed and sensitive feel: the guitar work floated cleverly around the track in a mixture of background ambience, occasional rhythm and punctuating strums which drifted over the mechanical rhythms. A unique and convincing vocal drew the listener in to a song about apartheid in South Africa in which the songwriting craft was mature and the subject matter topical. The music lacked any of the clichés of its contemporaries, using guitars, drums and synthesizers in alternative ways. Reviewing 'African and White' and other early tracks, Peter Martin described the band in *Merseysound* as "Funky scientists concocting sparse rhythmically interesting hypnotic clean songs to awake the nation."[38]

Despite only reaching the lower reaches of the charts, 'African and White' went on to sell over a quarter of a million copies (including re-releases). It caused a stir and became one of Liverpool's favourite tracks in the early 1980s without being a massive chart hit.

Following the moderate success of 'African and White', Inevitable Records released a second single, 'Scream Down at Me', which revealed a different style of writing: the hypnotic rhythms were still there but the track was angry and disorienting. A malevolent feeling was captured without resorting to distorted guitars or screaming vocals. Although Gary and Eddie claim to be unhappy about its release, 'Scream Down at Me' set the precedent for China Crisis's distinctive take on the world with songs that set them apart from other bands. The Inevitable Records phase turned out to be a brief transitional one, and the band eventually signed to major label Virgin Records, a move that was to lead to chart success.

Their breakthrough hit 'Christian' was an unusual song to make it into the charts: it was not as immediately appealing as 'African and White' and bore no similarity to the music dominating the hit parade at the time. Gary explains how this song became an unlikely choice for a single and how their distinctive style often caused issues with professionals who were trying to record the band:

> Virgin Records had not really made a decision on what track should be the next single. In fact, we had walked out of quite a few

recording sessions when making the first album, saying "We are not working with him!" So we had put three singles out by then and not had chart success with any of them.

We were at the record company offices one day and one of the girls from telesales said, "I know what your next single should be." The telesales staff all loved 'Christian'. Nobody at Virgin or even me and Ed had thought of that track as our next single. Virgin decided to go with the telesales staff and released it as the single. It took about eight weeks after Christmas to make it into the charts before we got the call from *Top of the Pops* . . .[39]

'Christian' stood out from other songs in the charts at the time; its appeal was its strange, otherworldly sound – what Radio Merseyside DJ Roger Hill described as "More of a mood which takes you over". Eddie Lundon explains:

And in the middle of Spandau Ballets, New Romantic bands and all that kind of stuff, we come out with a fucking big ballad! [laughs] . . . In many ways, though, that was going against the grain as well. Just like 'African and White' was going against the grain, it was quite political. It used unusual sounds, sounded quite fresh, and 'Christian' itself, to this day I still believe it was unique when it came out. Everyone was focused on the Durannies or the Spandaus and all that kind of stuff with an up-tempo New Romantic thing. Then we come in and do a ballad – no one was doing ballads at the time, no one. I'm not talking like your power ballads – again, it was kind of eerie, you know with the fretless bass, synth sounds, and just the little guitars picking away and the beautiful melody. So, again, it was different sounds, and it was unusual for a ballad to come out at that time. It kind of worked in our favour.[40]

The band had not completed the conventional "apprenticeship" route of regular gigs: they had done some early shows with their original line-up but were by no means the finished article. So the band that was summoned to appear on national television for *Top of the Pops* on 27 January 1983 consisted of two young lads who were used to playing tracks in their bedrooms. The quiet dreamy ballad combined with a static performance by the duo left *Top of the Pops* producers struggling to work out exactly what to do with them. There was little movement on stage and no other band members to focus on: just the two lads miming, so the television crew pumped out some smoke and had a couple of dancers swaying in the background. While the New Romantics of the day dressed flamboyantly and gyrated wildly, China Crisis tucked their shirts in and buttoned them to the top. Offering no feast of visual delights, just a hauntingly beautiful ballad that went against the grain of all the other music on the show that night, China Crisis stood out.[41]

'Christian' received mixed reviews. Adam Sweeting of the *NME* wrote: "'Christian' is a pretty fragile song attached to a rather revolting video".[42] Nonetheless, the song reached number 12 in the national charts after sustained national airplay.

Their debut album, *Difficult Shapes and Passive Rhythms: Some People Think It's Fun to Entertain*, was symptomatic of a band that had gone from formation to releasing records on a major label in a relatively short period. As such, it presented an eclectic set of songs quite unlike one another and produced by a variety of different individuals, including Steve Levine, Peter Walsh, Jeremy Lewis, Gil Norton and China Crisis themselves. The album established China Crisis as a band that was different and innovative, although Gary denies this being a conscious effort:

> It wasn't a conscious decision that we're gonna work in our bedrooms and be different from everyone. What everyone else was doing didn't appeal to us that much. We were quite happy just being us and we were learning from all the Enoisms and the Bowieisms and from people like OMD and Kraftwerk. You didn't need to have a band. You could just record and play with machines and if you think about it, you know a portastudio meant four tracks plus recording on a cassette, which is all very accessible so we were actually making music and mastering it onto a cassette deck so we could go home with all these tunes that we'd recorded. Imagine what a thrill that'd be. We made great-sounding recordings which just spurred us on and on.[43]

The second album, *Working with Fire and Steel (Possible Pop Songs Volume Two)*, saw Mike Howlett installed as producer. Any expectations that this album would be more consistent in terms of genre were unfulfilled and another mixture of songs with contrasting styles was the result. Only the two singles 'Tragedy and Mystery' and 'Wishful Thinking' bore any resemblance to mainstream pop music. Other tracks were the sub-reggae vibe of 'Papua', the ballad 'Soul Awakening' and a memorable electronic folk song called 'The Gates of Door to Door'. An album bursting with such a variety of ideas was a challenge for any producer but Mike Howlett was equal to the task. Each track was addressed individually and had a life of its own. Peter Martin wrote in *Merseysound*: "China Crisis are helping to reawaken the decrepit institution of pop and are carving their name on the new pop revival."[44]

China Crisis continued to evolve in terms of style and delivery. Their songwriting never remained static and their third album with producer Walter Becker became their most successful in terms of sales. Their sound was now more mainstream and defined. Becker demanded more from the band in terms of writing and performance, an issue that the producer faced head on, as Gary explains:

Walter was a strict taskmaster and Steely Dan were known in the industry as studio boffins. We had an amazing drummer with Kevin Wilkinson and a great bass player in Gary Johnson, but Walter put us through a steep learning curve. He said, "You guys are great songwriters but you are not top-quality musicians." I knew Kev and Gaz were – but we weren't. Ed and I were not great musicians, we were self-taught. We also taught ourselves how to write songs. So Walter made us think that we were not making records amongst ourselves. He showed us how we should use every available musician and instrument to make the songs the very best they could be.[45]

What remained unique about the band during the Becker phase was the songs' unusual subject matter, an aspect actively encouraged by Becker. In fact, this was a factor that had drawn him to produce the band in the first place, having been intrigued by 'Papua' on *Working with Fire and Steel*, a song about the hydrogen bomb tests in the South Pacific. Singles from the Becker-produced album, entitled *Flaunt the Imperfection*, included 'Black Man Ray' and 'King in a Catholic Style', neither of which have orthodox pop song lyrics. Despite the album's commercial success, the national music press remained unconvinced, Ted Mico writing in *Melody Maker*:

China Crisis, a group that has elevated mundanity to lethal proportions . . . China Crisis are about to unleash another clutch of finely chiselled melodies encased in the armour of inconsequence and wielding all the vehement emotional qualities of a ripe black pudding.[46]

Despite the stinging criticism, *Flaunt the Imperfection* charted in seven countries around the world and received a gold disc for its sales in the UK. The band continued to enjoy international success during the 1980s, and two albums – *What Price Paradise* produced by Clive Langer and Alan Winstanley, and *Diary of a Hollow Horse*, again produced by Walter Becker – provided more well-crafted songs of a high quality. Unfortunately, the latter two albums surprisingly failed to deliver the commercial success of their earlier work, despite featuring classic tracks 'Arizona Sky', 'June Bride' (*What Price Paradise*), 'St Saviour's Square' and 'Red Letter Day' (*Diary of a Hollow Horse*). Conversely, reviews in the national music press were more positive. "The Legend", reviewing *What Price Paradise* for the *NME*, said: "At their best 'Arizona Sky' is well worth following with its smooth, mellow, guitar chiming sound."[47] Eddie Lundon ascribes the better reviews but poorer sales to two main factors:

Firstly, I think by then that the record company may have had enough of us and weren't fully committed to promoting the albums as well as the earlier ones. And the second thing was that the albums were released at a time when the rave scene and Manchester indie dance scene was prominent and we were not part of that. We had received mixed reviews in the past even when we were successful but when our sound did not fit in with the indie dance scene the reviews got better. There is no point taking too much notice of the music press. We have never really listened to them or taken any notice of what they had to say.[48]

Since the late 1990s, China Crisis has concentrated on live performances all over the world which feature original members Eddie and Gary supplemented by a variety of other musicians changing over the years. They continued to write but remained unconvinced that there was public appetite for a new album. However, they decided to test that proposition in 2014 via the Pledge Music website, which gave them an overwhelmingly positive response. The band returned to the studio to record the *Autumn in the Neighbourhood* album, which was released in 2015. Although it was their first studio album for 21 years, some of the songs were based on ideas that had been worked on by the original line-up. Gary explains:

I always wanted to make another record. I thought Ed and I were a good writing team. We had started writing an album in the '90s. It gave us chance to finish some of the recordings which were started with the classic China Crisis line-up. So five of the tracks were with the original line-up and the rest are augmented with new songs. We always continued writing. It is not something you forget to do. Some people are so successful that they do not feel the need to write anymore. We are not like that.[49]

Over two decades had passed since their previous album but the quality and variety remained consistent. As older and wiser songwriters, the subject matter covered an even broader spectrum. The work ethic and resilience of the band are just as strong, if not stronger, than in their youth. Gary and Eddie are comfortable with what they produce and are no longer under any pressure from record companies to conform. Negative and positive reviews are both received with indifference. They were never a band that conformed and were consistently stubborn about what they wanted for their songs – in fact, belief in their songs is what united China Crisis in the first place, as discussed in the previous chapter with regard to the model of resilience. Their process remains the same. Gary explains how China Crisis songs are created through a mixture of inspiration, vigilance and sheer hard work:

Inspiration is around us all day and all the time and in all manner of situations but the actual writing is a process of sitting down, mostly with an instrument, and working hard. That means putting the hours in sitting there and playing. Usually, if you do that enough and work hard, some words will pop into the process as you are playing something. That becomes the foundation of a new song. Now it could be something in your subconscious or something welling up inside you or something you have seen that day. It could be anything. What you do then is to be vigilant! You are ready for that to happen! It is not that it happens all the time. It is a trick which we taught ourselves to do. Even as young as fourteen or fifteen, we were listening to music that other people were making and listening how they were putting all the elements of their songs together. Then by the time we were sixteen or seventeen, by trying to learn from other people's songs we had taught ourselves that actually this is how you write your own songs. You sit there and diligently work and work and that is how it happens.[50]

*   *   *

All the bands featured in this section of the chapter had in common a divergent way of thinking which ultimately defined them as different. This allowed them to create songs that took the listener to new places not visited by mainstream pop songs. Decades later, the bands continue to produce high-quality tracks in a variety of styles.

2. Attitudes (wanting to be "someone")

Gay icons in leather knickers. Seagulls live in smelly transit van.
Man on stilts dances to Echo and the Bunnymen. Wah! blow John Peel's socks off.

The second aspect of Norman Jackson's view of creativity is concerned with attitudes. The traits of creative attitude centre on: curiosity, a willingness to explore, and risk taking. This creative attitude is also complemented by enthusiasm, determination and obsession (Jackson 2011). Roger Hill believes that there were dominant personalities who were destined to be members of seminal bands and were always going to be noticed either through controversy, fashion or personality. The four bands featured in this section all have such distinctive personalities in their line-ups. Roger comments: "The bands were also ego-led with individuals who would not allow themselves to fail . . . even if they had to redefine the notion of failure."[51]

Frankie Goes to Hollywood, A Flock of Seagulls, Echo and the Bunnymen and Wah! were all bands who enjoyed international success and had individuals in the bands who were determined to be successful. Each band had an idiosyncratic image and a distinctive sound.

Frankie Goes to Hollywood had an irresistibly gritty sound forged from the heartbeat of the band's backline of Pete Gill on drums, Mark O'Toole on bass and Brian Nash on guitar. The band was fronted by two enigmatic and flamboyantly gay vocalists, Paul Rutherford and Holly Johnson. They oozed controversy, character and curiosity even before they had struck a note. Paul Lester (2014) wrote in *The Guardian*: "They were a one-off: two self-styled 'ferocious homosexuals' up front, backed by three prototype Liam Gallaghers, who were known as 'The Lads'."

A Flock of Seagulls emerged with distinctive hairstyles and fashion sense which complemented their particular brand of power pop. Mike Score had the face of a pop star and was always going to be noticed. In an article for *Trouser Press* in 1982, Mike compared A Flock of Seagulls to their contemporaries in Liverpool at the time and outlined their determination to succeed commercially: "We were aggressive/new and they were laid-back/new. We went to London and gigged there for six months. We set a policy not to play Liverpool for at least a year, until after we got signed to do the first album" (Goldstein 1982).

Echo and the Bunnymen had an air of mystique and a coolness epitomized by their enigmatic lead singer Ian McCulloch. Their quirky beginnings as three skinny indie kids with a drum machine playing the Everyman Bistro on Friday lunchtimes could not hide the dominant personalities that shone through their music. According to Chris Salewicz writing in the *NME*:

> McCulloch is the man, the group's ace face and teen heart-throb even though in profile he's really a bit chinless. He is the front man for this welter of sound which contains every emotion you can think of and is so much more than the sum of its parts.[52]

Wah! featured Pete Wylie. Pete was a charismatic character on the Liverpool music scene and was destined to be famous. Inevitable Records boss Jeremy Lewis said of him: "Pete had talent, attitude, personality and desire. He was always going to succeed."[53]

Frankie Goes to Hollywood

Frankie Goes to Hollywood were arguably the last great pop sensation to dominate the British music charts. Barney Hoskyns (1984) describes the astonishing success of the band:

> That a group should make the fourth-best selling British single of all time with their first release is remarkable; that they should

follow it up with the eleventh best-selling British single of all time is freakish. Phenomenon is the only word for it: Liverpool's Frankie Goes to Hollywood, like Michael Jackson, have made people buy records again.

The nucleus of the group emerged from the Eric's post-punk scene. Lead singer Holly Johnson was the former bass player with Big in Japan and had also released two solo singles. Frankie's original backline of Pete Gill on drums and Mark O'Toole on bass had been in a band named Sons of Egypt. Paul Rutherford from Hambi and the Dance subsequently joined, and finally Brian Nash on guitar united with his old friends and the famous record-breaking quintet was born. Johnson reported that the band's name is derived from the headline "Frankie Goes Hollywood" which appeared in the *New Yorker* magazine, regarding the emergence of Frank Sinatra as a film star. However, the *New Yorker* magazine piece was actually a pop art poster by artist Guy Peellaert, famous for designing David Bowie's *Diamond Dogs* album cover (Nash 2012).

Figure 7: Brian Nash of Frankie Goes to Hollywood (left) on the set of the **Scouse Pop** TV programme in November 2015, pictured with producer Neil Duffin (centre) and the author (right). Photograph by Clare Chabeaux

The meteoric rise and burnout of the band was startling even by the pop industry's standards of transience. The band certainly took risks and courted controversy but their impact on the pop scene cannot be overstated. Their first three singles all went to number 1 in the UK charts despite controversial subject matters of sex, global destruction and religion, respectively. Their Scouse traits of humour, self-deprecation and an ability to make an incisive comment only added to their appeal. They were larger-than-life characters who were able to take pot shots at the world with a tongue-in-cheek sarcasm and sardonic humour that resonated with youth. Richard Cook writing in *NME* reviewed their first album: "It is of course brilliant . . . It can't be crystallized into a neat menu of responses . . . they are in every area a pop phenomenon."[54]

From a public perspective, Frankie Goes to Hollywood was a musical phenomenon. The most obvious difference from other bands at the time was their structure, with the three "lads" on the backline forming the heartbeat of the band and two gay frontmen coordinating a dramatic performance. Holly Johnson and Paul Rutherford pushed the boundaries of decency in the 1980s as reported by Paul Lester in *The Guardian*: "Frankie are the most scandalous affront to decency since the Sex Pistols and the biggest band, Liverpudlian or otherwise, since the Beatles."[55]

There were relatively few openly gay celebrities in the public eye at that time, significantly fewer than today. However, the unconventional mix of heterosexual and homosexual band members with swagger, personality and attitude clearly had huge appeal for their adoring fans which included an army of teenage girls. Guitarist Brian Nash has a different view of the outrageous clothes and stage antics:

> We were into Mad Max and that is where some of the clothes style came from. It was all about dressing up, and if Paul and Holly wanted to go on stage in leather knickers then that was fine with us. As for the gay thing, we were in conservative times. If Frankie had started now then nobody would have batted an eyelid. But in those days Boy George said he would sooner have a cup of tea than sex and George Michael always had a pretty girl on his arm. But we were different from them: we were not playing a career game, we were just out there having a laugh. When the early Frankies played it was like Mad Max. We were here to invade the audience but it was with our guitars and our music.[56]

Paul Morley, whose label ZTT had signed Frankie Goes to Hollywood, commented in *The Guardian*: "Heterosexual Scouse energy and this very exploratory gay energy, all mixed up in one place. It was a ridiculous formula and you couldn't have planned it – it was too toxic."[57] This was followed by the epidemic of Morley's inspired "Frankie Says . . ." T-shirts, which sold in their millions, matching the record sales. There was a unique presence about the band which was exploited in an astute manner by ZTT.

Much of Frankie Goes to Hollywood's success could be attributed to the excellent production of ZTT co-founder Trevor Horn. However, an obvious difference between the manufactured bands prominent in today's corporate pop world and Frankie Goes to Hollywood is that the latter existed as a band well before Trevor Horn stamped his distinctive sound on them. Indeed, the band had a look and an attitude driven by ambitious personalities which Horn recognized and felt was workable for the label. The band also had the songs in place that defined their musical direction.

ZTT were able to present the band to the world as individuals who were always destined to be successful. They had a unique formula. Brian Nash comments:

> You fancy it because you can play a guitar, but fame was no more likely than playing centre forward for Liverpool. At best it was just your aspiration to have fun and do a gig and maybe at the back of your mind is "It would be great to get on *Top of the Pops*", but I didn't think realistically that's where I am going and that is where I'm going to end up. It's about talent but also about being in the right place at the right time.[58]

The packaging and promotion was sophisticated and precisely executed by ZTT. Frankie Goes to Hollywood was a bizarre mix, a one-off spectacle, but the strangeness of it all worked well creatively and commercially to achieve spectacular success for a couple of years in the mid-1980s. The usual questions were asked about how much of the creative process and success was a reflection of the band, or the genius of the producer. Brain Nash explains:

> Having a good producer is important. There is a world of difference between going into a recording studio and recording your song and going into a recording studio and making the record. They are two separate things. We heard the new version of 'Relax' for the first time sitting in the manager's car on Hanover Street. When it came on the car stereo we looked at each other and said, "That's what we thought it could sound like." It didn't sound like what we had originally recorded: it sounded amazing! Even when I listen to it now, sonically it still stands up.[59]

However the enthusiasm, determination and obsession rapidly morphed into acrimony and despair as ZTT brought their own interpretations to the songs' core concepts, which the band felt had been impaired rather than developed. This naturally led to tension and at times bemusement. Brian Nash explains:

> The band's first suggestion for the video of 'Two Tribes' was about a gang of skinheads smashing up a Rolls Royce, showing the working classes and the upper classes. But I asked, "Who is going to buy a Rolls Royce to smash the fuck out of?" The label said that they couldn't afford a Rolls Royce in the budget. I remember hearing the

ideas for the video from the record company and asking, "Do we have to be in it?" By then we had done three 'Relax' videos and it was boring hanging around all day doing something you don't feel very comfortable with.[60]

Issues regarding creativity continued with the third number-1-selling single 'The Power of Love'. Former members of 10cc Kevin Godley and Lol Creme directed the video to accompany the haunting ballad, a very different video from their first two for 'Relax' and 'Two Tribes', this one depicting the assumption of the Virgin Mary and the Nativity story. It was a fully costumed video, religious in content and a surprising departure for a band that had scandalized conservative 1980s Britain. 'The Power of Love' is now firmly established as a perennial Christmas song. However, the video's visual interpretation did not meet with the band's approval, as Brian Nash explains: "The song was nothing to do with religion! I remember seeing the video and dying . . . thinking what a load of shit!"[61] Brian recollects that the band members did not feature in the original version and were added later as a response to their complaints to the record company. They eventually appeared on the official video as characters on the outside of a picture frame that surrounded the drama of the Nativity story (Nash 2012).

Frankie Goes to Hollywood, regardless of ZTT, were always creative in their attitude and their success was astonishing. Many commentators in the music press have cited the quality of ZTT's marketing strategies and how music journalists employed by the label had stage-managed the most successful band of the 1980s. However Brian Nash points out:

> If it was all down to the brilliance of their marketing strategies, then why did it not work for the other bands they signed to their label? Why were they not able to have the same success as Frankie Goes to Hollywood?[62]

The success of Frankie Goes to Hollywood was indeed spectacular. 'Relax' is the sixth-biggest-selling single in UK history and remained in the charts for a whole year. They also stood at number 1 and 2 in the charts with 'Two Tribes' and 'Relax'. This was a feat last performed by the Beatles in the 1960s with 'Hello Goodbye' and the *Magical Mystery Tour* EP. The mix of art, controversy and commerce resulted in the brightest and loudest firework to explode in the UK music scene during the 1980s.

The band became world-famous and achieved commercial and artistic success beyond the boundaries of any other British band in the 1980s. Characteristically Liverpudlian in attitude and personality, they merged creative attitudes with a desire to succeed and cemented their place in pop history.

A Flock of Seagulls

Figure 8: Frank Maudsley of A Flock of Seagulls (centre) on the set of the **Scouse Pop** TV programme, September 2016, pictured with Neil Duffin (left) and the author (right).
Photograph by Kayleigh Heaps

The characteristics of A Flock of Seagulls were pop creativity and a distinctive fashion style. The unusual musical influences of the individuals in the band resulted in a unique sound. The band had an impact both nationally and internationally and became more successful in the US than in the UK. Their album track 'DNA' won a Grammy award in 1983 for the best rock instrumental performance. They were also nominated for two further Grammys, a feat no other Liverpool band of the 1980s could equal.

A Flock of Seagulls became household names in the US and the band is mentioned in sitcoms such as *Friends* and *Two and a Half Men*. They were also referenced in the 1994 cult film *Pulp Fiction* and their song 'I Ran' is used in the 2016 film soundtrack for *La La Land*. Their iconic hairstyles and British 'rocky' edge made them palatable to the more conservative American music market.

The 'Thanksgiving' episode of American sitcom *Friends* (1987) has a scene in which characters nostalgically recall the 1980s. A flashback episode includes the bizarre Flock of Seagulls "waterfall" hairstyle sported by Chandler Bing, one of the male characters: the volume of the canned laughter is turned up as Bing enters the room with a gelled quiff resembling some of the River Mersey's more powerful wave formations.[63] As the sitcom suggests, the Flock of Seagulls waterfall hairstyle was copied by teenagers across the US and their fashion and sound became embedded in the pop culture. This style did not escape criticism from some sections of the music press. Tim Russell (2017) reminisces on their impact on pop culture in the early 1980s: "Thanks to their admittedly preposterous haircuts, featured in some of the most cringeworthy publicity shots of the 1980s, Liverpool synth-pop quartet A Flock of Seagulls have become a byword for the perceived excesses of the decade."

The hairstyles and the music were born in a hairdresser's salon in Liverpool where Mike Score made his living cutting, styling and shampooing. The shop building also doubled as a rehearsal space for the band. The band's drummer Ali Score reminisces:

> Liverpool at the time was hotbed of music that was all different ... An exciting time ... If you wanted to do anything or be anybody, then you had to be in music. Mike was a hairdresser and Frank worked for him. Paul was an apprentice auto mechanic. I was an electrician. I was getting well paid; I had a good job as an electrician. Mike's hairdressers shop was also doing well. We were surviving. After hearing other local bands, we thought we'd try and do music of our own. We had a guy playing drums and he left his kit in the shop. Then one night he didn't turn up so we tried out the equipment as a band and it worked. We were happy-go-lucky. I think we just developed as people, and as musicians. We just developed our own style. It was a transition. I like heavy rock music so my playing was influenced by that and listening to all kind of things. We all had different influences and the music just naturally emerged.
>
> In the early days of the band it was just guitars. We didn't have synths to start with. The use of synths came later because they were only just being manufactured. The big guitars and the synths helped to define our sound. We always had a plan and we knew we could play.[64]

The first guitarist in A Flock of Seagulls was Willy Woo. He gave the band a more conventional rocky edge which made their early songs sound more heavy rock and less pop-focused. When Willy left the band, Paul Reynolds replaced him on guitar. Paul's unique guitar style in combination with the addition of new synthesizer sounds formed the bedrock of the definitive Flock of Seagulls sound. Bass player Frank Maudsley describes the change of guitarist:

> Mike and Willy did not see eye to eye on the music. Willy could play 25,000 notes a second and Mike did not want that. He tried slowing him down and asked him to play a more definitive riff for 'I Ran'. This went on for a while and one day we just got a little note through the door from Willy saying that he had left the band. A couple of weeks later, I was going home on the bus and I saw a

young lad with a guitar in a bin bag tied up with string at the top. I had heard that he was in bands so I asked him to come along and have a jam with us and that was Paul Reynolds. He was sixteen years old at the time.[65]

Managers Tommy Crossan and Mick Rossi spotted the potential of the band having seen them playing in some of Liverpool's less prestigious venues. Maudsley recalls how the Seagulls latched on to the prospect of having managers based in London in their attempt to obtain a record deal:

> Tommy was the sound guy for Liverpool band the Yachts. We gave him a tape and we were made up that he had connections in London. Tommy said, "Come down and have a chat with us." So we packed all of our personal items into a transit van and went and camped outside his house in the van. We all lived in it. It was a horrible van and it stank![66]

The band were determined to follow their dream and their strong personalities made sure that they would succeed at all costs. Alan Bennett was not the only inhabitant of London with someone living in a van outside his house.

Tommy Crossan and Mick Rossi were impressed by the determination of the band as well as their music and managed to secure a deal with Jive Records to release their first single, 'Telecommunication'. It became popular on the American dance scene. Other tracks they had recorded fell into a wide variety of categories such as rock, pop and New Romantic, and so Crossan and Rossi saw that the band could be marketed in a variety of ways. Initially, they toured with Squeeze, who were in the top 5 in the US billboard chart. As Squeeze started to drop down the charts, A Flock of Seagulls started to rise with 'Telecommunication' eventually becoming a top 10 hit in the US. The band continued to support Squeeze even though they had now eclipsed them in terms of popularity. The Seagulls accepted that they were learning their trade and that determination, as well as a strong work ethic, would eventually prevail. Their strategy paid off and A Flock of Seagulls were rewarded with some support slots on the Police's 'Synchronicity' world tour – one of the highest-grossing tours of the 1980s. Frank explains:

> We played so many gigs. It started off in clubs and wine bars. The earlier gigs were packed out. We called them sweat boxes because the moisture dripped off the walls. I lost so much weight playing the gigs. Sometimes we would do two a day – a matinee *and* a night-time gig. Then gradually we went to bigger and bigger venues ending up in concert halls.[67]

Their creative use of huge guitar sounds, electronic beats and memorable pop refrains were complemented by enthusiasm, determination and obsession. The work ethic of the band was admirable: they gigged solidly in the US until they had deafened the American public into submission and broke into the billboard charts. As Ali Score comments:

> The biggest thing was we worked hard. We played every night. In the early days we played 120 shows in a row in the States, night after night. We were determined that they were going to like us whether they wanted to or not! It was sheer hard work and bloody-mindedness.[68]

Frank Maudsley also comments on the sheer determination of the band to work hard and become a success:

> You can take on the mantle of "I want to succeed" and the more you keep working at it, in anything, the more you will progress. Hard work means you become more of a unit and the chemistry in the band starts to work. You can pre-empt what the other players are going to do next.[69]

As mentioned above, American audiences copied their fashion sense, the mixture of an unusual sound and an unusual look offering an appeal to American teenagers, as Ali Score explains:

> The hair was a big part – people had to have something to focus on. Our fashion was a factor and the music was a factor and it just all came together. I was jeans and a T-shirt man but Mike and Frank used to go down the high street and say, "I like that but it's a girls' shirt, but I think we can get away with wearing it anyway."[70]

Frank openly admits to this cross-dressing phase as an attempt to create an image for the band that would set them apart from others. Their distinctive style also started to have an impact on youth culture and appearance in the US, as Frank explains:

> I would go shopping in Chelsea Girl and buy shirts with buttons across the shoulders because they looked a bit futuristic. I would also buy harem trousers from there and put them together with a pair of winkies [winklepickers]. No one in America had seen anything like it. They were all long hair and boots with checked shirts and heavy metal T-shirts underneath. All the clothes I wore in the band were female clothes. We would be walking down the street in America looking like proper nancy boys. But they loved it

and kids in the audience would start copying us in the things that we wore. They also had the haircuts and would do a waterfall sign with their fingers.[71]

The band was also in the right place at the right time to deliver something unconventional: that is, in the US when MTV was in its infancy. The most powerful medium for music pre-MTV was the radio: and in the early 1980s sustained airplay was the way to achieve a hit record, so the look of bands was largely secondary. Many bands sounded good but had little visual appeal before MTV and still managed to secure massive hit records. A Flock of Seagulls' breakthrough was achieved by gambling some of their early resources on making a video. By modern standards, it was mediocre, but MTV still had a limited supply of pop videos from bands, so when an odd-looking and strange-sounding band appeared in their in-tray, they played the video on repeat. A 1983 review in *Rolling Stone* commented:

> Among other groups that enjoyed substantial commercial break-throughs were Duran Duran, Adam Ant, Haircut One Hundred and, most startlingly, A Flock of Seagulls, who turned a quick two-week tour into a six-month stay in the States and wound up with a gold record. "We used dance-club play to get AOR airplay," says Arista president Clive Davis. "It helped that Flock used guitars and a real drum sound. But the barriers are coming down; these groups were in the forefront and broke through the barriers" (Connelly 1983).

A later retrospective review in the same publication stated:

> A Flock of Seagulls were the perfect band for 1982. They had crazy haircuts, a near-perfect New Wave single and a video for MTV. The video [for 'I Ran'] . . . looks like it was filmed over the course of about 10 minutes inside a trashcan – but that didn't matter. MTV played the hell out of 'I Ran (So Far Away),' and before they knew it, A Flock of Seagulls were opening up for the Police at stadiums (*Rolling Stone* 2012).

Frank Maudsley acknowledges the power of MTV and the use of the pop video. But he defends the band, claiming that it was the strength of the music that made A Flock of Seagulls a hit: "Although the video was cheaply made, the song still did really well despite the video. That to me shows that the song must have been good."[72]

In hindsight, A Flock of Seagulls achieved the success that their hard work deserved. Groundbreaking use of electronic instrumentation mixed with a New Wave guitar style ensured a different sound, the development of which was partly due to the excellence of Mike Howlett and Bill Nelson's production, but also due to the variety of musical influences within the band. However, the main ingredient was the attitude and determination of the individuals involved. Frank Maudsley sums this up:

> I was always up for it and game for anything. Some people are not flexible like me and won't do things because they can't be bothered. I wasn't a yes-man but I always thought you have to try. You have to work at things and have a bit of give and take.[73]

Echo and the Bunnymen

Figure 9: Ian McCulloch of Echo and the Bunnymen. Photograph by Denise Hodgkinson

Echo and the Bunnymen were establishing a following in the city by the late 1970s. The comparisons made between the developing style of the band and that of the Doors were a little overstated and perhaps too focused on the impressive vocal style of Ian McCulloch, whose voice had a passing resemblance to that of Jim Morrison, while the guitar-based music had '60s psychedelic undertones. However, the assumption that the Bunnymen were derivatives of the Doors does not stand up to scrutiny. The first obvious difference was that the early Bunnymen used a rhythm machine; secondly, Les Pattinson's bass lines were busy and complicated to compensate for the lack of a drummer; and, thirdly, Will Sergeant's guitar craft was quite different from Robby Krieger's, avoiding standard riffs and presenting a unique style which was as melodic as it was menacing. The sound, delivered in fits and starts, weaved in and out of the general groove. The original material was as bewildering as it was wonderful: there was nobody around that sounded quite like Echo and the Bunnymen. Local and national music press were quick to recognize that the band were different and possessed creative attitudes. Johnny Rogan of *Record Collector* wrote: "Many people would contend that Echo and the Bunnymen are the most important group to emerge from Liverpool since the Beatles."[74]

Their sound was a product of a variety of ideas and influences brought by the individual members of the band – an eclectic mix with an obvious reference to '60s psychedelia but not restricted by genre or instrumentation. Ian Pye reviewed their 1980 gig in Norwich for *Melody Maker* and commented:

> Despite a cold, Ian McCulloch's voice still reached the ethereal peaks of the album [*Crocodiles*], while Will's understanding of electronic sound can be sublime on either attack or reflection. Les Pattinson's bass lines are becoming thunderous in places, always original and cleverly at variance with the twin guitars that look for anchorage in Pete De Freitas' rushing drums . . . at their best they are capable of awe inspiring, shimmering magical, warp factor ten rock.[75]

The Bunnymen became the early-'80s epitome of cool: a unique, intense sound accompanied by a distinctive look for all seasons with an unlikely combination of sunglasses, overcoats and stylized haircuts. Early interactions with the press had left some music critics angry and dismissive towards the band, with some interviewers finding the band difficult to relate to and deliberately obstructive. Deanne Pearson described her attempt:

> Echo and the Bunnymen haven't had a lot of press attention since their formation over a year ago, and vocalist Ian "Mac" McCulloch could be one reason why. "Form your own opinions," he says between yawns, "make it up". As far as he's concerned this could be the start and finish of the "interview" I've travelled 170 miles to conduct. I thought seriously about not even bothering to write this piece but decided the band deserved more, not least because Echo and the Bunnymen's music is exciting and positive where Ian McCulloch is arrogant and negative.[76]

Although some journalists found the band's attitude difficult, their desire to succeed was evident for observers of the music scene in Liverpool. According to Jeremy Lewis of Inevitable Records:

> There were a few big personalities in some of the bands in Liverpool at the time. Pete Wylie, Pete Burns, Ian McCulloch, Julian Cope, for example. They had an attitude about them and somehow you knew that eventually they would be successful. They were real characters and had charisma even if they did rub some people up the wrong way at times.[77]

Eventually, the determination of the Bunnymen paid off and their single 'The Back of Love' charted in 1982. A cause for concern at the *Top of the Pops* studio was to how to present the band in the context of the other more mainstream artists performing on the show. In the end, the cameras focused predictably on the inscrutable McCulloch with the trademark overcoat and coiffured hair, but, inexplicably, they considered it appropriate to include a manic dancer, on stilts, in the audience. The circus-style performer gyrated wildly during the track as the band played on trying to maintain an aura of cool. The inappropriateness of this choice was laughable: mainstream at the BBC were clearly having difficulty working out what the band was about.[78]

Despite often being associated with the attitude and ego of its lead singer, the essence of the band's uniqueness lies in the contributions of all its members. The vocals and image of the frontman were predominant but were supported by great tunes and a unique style. Drummer Pete De Freitas, in an interview with John Fun, described the creative process: "We all come from quite different musical tastes, but somehow we manage to fight our way through to one thing that satisfies all of us."[79]

By 1988 Will Sergeant had become disappointed with McCulloch's lack of communication and repeated failure to turn up for rehearsals and soundchecks. When the Bunnymen consequently broke up in 1988, McCulloch embarked on a solo career under the assumption that the band could not possibly go on without him. However, Sergeant and Pattinson replaced him with Noel Burke, the singer from Belfast outfit St Vitus Dance. Following the tragic death of Pete De Freitas in 1989, the Bunnymen recruited Damon Reece on drums and Jake Brockman on keyboards to complete a new line-up. Noel Burke commented on the new band formation:

> Will wanted someone who could write lyrics and contribute to the writing of the songs. He said that we don't just want a singer. We know you can sing from your records with St Vitus Dance. We knew that we would get the inevitable negative comparisons when Mac left. If I was looking at it from the outside I would have been just as judgemental. People would say, "Maybe they are just carrying on for the money" but Will and Les wanted to keep the name because they started the band and why should they give it up just because one member decided to leave? I supposed it was "we'll show him" sort of thing – and it would probably annoy him! I think it was a little bit of that. From my point of view I thought, "Am I going to give up this chance of joining the band because of all that?" So I thought, "No! I want to carry on."[80]

In terms of the creative process, it was business as usual, and the band carried on without McCulloch while retaining the name. They started work on their new album, *Reverberation*. Noel Burke describes the creative process:

It was all about everyone chipping in bits and pieces. Some songs would start with a bass line played by Les . . . then Will would add a bit of guitar, I would add a few more chords . . . There would be three or four ideas there that we could roughly demo instrumentally. Songs like the single 'Enlighten Me' started off as just playing an E chord through an effects unit. It then developed into a groove. The rest of the band just chipped in their bits and the song evolved. I wrote all the lyrics. That's the way it was with the band. That is why everyone is credited on the album.[81]

The Bunnymen had a working formula and it continued to function during the writing and recording of the *Reverberation* album and the subsequent album tour. However, the album received a predictably poor response from a music press that had already made their mind up before a note had been played. Dan Gibson (2008) was typical: "The band shouldn't have even continued to soldier on after Ian McCulloch left . . . [*Reverberation*] is possibly best known for Johnny Marr's dismissal of the album as being by 'Echo and the Bogusmen.'" Peter Marks (2015) reflected on the changed line-up: "While Mac readied his first solo album, Will, Les and Pete had made preparations to soldier on without him. This alone made the press viciously turn on them and led many 'fans' to turn up their noses in disgust."

In retrospect, *Reverberation* is still a most credible album, having been created in the same way as all the other material. It has a guitar-based organic sound with the familiar psychedelic influence and a moody vocal with interesting lyrics. Peter Marks (2015) concludes his retrospective article by saying:

If they'd bothered to put aside their prejudices and listen they'd have been transported to a glorious Technicolor fantasy land . . . 'Gone Gone Gone' is about as perfect an opener as you could have hoped for . . . The musicianship is first rate and Noel holds nothing back in either his words or with his singing. He was a soulful tonic for Will and Les. The guy carved out his own territory in the band and blended into these songs seamlessly.

However the new line-up lasted only two years before Echo and the Bunnymen disbanded. McCulloch and Sergeant reunited in 1994 to become Electrafixion.

The mystique and cool that surrounded the Bunnymen was transmitted through their intensity and the aura of difference that they exuded. This "difference" seemed to be a natural and organic process for the Bunnymen; in a VH1 interview from the time of the formation of Electrafixion, Will Sergeant said: "We prided ourselves on doing things which were against what you were supposed to do in the music business. We didn't have to think 'let's be weird' because that is just how we write."[82] Whether they were, as

McCulloch claimed, the best band in the world is debatable. However, they have left a legacy of the many bands that have followed and imitated this iconic Liverpool group. The Bunnymen still sell out stadiums: their music has a resonance that continues to attract devotees. McCulloch and Sergeant continue to mesmerize their audiences while sticking to their musical principles and keeping a healthy distance from the music business machine. As McCulloch commented in an interview with John Fun about the band's creative process: "Music should be about magic not entertainment."[83]

The Bunnymen's style developed over the years and their music is now considered classic pop. Their *Ocean Rain* album recorded at Amazon in Kirkby is rated by Amazon Studios former owner Jeremy Lewis as the best album recorded there. Thirty-five years after they had begun, they headlined the Liverpool International Music Festival in Sefton Park in 2015, accompanied by the Royal Liverpool Philharmonic Orchestra – a musical collaboration that lifted their work to a different level of complexity and quality. It was an emotional return for local lads who had become internationally acclaimed musical icons. A stunning set sent the audience home singing through the park and debating which song was the best Bunnymen track ever. The arguments continued into the pubs and restaurants in Lark Lane during a balmy Bank Holiday Monday.

Wah!

Figure 10: A publicity shot of Wah! Heat from 1980: (left to right) Carl Washington, Rob Jones, Pete Wylie and Ken Bluff. Courtesy of Rob Jones

Pete Wylie was always destined to be someone. His brash confidence and cheek were complemented with effervescent Scouse wit and a true affection for Liverpool. Wylie had been one of the legendary Crucial Three, along with Julian Cope and Ian McCulloch. Pete went on to form Wah! Heat, and subsequent variations Shambeko Say! Wah!, Wah! The Mongrel and JF Wah!

Figure 11: Julian Cope plays keyboards for Wah! Heat at the Everyman Bistro, Liverpool, in 1979. Photograph by Rob Jones

The context for Wylie's music was unmistakably Liverpool as revealed in his biggest hit 'The Story of the Blues' (1982) about standing up in the face of adversity and social strife in Liverpool. His 1998 song 'Heart as Big as Liverpool' was written in response to the tragic events at Hillsborough in 1989 where ninety-six Liverpool football fans lost their lives at a football match. Vivienne Mellor Schwartze (1985) wrote: "Pete is a real 'laugh a minute' Scouser. Everything about him is stamped 'Made in Liverpool'. The city has toughened him and trained him to take the knocks" (Schwartze 1985: 137).

Wylie's defiance is clear in the early singles 'Better Scream', 'Seven Minutes to Midnight' and 'Some Say'. These songs epitomize Wylie's stance as a grass-roots alternative spokesperson on the social and political events of early-1980s Liverpool. Wylie, in an interview with Steve Sutherland, said:

> Boys from the Blackstuff influenced me a lot because it was reflective, making points to people who wouldn't normally consider politics. Me mam and me dad, for example, who when a party

political broadcast comes on telly on behalf of the Labour party think "Oh let's watch *MASH* on the other side."[84]

Wylie had a strong opinion on the way Liverpool had been treated and perceived, and supported a number of events to help causes such as Liverpool People's Festival and the Hillsborough Support Group.

Jeremy Lewis of Inevitable Records comments on Pete Wylie's early work:

> At that time the band that stood out were Wah! They really had an edge and were a great-sounding band. Pete Wylie just wrote great songs – end of! 'Seven Minutes to Midnight' is a really seminal record of the time. Although it never got into the main charts, it was a song we thought we just had to release. Pete had a big personality. He had a quality about him and was a star in the making.[85]

The grand emotions captured in the early material characterized the mood in the city during the early 1980s. The songs were all of epic proportions and resonated with experiences of others at that time. Wylie's early work was championed by Radio 1's John Peel, who supported Wah! from the outset, playing the guitar-based indie-sounding tracks on his Radio 1 evening show. Peel continued to support Wylie through to his crossover into mainstream commercial success when Wah! became more palatable daytime fodder. It was Peel who described their hit single 'The Story of the Blues' as the kind of record that "knocks your socks off" (quoted in Hann 2013).

However whether Wylie was making it all up as he went along or if he had a master plan to achieve his self-proclaimed full-time legend status is debatable. The answer probably lies somewhere in between the two. Wylie certainly seemed to know which musicians he wanted in his band and exactly how he was going to get them. Drummer Joe Musker, who replaced original drummer Rob Jones, explains how he became drummer with Wah!:

> I had just left a well-paid position as drummer with a '60s hit recording band from Liverpool called the Fourmost. I was looking at doing something completely different when I met Pete Burns and formed Dead or Alive. I then met Pete Wylie at a gig where I had just performed. He shouted to me, "Hey mate you're a great drummer! But the band [Dead or Alive] are crap! How do you fancy playing with my band?"[86]

Wylie's determination to succeed meant that he was not worried if he offended Pete Burns by poaching his drummer. Wah! seemed to arrive on the scene with a ready-made musical identity and with something desperately important to say. The music was compelling and challenging. Joe Musker describes his involvement and the creative process:

Pete had already written the songs which we recorded and played on tour. I sensed right away that it was his way or nothing. Washington and Bluff played everything he wanted. I remember a song from the *Nah Poo* album coming together from a jam of a rhythm that I had written. The song was called 'The Death of Wah!'. I played some accented triplets around my kit just on the toms and an accented bass drum beat . . . All the lyrics and every song was written by Pete Wylie. Wah! already had their musical identity when I happened to work with them.[87]

Certainly, Wylie seemed to know what he wanted musically. Producer Gil Norton recollects one of his early sessions with the band:

Pete was going into the studio to record a live guitar track for a particular segment of the song. He said to me, "I am going in to do a seven-second guitar solo. If any of the notes sound in tune, then stop me and I will do it all over again!"[88]

By 1981, Warner Bros had signed Wah! and released their album *Nah Poo: The Art of Bluff*. Their biggest-selling single was 'The Story of the Blues', which reached number 3 in the UK charts. Wylie continued to write the big songs full of emotion and had further chart success with 'Come Back' and 'Sinful'. A musical innovator who used emotion as his first point of contact, his epic 'Heart as Big as Liverpool' is still played at Anfield, home of Wylie's beloved Liverpool Football Club.

3. Effects

Ian McCulloch refuses to sing so Julian Cope becomes singer by default. Pete De Freitas gets an ear-bashing from Gladys Palmer. U-turn by Gladys sparks the post-punk renaissance. Limousine for McNabb at LA airport. Rock 'n' roll replaces haircuts and synthesizers for the La's.

The third element of Jackson's framework of creativity is *effects*. This is when new ideas and innovation lead to change. The three bands in this section, the Teardrop Explodes, the Icicle Works and the La's, were uniquely Liverpudlian. The variety and versatility of the writing and instrumentation created exemplars of how the classic pop song could be further enhanced beyond the anthems of their psychedelic predecessors in the 1960s. The inclusion of a varied range of influences and lyrics with diverse subject matter made the bands different from mainstream 1980s pop. This redefinition of psychedelia had an effect on other indie-style bands that followed. Icicle Works tracks have been covered by artists such as Rhydian and their music has been used in various films, while the music of the Teardrop Explodes was recognized in the 2010 *MOJO* Inspiration Award. The La's have been covered by many other artists following their one and only album release, including by Robbie Williams (B side to the 'No Regrets' single [1998]), Sixpence None The Richer (single: number 32 in the Billboard chart [1999]) and the Boo Radleys (1993 soundtrack to the film *So I Married an Axe Murderer*) – in all three cases covering their most famous song, 'There She Goes'.

Klaus Schwartze, who identifies the Teardrop Explodes and Echo and the Bunnymen as two seminal bands at the forefront of the "Scouse Phenomenon", documents the incestuous nature of many of the bands on the Liverpool music scene and the interchange of members among those two bands (Schwartze 1985). The La's also had a fluid line-up. The effect on pop music was significant, because not only did the musicians influence each other as they moved among their local bands, they also influenced the wider pop music scene around the world.

The story of how this family of Liverpool bands was able to spread its musical influence has humble beginnings in a cellar of a house in a suburb of Liverpool called Kensington. The story also revolves around a teenager called Dave Palmer ("Yorkie") and his long-suffering mother Gladys Palmer, who allowed a disparate group of fledgling musicians to rehearse in her house despite complaints from neighbours and visits from the police.

Gladys Palmer's cellar

Figure 12: Dave Palmer in 2015. Photograph courtesy of Dave Palmer

The members of the Teardrop Explodes were contemporaries and friends of Echo and the Bunnymen. Both bands rehearsed in the Palmers' cellar, while Gladys remained oblivious to the impact that her guests, disturbing her evening TV viewing, would later have on British pop music. The two pioneering bands shared the same space but produced quite different styles of music. Dave Palmer recounts how he became acquainted with them:

I had spotted Julian [Cope] around the Mathew Street area of town. He was a familiar face in the music scene. Then one day I saw him near where I lived. Julian had moved in not far away from me and I remember as a school kid shouting over to him in the street, "Are you going to see the Adverts at Mountford Hall tonight?" (Not realizing that the Adverts were considered uncool at the time.) He said, "No, I'm going to see Pere Ubu at Eric's." Well, I didn't know who Pere Ubu were. After that, we just struck up a friendship. He took me under his wing and tried to educate me about cool music. We used to go around to each other's houses and we ended up making tapes. They were stupid jam things with me hitting a tea set and Julian screaming into a mic. Then I bought a bass and he taught me how to play it. The first bass line he taught me was 'Mongoloid' by Devo. Then one day he said to me, "I've got a band together. Is there any way we could rehearse in your cellar?" So I asked my mum and she said, *"Absolutely no way!"*[89]

At this crucial point, the Liverpool musical renaissance could have stalled. However, for reasons known only to her, Gladys had a change of heart and allowed an incongruent band of musicians called A Shallow Madness into her cellar. Dave takes up the story:

Then a couple of weeks later she said, "OK we'll give it a try." So then the band members started to move things into the cellar – a little guitar amp for Mick, then a drum kit, then Julian's bass and Paul Simpson had a little cheap organ which didn't work unless you put four bricks on top of it to make it work. We then ran a lead down into the cellar because there was no electricity down there – and then they stayed . . . for about TWO YEARS![90]

The patience and kindness displayed by Gladys Palmer was remarkable. Dave suggests that this is just what Liverpool people do to encourage their children and friends to enjoy themselves and be creative. So the plot thickened in the Palmer household, as Dave relates:

Then Julian said that there were some of their mates who were starting a band. He asked if it would be all right if they shared the cellar. His mates were Echo and the Bunnymen, and because they didn't have a drummer, they could rehearse in the evening and keep the sound down so it didn't disturb my mum too much. That worked quite well until they got Pete De Freitas in on drums. So then they had to share the daytimes and sort out who did what and when. I don't know how my mum put up with it. The glasses cabinet would vibrate every time the bands played and she couldn't hear the telly. I remember when Pete joined the Bunnymen on drums because the rest of the band had to make themselves louder in order to be heard. My mum wasn't happy with the noise level so the next time Pete turned up for rehearsals she was ready for him. He was only a young lad and my mum answered the door and laid in to him saying, *"So it's you is it?! Can't you play those fuckin' drums any louder?!"* Pete looked shocked and terrified. My mum saw the horror in his face and realized that he was shaken ... She stopped and just smiled at him, and then we all burst out laughing.[91]

This anecdote about musical legends the Teardrop Explodes and Echo and the Bunnymen being scolded by Dave's mum is an amusing detail about their humble beginnings, but the local music scene indeed owes much to her tolerance. The rise of the Teardrop Explodes was a spur to other bands in the city. They sounded new and exciting, and were attracting national attention. However, their formation and rise to prominence was far from straightforward.

The Teardrop Explodes

Figure 13: Julian Cope of the Teardrop Explodes at the System Club, Liverpool, in 1980.
Photograph by Colin Howe, digitalised by Dave Williams

Paul Simpson (keyboards) was one of the original members of a band called A Shallow Madness, along with Julian Cope (bass), Ian McCulloch (vocals),

Mick Finkler (guitar) and Dave Pickett (drums). Paul was among those Gladys Palmer kindly tolerated rehearsing in her cellar. He recounts his early Teardrop Explodes days and how he suggested the band's name:

> I met Kath Cherry's boyfriend Julian Cope through Eric's. Julian was a lovely bloke and the poshest person I had ever met. He was so enthusiastic. He was at C. F. Mott Teacher Training, and as we were both seeing girls from the college we would see each other around. We also knew Mick and Dave who would form the rest of the band at the time.
>
> When we were searching for a name for the band, I was flicking through a Marvel comic and I commented on this phrase "The teardrop explodes". The phrase had nothing to do with the storyline, but when I read it out Julian immediately said, "That is the most psychedelic name I have ever heard in my life; it's amazing." The rest of the band all thought it was a rubbish name, but Julian liked it and the name stuck. Originally, Ian McCulloch was the singer and Julian was the bass player. We were called A Shallow Madness at the time. I couldn't really play keyboards then but all the other positions in the band were filled, so I bought this forty-quid organ. I wanted to be more experimental with the sound, as I was into Brian Eno at the time. Julian and I were also into Pere Ubu and early Fall. I saw A Shallow Madness as left-field.[92]

Retrospectively, the events that led up to Julian Cope[93] becoming lead singer in the Teardrop Explodes appear surreal. A Shallow Madness boasted three of the most iconic voices to emerge from the Liverpool scene in the 1980s. Paul Simpson, Ian McCulloch and Julian Cope would all go on to become lead singers in their own respective bands: the Wild Swans, Echo and the Bunnymen and the Teardrop Explodes, the three impressive voices being distinctly different in style and tone. However in A Shallow Madness Paul Simpson was playing a keyboard, Julian Cope was playing bass and Ian McCulloch appeared not to be doing anything. Paul Simpson explains:

> Mac was not turning up to rehearsals and when he did, he hadn't written any words and sometimes he just refused to sing. Weeks and weeks were going by and nothing was happening with him so we sort of sacked him. We were then looking for a new singer and Julian said, "Well I'll do it!" We looked at him and said, "You are joking, aren't you? Forget it!" but he really wanted to sing. We thought that he was rubbish and didn't really like his singing or his words but eventually he became the singer by default. We just accepted it and carried on.[94]

The band continued rehearsing and Cope took on the singer's role. They started to write some original-sounding tracks but attempting to find the source of the originality of the Teardrop Explodes' early work is confusing, as the songs seemed to emerge from a variety of sources and directions. Paul Simpson explains:

> When Mac was the singer [in A Shallow Madness], he would come along with some chords and words to work on and everyone would contribute to the writing. They were initially daft songs like 'Space Hopper' and 'Robert Mitchum', and some of the things Julian subsequently recorded on his *Floored Genius* album. I didn't like them that much. They were a bit too tongue-in-cheek. I wanted to be taken more seriously because initially our material was all left-field. Mick was into Captain Beefheart and we played on cyclical riffs and rhythms, but by the time we had become the Teardrop Explodes and 'Sleeping Gas' was recorded, Dave Balfe had come on board and he was itching to join because he could actually play the organ. It was different from me because I was just playing noises. He recorded the session and said that he thought he should play on it. I objected because it was turning into something different and it was a long way from where our original roots were.[95]

However, Paul Simpson's iconic look was so distinctive that he rivalled Cope as the focus of the band. Paul decided to leave and went on to form another Liverpool band, the Wild Swans. They, too, rehearsed in Gladys Palmer's cellar.

Dave Balfe had originally played with various Liverpool bands such as Radio Blank, Big in Japan and Dalek I Love You. Balfe was also the co-founder of Zoo records with Bill Drummond who also played in Big in Japan. When Paul Simpson decided to leave the Teardrop Explodes, Balfe was quickly installed as keyboard player, bringing a more melodic and pop influence. In January 1979, they recorded a session for John Peel on BBC Radio 1 and the next month released their first single, 'Sleeping Gas', on Zoo Records.

The band recorded further singles with Zoo before they stormed into the charts in 1981 with 'Reward'. By then, the whole of the original line-up had been replaced by frontman Julian Cope. Their most commercially successful line-up was: Julian Cope on bass and vocals, Alan Gill on guitar, Dave Balfe on keyboards and Gary Dwyer on drums. Their sound was upbeat and exciting and the songs were more commercial versions of the original songs from the 1979 Peel sessions. Ian Wood described the Teardrop Explodes as having "A melodic vision all of their own . . . I think that Teardrop Explodes are the proof I have been awaiting that a new dawn has broken on the Liverpool scene."[96]

When 'Reward' charted in January 1981, the band appeared on *Top of the Pops* with Cope dressed in a flying jacket and surrounded by a band with no obvious dress theme.[97] Although 'Reward' was a commercial pop success, nothing on *Top of the Pops* at the time corresponded to it. There were no signs of trends being followed. Dave Balfe explains the band's thinking at this stage:

> A major part of the music scene at the time was that you had to be innovative. It goes back to the Beatles who over their recording life showed a definite development and so you didn't just do what you were doing two years ago. You did something different. When punk happened, it became culture Year Zero. Bands did not want to do what had been going on before. No more tired rock clichés. At first, punk was quite an arty thing with Television, Patti Smith, Talking Heads and Blondie, not just the Sex Pistols, Buzzcocks and Clash. Then within a year even punk had become clichéd. It became loud, brutish and too fast. Those of us who were there at the start of it said we can't just do that again. It would be pathetic. We were left with an arena to move into where there were very few things that you could do. So you had to be innovative. We were all fairly incompetent musicians but that was useful for innovation because when you were in a three-hour rehearsal, you could come up with new things instead of relying on taught riffs. We were trying to assemble something half-decent that wasn't like anything else.[98]

The Teardrop Explodes were influential in the early 1980s. Although their success is often attributed to Cope, the effects of other members of the band, in terms of their influences on pop music, remained evident long after the band had split up. Paul Simpson found a spiritual home with his band the Wild Swans and its inspiring and uplifting brand of music which was appreciated more abroad than in the UK. He is adored in the Philippines, where his music is regularly played on radio stations and imitated by admirers. Teardrops' guitarist Alan Gill became involved in a variety of innovative musical projects and wrote the film score to highly acclaimed independent movie *Letter to Brezhnev*. Dave Balfe became a major influence on the music industry as writer, producer, manager and influential figure in the Britpop movement in the 1990s.

At the height of their success in 1981, Gill left the band. Despite this setback, Cope continued to perform as the Teardrop Explodes until 1982, which included a tour of Australia garnering positive reviews – for example from Brett Wright, who described them as "The leading lights of English neo-psychedelic or mind expanding music".[99] However, the band was not destined to last: Paul Morley's article in the *NME* on 31 January 1981 was entitled "Teardrops implode" and indeed predicted the eventual end of the band the following year.

Although they only recorded two albums, the Teardrop Explodes left a permanent mark on British music. Julian Cope subsequently developed and reinvented himself in several remarkable solo musical regenerations and also became an antiquarian and author. The band's effect on musical development was recognized in their 2010 *MOJO* Inspiration Award. The award was presented to Dave Balfe by Alex James from Blur, the very band Balfe had steered to stardom. Gary Dwyer and Alan Gill were also in attendance but Julian Cope was not, which allowed Balfe the opportunity to make this amusing quip when picking up the prize: "I will keep this here for Julian . . . until he learns to accept his award!"[100]

The Icicle Works

Figure 14: An early publicity shot of the Icicle Works, taken at Liverpool Polytechnic (now John Moores University) in 1981: (left to right) Ian McNabb, Chris Sharrock and Chris Layhe.
Photograph by Colin Howe, digitalised by Dave Williams

The Icicle Works were a Liverpool band formed in 1980: a three-piece outfit featuring Ian McNabb on vocals and guitar, Chris Layhe on bass and Chris Sharrock on drums. The band was named after the 1960 short story *The Day the Icicle Works Closed* by sci-fi writer Frederik Pohl. They were a hard-working band and would regularly gig in Liverpool during 1980 and 1981 at venues such as The Masonic and Brady's. Their early work divided opinion. They have latterly been described as neo-psychedelics, having risen to prominence shortly after the success of Teardrop Explodes and Echo and the Bunnymen. Penny Kiley claimed that the band's musical references to artists such as the Byrds and Neil Young was overly ambitious, leading to: "Over the top psychedelic trappings, tongue in cheek pretentiousness and a magnitude of scale that a pop group should not have dared to attempt".[101]

However, they were not derivatives of their two Liverpool predecessors. John D. Hodgkinson takes a different point of view from Kiley and describes their music thus: "Evocative and excites the emotions . . . The Icicle works are a group continually asking questions of the listener."[102] During the early 1980s, the national music press tended to judge every band emanating from Liverpool in the context of the main bands on the Zoo label. John Robb described them as "A solid gel of Liverpudlian pop and American acid rock".[103] Although lead singer Ian McNabb acknowledges the influence of the Teardrop Explodes and Echo and the Bunnymen, the Icicle Works were determined to be different and develop their own unique style. McNabb recognized that, to achieve success, the Icicle Works needed their songs to be big, innovative and appealing, matching the high standards set by the best of Liverpool's new pop icons. There was intense competition between the bands in the city and it was a challenge to produce better material than the prestigious rivals. Their first single, 'Nirvana', was released independently and charted at number 15 in the independent charts in 1982. It attracted interest from the Beggars Banquet label and their impressive-sounding music began to gain popularity. McNabb explains the writing process at that time:

> A lot of bands sound similar these days. You couldn't do that back then. We ditched a couple of tracks because they sounded too much like other people. Teardrop Explodes and the Bunnymen were influences but I think you arrive at your own sound naturally. Even people who aren't very good have their own sound because everyone's voices are different and everyone plays differently. Our first album is the one we worked the hardest on for the longest amount of time and the one I am most proud of.[104]

The fact that the Icicle Works were a three-piece did not limit them in a live context as the clever instrumentation, immense drumming and convincing vocal made their sound remarkably full. Their studio work produced huge, dramatic, and at times orchestral, layered tracks which took the classic big pop song a stage further. McNabb explains how the songs developed and how they carved unique elements into their work:

> Whenever anything sounded like something else, we ditched it by a process of elimination. But sometimes we still sounded like other things from that time. So we added something that was a bit weird, like a different drum pattern, an unusual instrument or something.
> Preference, self-belief and luck have more than fifty per cent to do with originality. We eventually got some breaks. We worked for quite a long time and didn't really get anywhere and then 'Birds Fly' was a hit. After that we got a Kid Jensen session and a few better gigs. Because there was quite a lot coming out of Liverpool at the time, people were keen and they would listen to you. They wanted the next Bunnymen, Teardrops or OMD. Then in early '84 'Love

Is a Wonderful Colour' was a hit. It took us about three years to make it, which isn't a long time but at the time it felt like ages.[105]

The Icicle Works rose to prominence in the UK with their grandiose single 'Love Is a Wonderful Colour' in 1984. But it was their second single, 'Birds Fly (Whisper to a Scream)', that was to break them in America reaching number 37 in the US Hot 100 chart. They were now enjoying national and international success with their unique brand of classic pop songs: another Liverpool band doing things differently and influencing others around them.

Following the release of 'Love Is a Wonderful Colour', the Icicle Works were summoned to appear on *Top of the Pops* in January 1984. In a repeat of the Echo and the Bunnymen scenario two years earlier (see above), there was uncertainty about how to present a band that didn't conform to expectations. The Icicle Works went about their work with the professionalism expected of a well-rehearsed and musically talented trio; they were dressed in black and conveyed the intensity and mystique required of their classic song. However, as they were a three-piece, there were some gaps on the stage which the *Top of the Pops* producers decided to fill with two dancers resembling extras from Wham's 'Club Tropicana' video. The male dancer, stripped to the waist, twirled to the left of McNabb, while his female counterpart looked on adoringly. To add to the incongruity, party balloons were despatched over the band.[106]

The band's rise was meteoric: within a year they went from playing local venues in Liverpool to being picked up by a limousine at Los Angeles airport to play concerts and TV shows in America.

The Icicle Works and their classic pop songs have influenced other artists including *X Factor* finalist Rhydian who featured 'Love Is a Wonderful Colour' on his 2011 album *Waves*. Their songs continue to be used in a variety of media: a cover of their song 'Birds Fly (Whisper to a Scream)' by a band called Soho was used over the closing titles of the 1996 film *Scream*. The same song was also used in the 2008 film *Garden Party* in a scene depicting a drive down Sunset Boulevard.

Ian McNabb continues to write, record and perform. His musical memoir, *Merseybeast*, was published in 2008. Ian's own take on his music was expressed in an early interview with John D. Hodgkinson:

> A lot of people don't know what we are trying to achieve ... Just a bit of confusion; which is quite healthy? It is like a big cauldron with things revolving in it and eventually something comes out and people dig it. Some people have to have things presented to them in categories but if they can't categorise it they shy away from it ... except for the intelligent people (Hodgkinson 1982).

The La's

Mike Badger prefers rock 'n' roll to haircuts and synthesizers.
Captain Beefheart should collect his royalties.

Figure 15: A publicity shot of the La's in 1985: (left to right) Barry Walsh, Mike Badger, John Power and Lee Mavers. Photograph courtesy of Mike Badger

The La's were noted for their distinctly different '60s-infused guitar style which was at odds with other popular bands dominating the British charts in the late 1980s. While the UK was mostly listening to established artists such as Cher, Billy Joel and Madonna, as well as dance music by Janet Jackson and De La Soul, the La's were a more indie-sounding prospect and had a passing resemblance to the Liverpool bands of the 1960s, rather than their 1980s musical contemporaries. Their guitar-based style and indie look set the tone for Britpop which emerged some five years later. The pursuit of guitar-driven pop was seen at the time by founder Mike Badger as a refreshing change from synthesizer-dominated pop. In this respect, their effect on what was to happen in the mid-1990s was sizeable. The Liverpool bands of the early 1980s did not make many musical references to their Merseybeat past, but the simple, tuneful, acoustic-driven arrangements of the La's had a clear link to the music of the 1960s.

The La's formed in 1983 when Mike Badger, who was then lead singer and guitarist, had a dream in which he was in a band named the La's. (The "la" in this case is actually the musical note, not Liverpool slang for "lads", as is often assumed.) Lee Mavers joined in 1984 as rhythm guitarist and eventually became songwriter and frontman. Phil Butcher was on bass briefly that year but was replaced by Jim Fearon within a month of joining. John Timpson was on drums. The La's had a fluid line-up: 24 musicians can claim to have been part of the band at some point (Macefield 2003).

Mike Badger claims that the music was about expression. It was a personal response to begin with, but turned in to something different when the band members provided their individual input. He explains: "The music was instinctive and intuitive. We never deliberately tried to be different. It was never contrived. We didn't think that we would make a particular type of song. We had a broad church of influences."[107]

The La's, along with Cast and Space, originated from a scheme targeted at reducing unemployment in Liverpool during the 1980s called the North Liverpool Musicians Resource Centre, which was designed to train unemployed people in Liverpool for work in the music industry. Mike Badger explains that, although the scheme had resource and staffing problems, it was a meeting place and a hub for musicians who would later form successful bands. The scheme's success turned out to be the convergence of a mix of aspiring musicians with diverse influences rather than the formal musical course it was offering. Mike Badger describes how the La's were formed and the influence of the variety of musicians emanating from the scheme:

> I got into the music of Captain Beefheart because I met him briefly at a gallery in 1980. I asked Lee whether he had heard of Beefheart and he said, "No." I left Liverpool for a few years and went to London and when I returned I met Lee and he said that he had been listening to a lot of Captain Beefheart. We took things further and started to record in the Attic Studios in town. We had a revolving door of bass players and drummers until we went onto this scheme called the North Liverpool Musicians Resource Centre. I was sent there by the Jobcentre on Allerton Road. There were about twenty musicians at the centre sent there because they were unemployed. Lee applied for the scheme but couldn't get on. They all had different musical tastes so when we started playing together some really interesting music started to happen. We didn't know at the time but all these musicians went on to be in the La's, Cast, Space and the Lightning Seeds. It was amazing really because we were treated badly. The scheme was supposed to train us up to do real jobs in the music industry but that didn't really happen.[108]

Paul Hemmings was also involved with the North Liverpool Musicians Resource Centre, and he also played guitar in the La's, the Lightning Seeds and Space. Paul describes how the mixture of musicians with their variety of influences and ideas was a positive factor emerging from the collective:

The building in Colquitt Street was amazing, really. It had its own Victorian theatre and the bands used to perform songs to each other. We were then supposed to go out into community centres and encourage others to play instruments. However, not much materialized. But, if nothing else, it was a place where we met other musicians and ideas and influences were shared. Looking back, it was a really exciting time as we learnt different things from each other and tried to do something different from one another. The bands from those days like the La's, Space and Cast all sounded different and yet were all closely related because many of the musicians in the bands were the same.[109]

The success of Liverpool bands during the mid-1980s led to much interest in music originating in the city, and bands with roots in this collective were catching the attention of the record labels: the La's in particular were intriguing with their light, uncomplicated sound. However, because the line-up of the band was in a state of constant flux, Badger decided to leave the band in 1986 to start another band called the Onset. Lee Mavers took over as lead singer and began to add some of his own material to the set. Mike describes the 1986 transition:

One thing I am really proud of is that when Liverpool was on the bones of its arse we brought back really good acoustic and guitar-driven music. The La's brought the rock 'n' roll back into the city which had been taken over by haircuts and synthesizers. It was an interesting consequence of the characters in the band and their inputs. It was guitar-based because Liverpool for a long time was a guitar city. The songs seemed to resonate with people's feelings at the time. After I left the La's the band became the vehicle for Lee's ideas. It was perfect for Paul [Hemmings] because he was a great guitarist and stepped into my shoes and within a few months they played in front of Andy McDonald from Go! Discs at the Everyman Bistro.[110]

The location was ironic: the Everyman Bistro on Hope Street was the very spot where he had renewed his acquaintance with Lee Mavers in 1984 and the La's musical direction was conceived.

Nonetheless, the process of delivering the La's hit single 'There She Goes' was complicated. The song is a guitar-based track with an infectious '60s-style melody. At first listening, it appears to be a lightweight "boy loves girl" song. However, in a retrospective article in *Rolling Stone*, James Sullivan (2013) argues that many people believed the pleasant melody masked a dark lyric about the euphoria of drug taking. (This interpretation had previously been disputed by guitarist Paul Hemmings [Macefield 2003].) In any case, it did not stop wholesome Christian American teen sensations Sixpence None The Richer covering the song and having a huge hit with it in the US. The song was also covered by Robbie Williams, the Wombats and the Boo Radleys.

Mike Badger explains the difficulties in making the song:

> It took quite a few attempts for 'There She Goes' to become a hit. I think it was released about three times before it made the charts. Steve Lillywhite did a good job on the album under the circumstances. I can't listen to that album now because I had been playing those songs since 1984. I wanted to move on. Imagine recording those songs five years later. They tried every permutation to get the sound that Lee wanted. Lee was a perfectionist. They even phoned Virgin and tried to get Beefheart. Virgin said, "If you can find him, let us know. Last thing we knew of Beefheart was he was in a trailer in the middle of the desert and if you do find him tell him that we have some royalties waiting for him."[111]

The song resonated with the record-buying public and 'There She Goes' achieved international success. It has made its way onto a number of film soundtracks, including *The Parent Trap*, *Fever Pitch*, *So I Married an Axe Murderer* and *Girl, Interrupted*. The most ironic use of the song (considering it was created by a band forged in a scheme to mop up the unemployed in Liverpool) was as a BBC 2 *Newsnight* TV soundtrack to Margaret Thatcher leaving Downing Street in 1990.

4. Feelings

The dust on Henry's mirror. The knobheads and foot-shooters succeed in the end. Jerry Kelly's collaborative auteurs.

The final part of this chapter centres on the fourth aspect of Norman Jackson's concept of creativity: *feelings*. In this respect, the music is all about expressing yourself. It feels like a personal response to begin with, but may turn into something different. The feelings may resonate with others. Such feelings can range from despair to elation and can make the listener feel euphoric or uncomfortable.

One element underpinning the success of the bands discussed in this book is that they were all able to convey intense emotion within their songs, a notable characteristic of Liverpool music during the period under investigation. The three bands in this section are the Christians, Black, and the Lotus Eaters. All three were melodic by design and produced songs that were reflective in nature. An ability to pull at the heartstrings and change the way the listener feels is a recurring theme in the following interviews.

The Christians

Figure 16: Recording the 'Ferry Cross the Mersey' charity single in 1989. The Christians (left to right Russell Christian, Henry Priestman and Garry Christian) in the studio with Paul McCartney (far right). Photograph courtesy of Garry Christian

The Christians were a band who produced melodic, thought-provoking songs. Henry Priestman, formerly of Yachts and It's Immaterial, had been recognized for some time as an accomplished songwriter. Before the formation of the Christians, during the mid-1980s, Henry had been writing an album of songs but, not belonging to a band, had no vehicle with which to present them to an audience. Henry claims that Radio 1 DJ Janice Long had suggested he try "that ginger lad from Manchester", by whom she meant Mick Hucknall. However, after a performance at the Larks in the Park music festival in Liverpool's Sefton Park, Henry met three singing brothers, Garry, Roger and Russell Christian. He recognized their potential and how his songs could be developed using their impressive vocals and ideas.

Nevertheless, the route to success was far from straightforward. Henry had recorded some tracks on a portastudio tape recorder which he hurriedly re-recorded in a studio with new vocals courtesy of the Christian brothers. Owing to Henry's songwriting reputation and the dominance of Liverpool bands in the charts, the Christians' demo tapes quickly circulated around record companies' A&R departments, which were eager to unearth another potential Scouse success. Some of the A&R scouts who had reviewed the demo tape said that they could not hear any singles in this first batch of songs – the same songs that eventually appeared on their number 1 album *The Christians*, which boasted five top 30 singles and subsequent album sales of over 1.6 million.

Despite the band not being ready to perform live, some A&R staff were eager to meet them. Henry recalls one such "audition" in his flat in south Liverpool which took place with no stage, props or PA. The Christians simply sang over backing tracks on a portastudio augmented by some basic instrumentation provided by Henry. The band was so under-rehearsed that they could not remember all of the lyrics. Henry recalls an ingenious solution: out of sight of the Island Records A&R scout, Henry wrote prompts in the dust on his mirror to remind Garry Christian of the lyrics to 'Forgotten Town'. In the end, Island Records were sufficiently impressed by the unorthodox performance that they signed the band shortly afterwards. A band was hastily assembled with Paul Barlow (drums), Mike Bulger (guitar, vocals) and Tony Jones (bass) to complement Henry on keyboards and Garry, Roger and Russell on vocals.

The first single released by Island Records was 'Forgotten Town' which reached number 22 in the UK charts in 1987. It expressed the feelings of the population of Liverpool at the time, with the Christian brothers' soulful harmonies reaching out to listeners imploring them to recognize the injustice and neglect that had been served on "forgotten" towns, such as Liverpool, over many years. The real stories of the much maligned and caricatured Scousers were finally articulated in this song. The subject matter was unconventional and felt personal and defensive about the city's plight. Henry explains: "I suppose you could compare 'Forgotten Town' to a protest song. It was how I felt and it seemed that others felt the same emotions of disappointment and frustration that I felt."[112]

The lyrics resonated with many inhabitants of cities across the UK who had seen difficult times during the 1980s. They were set over a strong melody and sung with conviction by perfect vocal harmonies which would not have been out of place on a classic Motown hit. The Christians' songs dealt with contentious issues that were rarely found in a standard pop song. Their hits, such as 'Hooverville', 'Ideal World' and the Isley Brothers cover 'Harvest for the World', contained well-observed commentaries on social issues. The band offered a brand of pop music that was unique for its time. Priestman describes the thinking behind the songs:

> We enjoyed using words in quite a weird way and didn't write songs about cars or girls. When people said the first album will do well, I thought, "How can it?" It's like nothing else. I couldn't see it doing well. It was soulful like the Temptations but with my influences. We admit we were influenced by the Temptations but we did not attempt to be an obvious copy of them. The mix of influences meant our sound was nothing like anything else in Britain at the time. The next thing was . . . we were on the front cover of *NME* and *Melody Maker*.[113]

The front cover of *Melody Maker* of 17 January 1987 depicted a pensive-looking Garry Christian under the caption "The Christians: A soul salvation".

The Christians went on to enjoy a sustained career of chart success which included ten top 40 singles (thirteen reaching the top 60) and two number 1 albums in the UK alone. They were generally well received by the national music press. David Quantick commented on the vocal style: "On 'Save a Soul in Every Town' he sounds like David Bowie does now but this is quite pleasant."[114] Alistair Thane also rated the band highly, being impressed by the quality of the songs and the harmonies: "1987 sees the group established as yet another international successful Liverpool outfit."[115]

The Christians also enjoyed success in Europe, the US and New Zealand. Their albums, *The Christians* and *Colour*, both reached number 1 in the UK. The main appeal of the songs an the basis of their success was their ability to appeal to the feelings of the audience and relate to their own emotions to the experiences of others. Henry explains:

> I think a lot of our success was due to the variety of emotions in our songs. Some were angry songs like 'Forgotten Town' and 'When the Fingers Point', and we can all relate to those feelings of frustration. Some of the other songs like 'Ideal World' and 'Words' were softer, more thoughtful songs which made the listeners reflect on the lyrics and the emotion of the melody.[116]

However, with the popularity of the band still high, Garry Christian decided to pursue a solo career and left the band and his hometown of Liverpool to move to Paris. This derailed the band's momentum, and the resulting hiatus eventually led to the disintegration of what was left of the original line-up.

Garry decided to perform again as the Christians in 1999, following the tragic death of Roger Christian from a brain tumour in 1998. Russell Christian left in 2005 leaving Garry as the frontman. Henry Priestman no longer performs on a regular basis with the Christians but made a guest appearance in 2012 at the Royal Court Theatre in Liverpool to mark the band's 25th anniversary.

Henry Priestman continues to perform with Les Glover and includes songs from his days in Yachts, It's Immaterial and the Christians. His music has featured in musicals such as *Dreamboats and Petticoats*, in a James Bond Xbox game, and Mark Nunneley's short film *Kismet Diner*. A thread is observable in his songs, which is a capacity to touch the emotions, and it is this that endears him to his adoring fans. Garry Christian continues to perform as the Christians and commands large audiences who come to enjoy the hits from the 1980s and '90s.

Black: A personal response since writing this book

As research began for this book, I was trying to arrange interviews with as many as possible of Liverpool's great songwriters and musicians from the Scouse Pop period. As with most research, it is never certain what you will discover. I had a vague framework to work with and an open mind about what the interviews might reveal.

I had known Colin Vearncombe from the early 1980s and remembered his first incarnation of Black, which was an indie-rock-inspired three-piece. We also met in the mid-1980s in rehearsal rooms in Liverpool called The Ministry, just after his record company had dropped him and his first marriage had ended. We discussed the ups and downs of our musical careers and life in general. He was calm, witty and intelligent. He always had a perceptive view of life.

Apart from attending his concerts in later years, I had no further contact until I embarked on this book. He was the second person to be interviewed. When I contacted him to explain that I was writing a book about the Liverpool music scene in the 1980s he immediately agreed to be interviewed. It was only after several emails that he asked about the book's focus. When I told him it was musical creativity, he replied "even better".

We met in a wine bar in Lark Lane. What was supposed to be a brief interview became a four-hour chat in which we discussed a multitude of issues and shared memories and opinions. Most of the conversation was not about music: it was about life. He was a man in touch with the things that make us tick: our emotions, frustrations, reality, anger and love. He had returned home to Liverpool for a family birthday celebration and eventually headed off.

The afternoon conversation in Lark Lane told me everything about Colin Vearncombe's character. Firstly, he remembered exactly who I was after almost 30 years; secondly, if he could help somebody, he just did it; thirdly, he was humble and polite. Finally, his most endearing quality, which underlies his wonderful legacy of songs, is that he was a kind man who understood people and life. His character and understanding shone through his songs, which continued to improve as Colin perfected his craft. The private tragedy for his family of losing him at such an early age is shared by his adoring fans because Colin died at the peak of his powers and meant so much to so many people.

Figure 17: Colin Vearncombe (Black) (right) on the set of the *Scouse Pop* TV programme in July 2015, pictured with the author. Photograph by Neil Duffin

When I recorded the first TV series of *Scouse Pop* in 2015, I asked Colin to feature in an hour-long episode.[117] He agreed without hesitation and enthralled the TV crew with his wit and humour. The session was filled with laughter and fun, and producer Neil Duffin and I received many complimentary emails following the broadcast. But we were just passengers on a ride through his wonderful life as Colin commanded the screen with a relaxed presence that made everyone feel engaged. It was the last full-length interview he was to give. I really wish this had not been the case. His memorial service in Liverpool's Anglican Cathedral in February 2016 was attended by over a thousand people. The bravery of his wife and son singing one of Colin's songs at the service was breathtakingly beautiful. We all miss him.

Black

Black's early days were as a three-piece leather-clad rock outfit consisting of Colin Vearncombe on vocals and guitar, Dane Goulding on bass and Greg Leyland on drums. The original set of songs was derivative of other bands in the developing Liverpool scene at the time and had more of a rock sound to them, as Colin explains:

> I was influenced by Echo and the Bunnymen at the time. They were my favourite band because I like melodramatic overblown pop music. I didn't know anything about the Doors and so wasn't aware of any allegations of plagiarism. When I listen back to the Bunnymen albums now you can tell who they were influenced by, but because of their limitations using a drum machine in the early days I suppose they ramped up their sound to be the best that they could be, which I suppose is all you can ask of anyone really. I still remember that it was a radical move to appear without a drummer because we had that heritage in Liverpool that we value high-quality musicianship and if you couldn't play then you had to get off the stage. But they were different and unique.
>
> In Liverpool around the early '80s we shared the idea that we were at the centre of the universe and for a short time the music industry were happy to go along with that. A few key journalists talked up the whole Zoo Records thing, and once you had the Bunnymen, the Teardrops and OMD, Liverpool began to appear really important to music nationally.[118]

Enthused by the local music scene Black continued to gig and eventually managed to release their first single 'Human Features' on local independent label Rox Records. However, Colin was not content with the sound of the band so the original Black line-up split up in the early 1980s with Colin deciding to pursue a solo career. This proved to be a metamorphosis as the style and direction were reinvented. Colin describes the process:

> Well at the time I would not have known what to do with an acoustic guitar. I had an electric guitar and an amp that I called the electric fire because that is what it looked like. But we were all knobheads. We were in our late teens and thought we knew what to do. In Liverpool we all seemed to get our five minutes of fame despite the fact that we were all foot-shooters because beneath the loud bravado there is a lack of self-esteem. Two hundred years of Catholicism is enough to undermine most people. Then I realized that quiet sounds can be big as well. It wasn't just about being loud.
>
> I used different musical collaborators. I am a writer not a music technician or knob-twiddler and I was introduced to a more technically minded guy called Dave Dix from the Last Chant who were a very interesting band. One of their members was Nigerian and he spoke pidgin and his hero was Fela Kuti and their music was a mixture of Fela Kuti's Juju style and the Velvet Underground.
>
> Pete Fulwell from Inevitable Records put me in the studio with Dave Dix. He wanted to expand what he could do in music and he was very interested in button-pushing and production and we just hit it off. It doesn't matter if he was messing around with the rusty innards of a bicycle or the sounds in the studio. He is a searcher. We were good astronauts together for a while. We used to do all-night sessions in the Eternal studio because we couldn't get in there during the day. It was booked for Wah! or the Christians. So we would work from nine until six in the morning and go home on the early bus with all the factory workers. It was great fun but it was hard and depressing at times. The small hours are hard. The hot water was off so you couldn't wash the cups properly and the tannin was building up and the ashtrays were overflowing and Dave's ashtray was like a pig pen because he aimed his ash from a distance. It was tough but when you are young you can only see the thing that you are aiming for and the road that you are on and you are fired with the dream. That was the thing about the '80s. It didn't matter about our circumstances: we didn't give a sod! We were going for it. The dole was called the unofficial Arts Council grant! We swapped musicians and instruments and you got done what you needed to do.[119]

Following his collaboration with Dave Dix, Colin signed with WEA in 1984 and the pair collaborated on two singles, 'Hey Presto' and 'More Than the Sun'. The songs were more interesting and thoughtful than those of the three-piece rock band. The singles raised interest but did not sell, leaving

WEA disappointed. A series of difficult events made 1985 a tough year for Colin. His mother became ill, his first marriage ended, he was injured in a car crash and he was dropped by WEA. Although at a low ebb in his life, he found the inspiration to write the song 'Wonderful Life', which he recorded over a weekend in "The Pink" recording studio owned by Liverpool musician Hambi Haralambous. Colin's collaboration with Dave Dix led to other notable material being recorded such as 'Sweetest Smile' and 'Finder'.

The transformation of Black had begun but it was far from a straight-forward transition to success. Colin had attracted interest from record companies before, but had failed to convert the interest into a solid deal owing to inconsistent live performances. Colin explains:

> There had been a buzz about me before and I had always blown it. Live had been a problem and I hadn't done enough gigs, to be honest, and I was better in the studio, really. It was in the studio where I learnt my trade. I have only just cracked the live thing. I'm a late developer![120]

Colin had completely changed his vocal style from his early days in order to expand his range of options.

> I started taking singing lessons and I only stopped ten years ago. I'm as good as I am likely to get now. I am not being arrogant but give me a room and an audience and I can perform. I am better now than I was in the '80s.[121]

The first recording of 'Wonderful Life' was released independently through Ugly Man Records. The first airing of the track was by local Radio Merseyside DJ Terry Lennaine, who used to host a show entitled *Keep on Truckin'*, featuring dance music and not associated with the more alternative styles of music emanating from Liverpool at the time. Lennaine also hosted another evening show that was popular on Radio Merseyside and it was on this that he unveiled 'Wonderful Life' with a prophetic preamble. He told his listeners that the track he was about to play was going to be an enormous hit and that a major company should immediately sign the band and release this song. He then announced that the song was by local band Black. The now familiar strains of the marimba-style percussive rhythm and string synth intro-duction was broadcast for the first time; a soulful vocal sang the melody with conviction – it was all a far cry from the Black of the early 1980s. The voice, the instrumentation and the quality of the songwriting had all undergone a metamorphosis to create original and serene-sounding music that engaged directly with the emotions of the listener. Terry Lennaine claims that he bet Colin £50 that the song would be a hit and these days jokingly complains that he never received his money.[122]

The song attracted the interest of A&M who signed Black and launched Vearncombe's international career. The first A&M single, 'Everything's Coming Up Roses', flopped but the follow-up, an atmospheric ballad entitled 'Sweetest Smile', became a UK top 10 hit. The song lacked an obvious chorus but had a mesmerizing and haunting feel, appealing to the senses with a mood of melancholy that drew the listener in. Colin's vocal performance was compelling. The fretless bass and legato strings supported the vocals and provided the accompaniment for a soprano saxophone that oozed sadness and melancholy. 'Sweetest Smile' was not an obvious choice for a single but, as Colin explains:

> A lot of pop music depends on whether you believe the singer. When Briggs at A&M decided that we should release 'Sweetest Smile' he said, "I'm not sure where it's going. I just know that when people listen to 'Sweetest Smile' their eyes go somewhere with it." It took people somewhere else in their lives because the feeling of melancholy was so strong. So that was a smart move by A&M. We let them release it just as it was and it went off like a rocket.[123]

The third single by Black was a re-release and remix of the original Pink studio recording of 'Wonderful Life'. At last the song was a huge success. Colin describes the process:

> Briggs at A&M took 'Wonderful Life' to Chris Thomas, and he said it didn't need a producer just a safe pair of hands to mix it and that's what they did. 'Wonderful Life', which ended up selling two and a half million copies around the world, was basically recorded for 200 quid in Pink studios in Liverpool over a weekend when Hambi was away. It was just mixed a couple of times because we could only afford a couple of days in the studio so we worked late just to get it finished. It was Steve Power and Dix who engineered and mixed it. Dix was very hands-on. I'm not sure if that was a good thing as he used to like to drink whisky late on in the sessions and I think you lose a few DBs top end for every unit of alcohol you consume. So he'd be messing around on the mixing desk at 3 am and I'd say, "Set the EQ before you drink you knobhead and if it sounds dull it's because you've been drinking! You arse!" So we used to argue a lot over stupid stuff. In fact, we used to argue even when we were in agreement.[124]

It it is actually quite refreshing to find that these poignant and soulful songs were made in an atmosphere of good-humoured juvenile banter. And so the £200 demo recorded at Hambi's studio became a massive hit worldwide, with the album of the same name, released in 1987, enjoying similar success, reaping commercial and critical acclaim. Colin describes the effect of worldwide success:

> When 'Wonderful Life' came out, we got to make the video that we wanted. It was the only one we got to make with the budget we wanted and that was the one that won all the awards. We got to look like what we thought our sound should look like. Record companies can be a bunch of interfering busybodies that charge exorbitant interest rates. As a bank, they are the worst bank that you could possibly go to. However, what other bank would give kids a million quid on the basis of a few songs? After 'Wonderful Life' became a hit, it rolled through the world country by country and we followed it because it is like your baby. I went around the world twice in two years. How I survived that I do not know.[125]

Colin continued to write and perform to a fiercely loyal fan base up until his tragic death in January 2016. On tour and in the studio he had been accompanied by the multi-talented Calum MacColl. Colin also wrote poetry, with two books published, and his artwork has also attracted positive attention – a genuine Renaissance Man. 'Wonderful Life' remains an anthem with an enduring appeal to the emotions and as such continues to be used regularly in TV commercials. Colin's music continues to impress with its intensity and emotional appeal.

The Lotus Eaters

The Lotus Eaters emerged from the Liverpool scene in the early 1980s as a hybrid of two local bands: the Wild Swans and the Jass Babies. The original line-up was Peter Coyle (vocals), Jeremy Kelly (guitar), Ged Quinn (keyboards), Alan Wills (drums) and Phil Lucking (bass). Their music is an apt reflection of Tennyson's classic poem from which they derived their name. In the poem, mariners serving under Odysseus and trying to find their way home land on an enchanted island and are greeted by "mild-eyed melancholy lotus eaters" bearing the fruit of the lotus. After eating the fruit the mariners fall into a trance-like state and are so relaxed that they are unable to make their way home. In some respects, this warm dream-like state is reflected in the band's soothing melancholic music. The intensity of the emotion in their songs resonated with the record-buying public and radio stations, and they enjoyed both national and international success. The band's formation was far from straightforward, however, and was a source of acrimony among the two bands who were the casualties of the reconfiguration. Jerry Kelly explains:

I was working as an apprentice electrician at the time and Paul and Ged from the Wild Swans had been off to Amsterdam; and when they came back they suggested that we should all go to Holland later that year. It was difficult for me to book a week off work but I agreed and took the time off. When it came to going they said, "Oh no! We can't go, because we haven't got any money." I felt a bit let down. I was then phoned by Peter Coyle to play on a John Peel session with the Jass Babies. When I listened to the material it was very heavy and there was no space in the tracks for my guitar. Peter asked me what I thought. I said this will not work unless you sack the band. I have worked well with Peter Coyle who is a great musician but it is not the same as working with a collaborator with another musical instrument. For example, I worked well with Ged Quinn when I was in the Wild Swans. He came and formed the Lotus Eaters with me. I did a terrible thing when we formed the Lotus Eaters because I convinced the entire band [the Wild Swans] to come with me and work with Peter and I convinced Peter to sack his band the Jass Babies. We then recorded the John Peel session.[126]

Figure 18: An early publicity shot of the Lotus Eaters from 1983: (left to right) Peter Coyle and Jerry Kelly. Photograph by Colin Howe, digitalised by Dave Williams

The session was recorded in October 1982 and led to the band being signed by Arista who employed Nigel Gray as producer for their first single, 'The First Picture of You'. The song received sustained national airplay and became the anthem for the summer of 1983. It became the Lotus Eaters' iconic song, giving them a UK hit single before they had even played a single gig. The band appeared on *Top of the Pops* on 23 July 1983 to promote the single. The mellow tones of a carefully crafted sound conveyed a dream-like quality which transported listeners to the feelings evoked in Tennyson's classic poem. *Top of the Pops* again failed to find a sympathetic way of presenting a band that was not the norm for the show and plonked two dancing girls in mini-skirts into the foreground, obscuring some of the band members. The dancers resembled those that had appeared with the Icicle Works on the same show, as described above. The atmosphere was entirely inappropriate for a song that demanded a sensitive treatment.[127]

The band recorded a second session for John Peel in October 1983 and their first album, *No Sense of Sin*, was well received by the music press. According to Lynden Barber, "The Lotus Eaters love to dwell on the bright side of life. Their spoken outlook is ubiquitously sanguine, drowned in hope drenched in sunshine."[128] Their sound was distinctive, with emotive sounds embedded in the tracks. It was able to express feelings in a manner unlike any other band at that time. Jerry Kelly takes the view that uniqueness was not their sole intention:

> As an academic I don't believe in uniqueness anymore. I wrote a paper a while ago called "The Collaborative Auteur". It is like with a film, the director has a vision but the photographer is not the cinematographer and he does not compose the music. As the notion of originality has been a driving concern, you do not want to sound like anyone else but you are reacting to them. I think creativity is a collaborative process and as a musician you have fertile ground to react with other musicians.
>
> In terms of trying to do something new, I don't think that the Lotus Eaters were truly original. I don't think you can say anything is truly original anymore and because you are playing chords you are playing within limits. However, there is a lot of scope for variation. When we are writing we are also hearing things all the time so it is difficult to know where those things are coming from. However, I was conscious that I did not want to sound like anyone else. 'The First Picture of You' was a song which appealed to the emotions.[129]

The Lotus Eaters enjoyed success with their album and singles and were admired in the Philippines and Japan. Their tours in the Far East were attended by fiercely loyal supporters that recognized the emotion in their songs and shared an empathy with their feelings. American journalist and owner of WXB102 New Wave Radio Station, Mike Sutton, articulates the emotional impact of the feelings in the songs performed by the Lotus Eaters:

> They sang of the sun and the windswept beauty of young romance, but they weren't afraid of enveloping themselves in the bleak embrace of despair. As a teenager attending high school in the Philippines during the mid-'80s, the Lotus Eaters captured the highs and lows of adolescence, from the dreamy innocence of 'The First Picture of You' to the crushed hopes of 'It Hurts'.[130]

3 Rainy-Day Music: Art Pop and the Scouse Romantic

In the days before social media and MTV, pop music on the radio was a dominant influence on youth culture – an aural rather than visual one (Shuker 2015). Smartphones, computer games and talent shows were either not invented or held little appeal. Radio playlists, although controlled, were less predictable and one could often hear something surprising and exciting even on daytime radio. There was a very limited diet of pop on TV: the BBC had its flagship show *Top of the Pops* once a week, with *The Old Grey Whistle Test* catering for the rock and progressive end of the market. Those who were young in the 1960s–80s can testify to the impact of hearing the excitement, energy and emotion contained in a three-minute pop song emerging from the speakers of a domestic transistor radio. The sound was all-important: the song had to stand out from the crowd and capture the attention of the listener; in the heyday of radio, the look didn't matter.

This is the context in which the successful Scouse Pop bands discussed here made the charts, some certainly because of the quality of their songs and not their appearance. Early television appearances by OMD, China Crisis and It's Immaterial testify to this: they had little in the way of an image or a floorshow – they just played unique and credible songs. The appeal was in the songwriting, the subject matter and the resonance they created with the listener: a triumph of substance over style.

The main strength of the Liverpool music scene was the abundance of songwriting talent. In the 1980s many local bands came up with classic tracks even on their debut releases. The early Zoo releases of the Bunnymen's 'Pictures on My Wall' and the Teardrop Explodes' 'When I Dream' are equalled by the excellent first singles of Wah! Heat ('Better Scream') and China Crisis ('African and White') on Inevitable Records.

Musicians and songwriters in Liverpool have consistently delivered sensitive, passionate and haunting songs. Many such songs are so direct in their appeal to the emotions that they become all-consuming. The listener is drawn in to the mood and romance inherent in the music and lyrics. One other aspect that distinguished Liverpool bands in the 1980s was the passion in their music. Despite the diversity of music coming from the city, a noticeable thread running through much of the output is the notion of "rainy-day music": songs in a minor key. The emergence of the "Scouse Romantic" was a defining feature of the Scouse Pop era. Roger Hill puts it succinctly: "There was such a variety of different-sounding bands . . . there was no single quality to them except the strange DNA which runs through Liverpool music which is a sense of Romantic young men presenting their credentials."[1]

This chapter will examine some of the songs that fall into the "Scouse Romantic" category. They are purely a personal choice, to be taken as examples of how the notion of romance can be represented in both conventional love songs as well as in less obvious concepts of romance such as spirituality, melancholy, sadness and ecstasy. The following describes the context in which the songs were written and the sentiments behind them.

'Ideal World': The Christians

Hope springs eternal when Mark Herman and Henry Priestman collaborate.

Henry Priestman and Mark Herman's classic track 'Ideal World', performed by the Christians, became a pop anthem in the late 1980s, eventually becoming the biggest-selling single from their first album, *The Christians*. Hull-born Priestman composed songs for the first album which were atmospheric, moody and contained elements of protest, all wrapped up in memorable tunes. The songs were socially aware and the lyrics contained messages, desires and moralities that held resonance in the 1980s and are just as relevant today. The thought-provoking 'Ideal World' reached number 14 in the UK charts in 1987.

'Ideal World' did not start out as a song about the iniquity of the South African apartheid regime. It was originally a simple love song called 'The Game of Love', which may explain the melancholic melody and the contemplative mood it creates. However, such a conventional love song would have been out of place on the album, so Henry and Mark changed the lyrics to make it more in keeping with songs such as 'Hooverville', 'Forgotten Town' and 'When the Fingers Point'.

Henry's schoolfriend Mark Herman is not normally recognized for his lyric writing but is more famously known as screenwriter and film director of classics such as *Hope Springs*, *Brassed Off* and *The Boy in the Striped Pyjamas*. He responded to Henry's concerns about the appropriateness of the song in the context of the album, and the pair came up with the poignant lyrics for what is now 'Ideal World'.

Lyrically, although the song carries aspirations for a better future, it is mixed with despair about the lack of compassion in the world. The melody is haunting and yet uplifting, disguising the distressing message in the lyrics. The tune has an emotional appeal, and its refrain creates a reflective mood. The song sits comfortably alongside John Lennon's classic 'Imagine' in the sense that it presents a wistful notion that the world could be a better place if only people could demonstrate a more tolerant attitude. Henry Priestman explains:

> 'Ideal World' was originally a straightforward love song called 'The Game of Love'. When we were looking at the composition of the first album we had songs like 'Forgotten Town', 'Hooverville' and 'When the Fingers Point'. These were all gritty protest-style songs so the notion of having a standard love song did not fit in with the flow of the album. It would have seemed out of place. The co-writer on the lyrics was schoolfriend and now film producer Mark Herman. We looked at the general theme of the band and considered other subjects which could reflect the emotion in the melody. The struggle against the apartheid regime in South Africa seemed to be a romantic notion which we felt passionate about. The chorus of: "In an ideal world we'd be free to choose / But in my real world you can bet you're gonna lose" just seemed to fit beautifully with the melody line.[2]

'The First Picture of You': The Lotus Eaters

Jerry moves and Peter dreams.

The Lotus Eaters' hit 'The First Picture of You' dominated the airwaves in the summer of 1983. It was Radio 1's most played track over the summer months and reached number 15 in the UK charts. Their lead singer was Peter Coyle, who was initially a progressive rock fan influenced by Peter Gabriel and Peter Hammill. However, his soft melodic vocals reflected a completely different style of singing. Jerry Kelly on guitar had a unique sound which provided light and ethereal counterpoint melodies to accompany Peter's voice.

The Lotus Eaters travelled to London to record their first Peel session in October 1982 and performed 'The First Picture of You'. It was a sumptuous track with a seductive guitar riff which enchanted the listener into the same dream-like state evoked in Tennyson's classic poem *The Lotus Eaters* (see Chapter 2). When the session was broadcast a bidding war ensued between rival record companies.

The sound displays similarities with the Wild Swans: the musicians were the same and the instrumentation was similar. The haunting melodic vocal, atmospheric guitars, piano and "vox humana" chorus combine to produce a sensual sound. This style is classic Lotus Eaters and reflects Peter Coyle's musical philosophy: "My dream is to write something that will touch you directly as though it came from your heart and soul."[3]

Jerry Kelly claims that there is no special meaning behind the song. The song is more of a feeling that takes over the listener producing a haunting sense of melancholy. 'The First Picture of You' is a quintessential example of the spirit of the Scouse Romantic. Its strength is in the melody and its ability to transport the listener to the gentle warm days of summer. Jerry explains: "Sometimes it is the rhythm in the music which moves people whereas we think melodies can move you in a different sort of way."[4]

'The Power of Love': Frankie Goes to Hollywood

An anthem for the festive season that has little to do with Christmas.

Amidst all the madness that surrounded Frankie Goes to Hollywood's momentous year of domination in 1984, Holly Johnson later remarked that his own favourite song was "'The Power of Love': the slow one . . . I was just pleased with it as a song. I thought it was a nice song that almost anybody could sing."[5]

The first broadcast of the song dates back to a John Peel session recorded in 1983. This recording was a more simple-sounding ballad and lacked the grandeur and production of the eventual single release. 'The Power of Love' credits all the Frankie Goes to Hollywood musicians as writers and demonstrates the band's more sensitive characteristics. The song was their third consecutive number 1 and was in complete contrast to their first two explosive dance-oriented singles. It is a soulful ballad with a spiritual core within the lyrics and the melody. The simple start with the quiet strumming of an acoustic guitar and a pure-sounding vocal sets the pensive mood and the quiet before the storm. The dramatic chorus has an uplifting feeling and a simple message about the nature of love. The orchestral sounds, the arrangement and the production make for a romantic record of epic proportions. However, even a stripped-down version with just an acoustic guitar and a vocal – as performed by Brian Nash in Episode 7 of the *Scouse Pop* TV series – has just as much impact and resonance.[6] It is essentially a beautiful Scouse Romantic ballad.

The song is predominantly associated with Christmas due to the accompanying music video and despite there being no direct references to the festive season in the lyrics. Brian Nash discusses the video, which features the assumption of the Virgin Mary and the Nativity scene:

> When we saw the video for 'The Power of Love' we were confused. We never saw it as a Christmas song. My contribution was on the

musical side so I never really knew what the song was about. I am still not sure exactly what the song is about. Holly's lyrics were based around a love song and, as far as I knew, and the rest of us knew . . . it had nothing to do with Christmas! The record company spent a lot of money recording the video in Israel because they wanted it to be "authentic". That is fine, but it cost us a fortune and they didn't ask us whether that was a good idea. The band was not even featured in the original version of the video. We were just stuck on later in the borders around the main shots.[7]

The song is still played every year around Christmas and is firmly established as a festive-season anthem. Holly Johnson, who wrote the lyrics, admitted in an interview with Laura Barton (2012) that the song did contain a personal religious element:

> I always felt that The Power of Love was the record that would save me in this life . . . There is a Biblical aspect to its spirituality and passion; the fact that, love is the only thing that matters in the end.

'Dark Clouds': Space

Tommy Scott loses his voice and asks a psychic to find it.

The original release of 'Dark Clouds' by Space was the final single taken from the *Spiders* album and reached number 14 in the UK charts in 1997. On first hearing, the song does not exemplify the notion of Scouse Romantic. The lightweight pop song with its semi-humorous video was not even one of the band's favourite tracks. Some years after the release, Tommy Scott openly admitted that it was not one of their greatest works:

> This is a little bit of advice for any musicians out there. If you have a song that is so cheesy that the whole band falls about laughing at it, then the song will not remain funny forever. When we recorded it and made the video for 'Dark Clouds', we laughed our heads off because we sounded like Kajagoogoo. It was dead cheesy and we ended up hating the song. Then we looked at other ways of trying to present the song. We even considered an '80s-style country and western version and that was even cheesier.[8]

However, the subject matter of the song is darker than the treatment suggested: it tells of two depressed and embattled individuals and their hope for escape. In the mid-1990s, dark clouds descended over the group themselves, ironically when they were enjoying a rich period of success.

Following two hit singles, this quintessentially English band began to meet with success in the US, which came as a surprise to many observers. But not to singer and songwriter Tommy Scott: "The Americans got us . . . They understood what we were about . . . after all it is the country of quirk. If you've got a good pop song with a good melody, then they get it and it really works."[9]

Following sustained airplay in the US, a North American tour beckoned, eagerly anticipated by their new American fans. However, this period was blighted by a series of unfortunate events. Firstly, guitarist Jamie Murphy quit the band for health reasons, which came as a great surprise to Tommy Scott: "I didn't know that Jamie had gone . . . we turned up in Canada and there was another guitarist in Jamie's place."[10] On top of this, the band members were feeling homesick, and for this reason drummer Andy Parle quit as well. To add to all this, bass player Dave Palmer suffered the loss of his mother Gladys (who had a pivotal role to play in the early days of Scouse Pop; see Chapter 2). The band was disintegrating before Tommy's eyes at the very point at which the challenges of international success were exerting their own pressures. Tommy comments:

> With all the setbacks it was hard. America was also a big culture shock. Before Space became successful, the furthest I had been was Wales. We were also quite shy and struggled doing all the "meet and greets" and we found that quite difficult.[11]

The final setback, which ultimately put an end to the American tour, was Tommy Scott losing his voice and being unable to perform. Whether or not this was a direct result of the collapse of the band during the tour is uncertain. Tommy believes it was: "The stress of all the events that had happened to us had affected me and my vocal cords had just frozen and I was told that my voice might come back or it might never come back."[12]

However, a silver lining was lurking behind this particular "dark cloud", and the story of how Tommy Scott regained his health is one that is very much of a piece with this bizarre band and its music. Tommy had tried medics and hypnotherapists but to no avail. In the end, it was Liverpool psychic Billy Roberts that changed Tommy's fortunes: not only did he cure Tommy's loss of voice he also predicted the exact date it would come back. Tommy recounts:

> The record company had taken me down south to someone who did hypnotherapy but it didn't work and I would pretend that I was hypnotized but I wasn't really! So back in Liverpool I met a friend called Billy Roberts who was a psychic. He was also a good guitarist from the '60s. He said "Let's just chill out", and he placed his hands close to my throat and he said that my voice would come back . . . and, on the day he said it would come back – it did! I don't know whether it was psychological or something but it worked![13]

Tommy's difficult experiences were sources of inspiration for many of his songs, 'Dark Clouds' among them. It is a cathartic process which means his innate songwriting creativity is at work even during difficult times. Tommy explains:

> I am a writer. I could always write a song. I was even writing when we were on tour and things were going wrong. 'Dark Clouds' is a song about depression. It is when the entire world is collapsing in on you. It was after the experience in America. I was depressed for ages after that.
>
> Even though 'Dark Clouds' was based on feeling depressed, it didn't turn out sounding like that when we first recorded it. When we first played 'Dark Clouds' to our producer it was a Sinatra style of song but the producer turned it in to a cheesy '80s-style pop song. But if you listen to the lyrics, it really is a dark song.[14]

When Space performed 'Dark Clouds' for the *Scouse Pop* TV series, that version was much more aligned with the original concept as written by Tommy Scott and Franny Griffiths. Here it was a slower-paced romantic ballad, augmented by a smooth-sounding cello courtesy of Satin Beige; it provided a wistful and memorable experience – art pop and the Scouse Romantic at work.[15] Nonetheless, Tommy claims that the best performance of this song was during a particularly emotional occasion in the city:

> The best time we ever performed that song is when we played it at the Hillsborough memorial concert at Anfield. One of the moments everyone remembers from that concert was that just as we finished playing the last notes of 'Dark Clouds' and all of a sudden the sun came out![16]

'Bible Dreams': The Wild Swans

Paul Simpson, Tommy Atkins haircuts and the Church of England's rousing hymns.

'Bible Dreams' was the second single released from the Wild Swans' 1988 album *Bringing Home the Ashes*. It is a grand pop song in true Paul Simpson style. His haunting baritone voice and cryptic lyrics are the most striking element of the Wild Swans' sound: he created a unique look and sound which resonated with the many followers of the Wild Swans in Liverpool and later around the world. According to Roger Hill:

> One of the truly unique and enduring characters in Liverpool from the Liverpool scene of the 1980s was Paul Simpson. He had

developed a unique look and sound which was very different from contemporary pop music at that time. His style was different, his music was different and his lyrics were poetry. His songs had that unique quality in which he was able to convey that image and sound of young manhood in a timeless way which set him apart from his peers.[17]

'Bible Dreams' presents notions of war, religion and young manhood wrapped in a glorious melody and driving rhythm. The song is built around a tight format of drums, bass, guitar and keyboards (string synthesizer) and yet sounds imposing in stature and almost orchestral. However, Paul maintains that the design of the Wild Swans sound was always within the simple conventional parameters of a band structure. When asked why the sound was not expanded into orchestral instruments, Paul replies:

'Bible Dreams' does have the heroic string synthesizer which gives the song a grand-sounding feel but its overall sound is based on the instrumentation we use in a band. I like that tight format. It does not limit the sound because we use the instruments in different ways. I am not against the use of different instruments: I just preferred that guitar-based sound for this track.[18]

Not all the influences and inspirations behind 'Bible Dreams' are the obvious pop music ones:

When I was a schoolboy, the songs I most listened to were hymns. The influence of hymns is still there in some of the Wild Swans songs. It is in the precise verses and rousing choruses and the type of symbolic or personal language used in the lyrics.[19]

Simpson's account goes a long way to explain the anthem-like quality of 'Bible Dreams'. The verse has a regular rhythmic precision like a melodic instruction while the chorus rises to take the emotions to a higher level. The lyrics refer to sacrifice, a chosen one and a bereft world awaiting redemption – the same themes to be found in a good old-fashioned Church of England hymn. Its impact and passion makes 'Bible Dreams' a 'Jerusalem' for the 1980s Liverpool generation. The lyrics would not be out of place in a Victorian Romantic poem: the appeal to the senses contained in the lyrics bears more similarity to the work of Blake, Keats and Shelley than contemporary pop music; and, to this author's ears, the music evokes colours that are bright and vibrant, reminiscent of the work of Pre-Raphaelite painters such as Rossetti and Millais. Paul Simpson confirms this observation:

People were intrigued by our style. Some said that we looked like we were from the 1940s. That was due to the baggy trousers and the Tommy Atkins haircuts. That wasn't really fair. We had more in common with the 1840s than we did with the 1940s.[20]

The notion of the Scouse Romantic is clearly evident in 'Bible Dreams'. It is a classic romantic triumph of the heart, sentiment and emotion over intellect and reason. It is an example of art and poetry combining with modern electric pop music.[21]

'The More You Live, the More You Love': A Flock of Seagulls

From alien invasions to Tennyson's views on love.

A Flock of Seagulls had created a new look and a new sound in the US in the early 1980s. They had been in the mainstream spotlight for two years before 'The More You Live, the More You Love' was released. The early subject matter of their songs was diverse, but the notion of romance as conveyed in conventional love songs had not been a major theme, although more alternative references to romance could be heard in 'Space Age Love Song' and 'Modern Love is Automatic'. Their debut long-player was a concept album with references to an alien invasion of earth and visions of a mechanical end to civilization. Lyrics related a science-fiction vision of a futuristic society made imperfect by the influences of tyranny through advanced technologies. There are even references to dragons!

The exciting combination of a new look, a new style of music and peculiar song themes made them a popular alternative to mainstream pop music, and A Flock of Seagulls remained at the forefront of US pop culture for two breathtaking years. As this period drew to a close, they released their last major hit from the *Story of a Young Heart* album.

'The More You Live, the More You Love' is one of those rainy-day songs that puts the listener in a wistful frame of mind. It is a reflective song containing all the classic elements of young love's dream, but with warnings that infatuation will eventually fade. The melancholic melody accompanies a lyric that speaks of self-survival and concerns about being hurt. It is advice to sensitive young men about the dangers of jumping head first into a relationship before really getting to know someone. The lyrics are fundamentally sad – all relationships will eventually fail and we will all suffer pain: "You'll put your heart in mortal danger / They all desert you in the end." To temper the harsh lesson that love hurts is the redemption contained in the unforgettable refrain, which explains that we all need love and we experience it throughout our lives. The more of life's rich experience we encounter, the more likely we are to be hurt. The consequence of living is the human cycle of love and hurt. According to bass player Frank Maudsley:

'The More You Live' was a bit different in tone to some of our other songs because some of our earlier stuff was a bit weird. I suppose 'I Ran' was about romance and being scared of finding someone you thought was out of your league suddenly becoming a possibility. 'The More You Live' is a romantic song. We all have relationships and some of them work and some of them fail. You always take that chance that you could end up getting hurt, but you can't go through life avoiding relationships because that is what life is all about . . . emotions experiences and love.[22]

'The More You Live, the More You Love' is an encapsulation in pop music of Tennyson's axiom that "'Tis better to have loved and lost than never to have loved at all".[23]

'L'image Craqué': Hambi and the Dance

Victorian villa in Ullet Road produces heartache for owner.

Hambi and the Dance were one of Liverpool's most passionate and quixotic bands to emerge in the Scouse Pop era. Their brand of romantic power pop was more intelligent, better written and more professional than that of all their Liverpool peers. Lead singer and writer Hambi Haralambous was slightly older than most of those on the scene at the time, with more life experience, greater knowledge and a more discernment in choosing the most appropriate musical elements to include in his compositions. Hambi drew inspiration from his time spent travelling through India as a youth, which was a spiritual and cultural experience for him. He explains:

> Before I became involved in music on a serious basis, I had travelled through India. It was a spiritual experience and I would stop at places on the way and play my Yamaha guitar and sing. Music was a big part of the spiritual life along with meditation, dance and prayer. I was doing the whole hippie trip of meditating and exploring the meaning of life. When I came back to England, I carried on my meditation and music in Liverpool.[24]

An advantage for his musical ambitions was his acquisition of a large Victorian villa in Ullet Road, Liverpool which had the potential to convert some of the rooms into a recording studio. This was the studio that became known as "The Pink" and was used by many Liverpool bands such as Frankie Goes to Hollywood, Dead or Alive, Black and A Flock of Seagulls. With the luxury of having his own studio, Hambi was able to take time over his songs and produce tracks of considerably higher quality than his peers. Every small piece of the musical jigsaw that made up his compositions was clearly defined and professionally executed, each detail carefully considered before being committed to tape. Hambi and the Dance had a unique and passionate sound which bore no similarity to other local bands. Andrea Miller wrote: "Hambi and the Dance are strange. Not weird strange or arty strange but quite unlike anything I have ever seen or heard before. A good thing."[25]

One might speculate that his youthful experience would result in an Eastern flavour in Hambi's music but this is not immediately apparent. At face value, the songs are reflective and powerful romantic pop songs with passionate lyrics. The musical landscapes are sensual and melodic by design. Hambi reveals that his influences included big-production Tamla Motown tracks from artists such as the Supremes. The influence of Berry Gordy's protégées is not immediately apparent to this listener, however, whereas Phil Spector's "wall of sound" – as in Ike & Tina Turner's 'River Deep–Mountain High' – is probably a more obvious reference. Hambi explains:

> One of my influences was Tamla Motown. I loved the big soulful ballads and well-crafted upbeat songs as well. The singers could all sing and the songs may have sounded simple but were very complex and well arranged and produced.[26]

He produced songs on a massive scale, with multiple melodies and counterpoints cleverly woven into a most vibrant and engaging sound. In many respects, Hambi set the bar for the Liverpool bands that followed him. Hambi and the Dance certainly did not have the chaotic and experimental sound of a group of lads having a go at putting something half-decent together.

Hambi's work at The Pink studio was much appreciated by Richard Branson, and Hambi and the Dance were eventually signed to Virgin Records in 1981, with an album entitled *Heartache* appearing the following year. All the songs were recorded at The Pink and oozed quality. The personnel was impressive: apart from Hambi Haralambous on vocals and guitar, there were Wayne Hussey of the Mission, music producer Steve Lovell, Gary Johnson (later of China Crisis), Steve Power (later the producer of Robbie Williams) and Paul Rutherford who would go on to join Frankie Goes to Hollywood.

Before the album's release, two singles came out in 1981: 'Too Late to Fly the Flag' and 'L'image Craqué', the latter being an intense romantic song. The vocal is passionate, screaming a fervent refrain accompanied by a counterpoint string synthesizer which adds more melancholy than Paolo Mantovani in reflective mood. The single garnered good reviews in *Merseysound*, the singles review of which stated: "'L'image Craqué' is high on atmosphere, passion and quality. It will go platinum, conquer the world and generally walk on water."[27]

The quality of the songwriting and musicianship was also attracting attention, and there was a sense that national success was imminent. John D. Hodgkinson wrote: "Hambi and the Dance are one of Merseyside's greatest hopes."[28] The 'L'image Craqué' single looked as though it would deliver the predicted success. The song created an intense atmosphere that drew listeners in and transformed their mood; and it had all of the elements of a truly classic pop song.[29] Sadly, radio stations largely ignored it and the song never received the recognition it deserved. Hambi explains the sentiments behind the track:

> It is about a young girl leaving the umbrella of her parents and moving out into the world. As the girl grows up she starts to enter into dangerous liaisons, as some young girls do.
>
> The idea for the song came from someone I knew at the time. I am not too sure why I wrote the song about that particular subject. It is not something I normally do. A lot of the things I write about come from my subconscious. I never deliberately sat down and wrote lyrics and then put music to them. We would normally put the music together through a jamming session. I would come to the session with an idea and then the band would develop it.[30]

Despite the quality and intensity of 'L'image Craqué', it failed to trouble the national charts. Virgin Records at the time were still a relatively small company: Richard Branson was still setting up his empire and living on a houseboat. Hambi offers an explanation for the lack of commercial success:

> I am not sure why the song did not take off as well as we hoped. The band at the time became a pawn in Richard Branson's empire. Geffen Records were keen to sign us. John Kalodner who signed Aerosmith really liked us. He kept coming over and watching us saying, "Come on, let's do a deal." So we ended up on Richard Branson's houseboat and Geffen wanted us to sign a deal and go straight over to America to tour for three months. They had a budget arranged. However, Richard would not let Geffen sign the band unless they signed some of the other bands on Virgin as well. At the time Virgin did not have any deal in America to release their records. So it never quite happened for us.
>
> On occasion, decisions in music seem the right thing to do at the time and sometimes the decisions can be difficult. After the first album, Virgin wanted to keep me but not my band. Nowadays that would seem reasonable to bring in the band as session musicians but back in the day I said, "No! This is it. This is the band. This is us together." So I refused to take up that offer. I wanted to keep the continuity going because we had been recording well together. 'L'image Craqué' was recorded over a day or two and mixed along with other songs at a later date.[31]

'Souvenir': Orchestral Manoeuvres in the Dark

Paul Humphreys becomes a contortionist to produce a hit record.

In the late 1970s and early '80s this author used to write articles and interviews for local fanzine *Merseysound*. I would cover Wirral-based groups in particular, and one of those bands that had quickly come into prominence was Orchestral Manoeuvres in the Dark (OMD). In just over a year they had progressed from being local lads performing on a Thursday night in Eric's to appearing on BBC's Thursday-night flagship pop programme *Top of the Pops*. By chance, I met singer and bass player Andy McCluskey at a gig in Wallasey's Dale Inn in January 1980. He was there to enjoy another Wirral synth-based band called the Games. I asked Andy if he would do an interview for *Merseysound* and he gave me the number of his manager Paul Collister. The latter turned out not to be keen on the idea because there had been a few letters published in *Merseysound* that were not complementary about the band. Despite this, Andy graciously agreed.

At the specified time, I arrived at OMD's recording studio, "The Gramophone Suite", passing through the music shop Curly Music on Stanley Street, armed with my Akai reel-to-reel recorder. Amused at the size of the recording device and my lack of professionalism, Andy and Paul kindly helped me in with the heavy recorder. One memorable aspect of the afternoon occurred before the interview. Paul Humphreys was experimenting with odd choral sounds and explained that the tapes were recordings of single notes sung by a choir. As samplers were unavailable in 1981, Paul was transferring the tapes onto individual tracks on his mixing desk. I thought little about this at the time, presuming that these choral drones would later feature on some bleak and industrial-sounding album track.

In the summer of 1981, with their popularity on the increase, the band released a single from the *Architecture and Morality* album called 'Souvenir'. It was a departure from previous OMD songs, being romantic and melancholy. The song began with the ghostly choir sounds with which Paul Humphreys had been experimenting. They had a warm, ethereal sound which drew the listener in. The vocal on the song was by Paul rather than Andy: it had a clear, naïve quality which matched the haunting melody and arrangement.

This song is another example of the notion of the Scouse Romantic. Although the lyrics are cryptic, the mood conveyed in the music is pure emotion. It is another of those rainy-day songs that invoke a pensive mood.

'Souvenir' was a huge success despite McCluskey's misgivings about its appropriateness as the first single from their most successful album. His concerns were understandable: the song was not representative of the album and so could set a misleading tone for future releases. However, the huge success of 'Souvenir' further increased the band's popularity and album sales rocketed. Andy explains:

Initially, I thought it was too pastel and too sweet. It wasn't my sort of song – it was radically different from all our other music and that bothered me . . . However, months later I got it – I realized that it was a beautiful ethereal melody.[32]

Paul Humphreys comments on the inspiration for 'Souvenir': "Some songs you labour over for months and months and some songs just arrive . . . and that song just arrived . . . After I had written it, it seemed like it had always been there."[33] Humphreys explains how the tape loops with which he had been experimenting became a prominent feature of the track:

I put the tape loops onto each track of our sixteen-track tape. Each track was a different note. I worked out what all the notes were and marked up the desk for each note. I became this contortionist and pushed up each of the faders to make chords with these single notes and the first pattern I did was the 'Souvenir' pattern.[34]

So this melancholy classic was created with an inspired use of tape loops arrived at through trial and error, with Paul Humphreys "playing" the Gramophone Suite mixing desk like a keyboard. The song remains OMD's biggest-selling single.

'Wonderful Life': Black

Colin's son travels the world and sends him a cheque every now and again.

The story behind Colin Vearncombe's classic hit 'Wonderful Life' has been discussed in the previous chapter under the more general synopsis of Colin's career. To recap, it was first released on independent label Ugly Man Records in 1986, and, despite low-key promotion by the label, enjoyed sustained airplay. It is one of those songs that is simple, sensitive and instantly memorable. Local and national radio recognized its appeal and several playlistings followed. Colin's recognition of the harsh realities of life, where hopes and expectations can suddenly come crashing down, is embodied in this ironic ballad. The song is laced with the sardonic humour often employed in times of despair. It was in fact written during a tough time in Colin's life, so from bitter experience emerges a striking, unique ballad that resonates with everyone. Many of us can relate to that weightless feeling when everything seems to stop and we feel alone spinning through life, detached from hope and struggling to face the mundane challenges of everyday existence. Colin explains the initial reaction to the track:

At first, I don't think people quite understood that the song was being sarcastic. That took them a few listens. Even later on, when it was used as the theme tune on the TV advert for the bank it was still being taken literally as though it was about people building a wonderful life . . . Well it wasn't . . . At the time I wrote it, I was broke and nothing seemed to be going well for me.[35]

'Wonderful Life' was later re-released by A&M Records after Black had registered a first hit with 'Sweetest Smile' in 1987. It subsequently reached the top 10 in the UK and became an international success, selling over 2.5 million copies. Due to the success of 'Sweetest Smile', A&M committed a significant budget to the haunting black-and-white video to accompany its follow-up. Colin returned to Merseyside to record the video on the promenades of New Brighton and Southport. The rollercoaster at Pleasureland in Southport is in plain view, as is New Brighton lighthouse. There is a detached other-worldly feel about the grainy, slow motion of the music video, which reinforces the melancholy and sadness in the song. Gerard De Thame directed the video and received an award at the New York Film Festival for his captivating work. Despite the irony, loneliness and melancholy in the song, it has an under-current of resilience conveying the need to stand up straight in the cold light of day and face the world. Ironically, the song marked a turning point in Vearncombe's career. Things were destined to get better, and out of despair came hope and out of hope came success:

'Wonderful Life' didn't take me that long to write. I just came back from the shops one day with an idea in my head and started to write it. We even recorded it on the cheap over a weekend in The Pink studio when Hambi was away. The irony of the song is that it became so successful and financially it has been a great support during my career. It is like a son you raise and one day let go to travel the world and every now and again sends you back a cheque.[36]

Artists who have one massive hit record often find it unfairly overshadows a career littered with great songs. As Colin explains:

At times 'Wonderful Life' became difficult to sustain because people liked it so much that they were not as enthusiastic about my other songs. I just resigned myself to the comforting thought that the song meant something important to them and as an artist that is all you can hope for.[37]

So, predictably, during Colin's latter tours with Calum MacColl, the fiercely loyal audiences would wait patiently for the hypnotic melody to arrive. Colin would often leave 'Wonderful Life' until the end of the set or even perform it as an encore. He would sing it *a capella*, and the sheer quality of the naked voice and sadness of the lyric would invariably stir his fans' emotions. The performances were among those rare occasions when noisy venues are reduced to complete silence, as Colin's voice cuts through the thick air. The audiences waited obediently in anticipation of Colin raising his arms to invite them to join in with the chorus. During his Liverpool gig in 2015, the odd tear was shed by fans in acknowledgement that one of their own had come home and brought his anthem with him.

4 Some Aspects of the Music Industry in Liverpool

This chapter attempts to capture some of the various outlets that supported the development of bands in Liverpool during the 1980s. It provides a snapshot of notable individuals who promoted the artists in various ways and focuses on four local record labels, two Merseyside record shops, local radio stations, a rock photographer, two local recording studios and Eric's club.

The record labels

In the UK during the mid to late 1970s there was a rapid increase in the number of independent record companies across Britain. By their nature they were localized and dealt with bands that were not mainstream or did not have major-label interest. Most of the material released was from newly formed bands (Hesmondhalgh 1996). Labels such as Stiff and Raw had started in response to the punk rock revolution. Liverpool had not fully embraced punk, however, and there were relatively few punk bands and independent labels compared to many other cities. This chapter will examine four local labels that emerged during this period: Zoo, Probe, Inevitable and Skeleton. Interviews with some of the characters involved in these labels will centre on how the labels were formed and why those involved with the labels were prepared to take a leap of faith on unproven bands playing music that challenged the commercial models of the day.

The context of the era with regard to pop music is important in under-standing the development of talent in Liverpool. Punk had given the major labels a shock: success could no longer be guaranteed using tried-and-tested methods of promotion and tour, backed by the labels' high finance. Street-level commerce had now combined with new music to produce hit records, and the guerrilla tactics of the new indie labels unsettled the majors (Hesmondhalgh 1996).

The major labels struggled to engage with early punk. The music seemed unwholesome, it was happening too fast, and they had no control over it. Realizing they were becoming out of touch with the fast-changing trends of the record-buying public, the majors opted for a tactical switch. Rather than developing new bands themselves, they either bought a band from an independent label or simply purchased the label itself. It marked a shift of power in the industry as the majors were forced to take notice of the independents and pay much closer attention to innovative and emerging trends. They had also lost control of the material DJs were prepared to play on radio stations (Hesmondhalgh 1997).

Local independent labels therefore became more important and more credible. And, as each new pop music trend emerged, it rendered the previous style obsolete. This made it difficult for the major record companies to plan ahead and produce a sustainable business model, never knowing what was coming next. This was a propitious environment for innovative bands evolving in Liverpool. If the industry was unsure what was going to be the next trend, any band could claim to be just what the record companies were looking for. It was an exciting time in British pop music, because it allowed for a variety of unorthodox styles and characters to come to the fore. But a realization that something different and quite distinctive was happening in Liverpool was slow in coming from the major companies, and it was left to the local labels to promote their oddly named and strange-sounding bands. The first Merseyside independent label to be examined here is Zoo Records.

Zoo

Bill Drummond nips to the shops and is never seen again.
Dave Balfe's big ball of brown plasticine and the sound of mating dinosaurs.
Dave Balfe has never considered writing a follow-up to 'Danny Boy'.

One of the most interesting local record companies was Zoo Records. Klaus Schwartze described it as "One of the most influential labels of the new Liverpool Rock scene" (Schwartze 1987: 162). It was the project of local musicians Bill Drummond and Dave Balfe.

David Balfe grew up in Thingwall, Wirral. He was a prominent musician in several Liverpool bands, starting with Wirral punk rockers Radio Blank. He then played with some of the bands associated with Eric's, including Big in Japan, Dalek I Love You and the Teardrop Explodes.

Bill Drummond was Balfe's partner at Zoo. Drummond came to Liverpool in 1975 to work at the Everyman Theatre as a carpenter and scene painter. He became the set designer for Ken Campbell's idiosyncratic production of the *Illuminatus!* trilogy. To Campbell, Drummond became "The man who went for Araldite". Allegedly, during a performance at the Roundhouse in London, Drummond declared that he was going to the shops to get some glue. However, he caught the train back to Liverpool and never returned to his job (Drummond 2014).

Figure 19: Dave Balfe at the System Club in Liverpool in 1980.
Photograph by Colin Howe, digitalised by Dave Williams

Balfe and Drummond met while playing together in Big in Japan and founded the Zoo label in 1978 in order to release their own EP *From Y to Z and Never Again*. Balfe then progressed to playing keyboards and co-producing the first Teardrop Explodes album, as well as being involved in producing early Echo and the Bunnymen tracks. Balfe and Drummond also managed both bands and consequently the label signed them and released their early work. In March 1979, out of the office of Zoo Records above the Chicago Building in Button Street, the debut single 'Pictures on My Wall' by Echo and the Bunnymen was released. The whole decision-making process of releasing records was based on the whims and fancies of Balfe and Drummond: it was purely a case of what they considered "good" – a gut reaction based simply on an emotional response to the music. However, one essential prerequisite – insisted upon by both Balfe and Drummond – was that the bands they signed had to be different from what was happening in music nationally and contain their own element of originality. Dave McCullough (1979) claims that "The Zoo selection process was determined by a mixture of luck and urgency rather than any set standards."[1]

Balfe recounts how he and Drummond selected bands for Zoo:

In those days we were immersed in a culture that was experimental. I did not look at the bands in a way that I would now. Nowadays I would be more Machiavellian. The Zoo label happened when I was twenty years old and Big in Japan had just split up. Bill asked us all "What are you going to do next?" and he then told us that he was going to start a record label. I said, "That's fantastic! Do you want me to do it with you?" He agreed, and that is how Zoo was formed. We started off with the posthumous EP with Big in Japan. This was to pay off a bank overdraft which the band had run up and it was successful in clearing the debt.

We both knew Julian Cope from Eric's. He had a new band called the Teardrop Explodes so we checked them out – and they were good! So we recorded 'Sleeping Gas' with them in the four-track Open Eye studios. We had no idea about the song we just thought that it didn't sound like anything else – so we considered that as a positive.

We decided to put it out – it really was that naïve. However, there is an awful lot of purity in naïvety. As I joke about my career in the music industry: I began as an inspired amateur and became an uninspired professional.

Then we signed the Bunnymen. I was the same age as the bands I was signing. The band was pretty basic and we shared equipment together. One of the reasons that the bands played at the same gigs is because they were all using my gear. So we did one of their tracks, 'Pictures on My Wall', at an eight-track and I remember thinking that this was a great song with lots of moodiness and atmosphere.[2]

This was a real gamble for Balfe and Drummond: releasing records that were quite different from the music being played at the time. There were no obvious outlets in terms of airplay other than John Peel at Radio 1, and the distribution infrastructure for independent labels was inconsistent. However, Balfe and Drummond remained true to their principles of innovation and difference despite the prospect of limited success and financial loss. They cobbled together DIY releases and attempted to control the whole release process in an ad hoc manner. Dave Balfe explains:

It was such a big part of music then that you had to be innovative. A lot of the musicians were incompetent and there is nothing like incompetence to spur on innovation. If you can reel off loads of riffs from here, there and everywhere very easily, then you are going to be referencing those riffs. Because we couldn't do those things easily, we would try to assemble something half-decent from our own resources and that didn't sound like anything else.

So we kept putting these records out . . . We found someone who pressed up records and we found someone with a print shop down the docks who printed up sleeves. A lucky thing was that my dad had bought me and my brother a car. Luckily, my brother failed his driving test so I could have the car to pick up records from London and literally sleeve the vinyl in the car after I had received them. I could take them to Rough Trade and drop off 25 here and 50 there – to places that liked it. Literally, Bill and I would make a record and we had no idea who would buy it. We would go into places and say, "Will you take fifty from us?" and we would have pressed up a thousand – and we didn't know whether we would be left with 750. BUT . . . we sold them! And people would come back and reorder. *Sounds* made both Bunnymen and Teardrop singles their Record of the Week. We just happened to be doing the right things at the right time – in a way that naïvety can make you more likely to succeed than craftiness and awareness. Craftiness and awareness always rely on precedent so you look to what has happened before and what is the right way to do things which have succeeded in the past. However, naïvety and ignorance made us just arrive at a situation where we just thought "we will give it a go" and in that way we were ahead of the curve.[3]

Zoo's early releases are now collectors' items and are considered groundbreaking. Although the releases were limited by budget, the quality and originality was making other record companies around the country take note. Zoo received overtures from broadcaster and entrepreneur Tony Wilson, who had his own label, Factory Records. Wilson had ambitions for a larger, combined north-western record company which would rival London counterparts. Jon Savage reports[4] that the two labels even agreed to a major concert to promote both sets of bands. The concert took place on the August Bank Holiday in 1979, in Leigh, Lancashire, which was equidistant between Liverpool and Manchester. It featured Echo and the Bunnymen, OMD, A Certain Ratio, the Teardrop Explodes, Joy Division and Supercharge, among others. Disappointingly, the event was not well attended, with the audience numbering under 500.

Notwithstanding ongoing proposals for a north-west super-label, Zoo decided to cash in on the interest in their bands by signing Echo and the Bunnymen to Sire and the Teardrop Explodes to Mercury.[5] This also signalled a parting of the ways for Balfe and Drummond, who they went on to forge their own separate careers in the music industry.

The Zoo label remains highly regarded and Balfe and Drummond became major influences in pop music in the following decade. Their publishing company, Zoo Music, signed the Proclaimers in 1987 as well as Drummond's own project, the KLF. Drummond's idiosyncratic career as an author, musician and artist is well documented and his work and his attitude have always remained decidedly non-mainstream.

Dave Balfe later joined forces with Andy Ross to form Food Records and steer artists such as Voice of the Beehive and Jesus Jones to international success. He signed Food Records to EMI in order to fund his projects, but retained creative independence. The partnership was successful in leading to Jesus Jones's international hit 'Right Here, Right Now'. In 1989, Balfe signed a band called Seymour, but then suggested that they change their name to Blur. He directed their first two videos and started to guide the band towards their ascendancy. However, he became disillusioned with pop music and the emerging Britpop Scene, sold Food Records and moved to the country with his young family. (Balfe was the subject of the Blur hit 'Country House'.) Here he reveals his feelings about the music industry and shows his fondness for the innovative days of the early 1980s:

> No one goes off and does something new anymore. It is always a blend of two different things: for example, we'll mix the Doors with Tamla Motown . . . It is like all the colours are already on the palette and it is just a matter of mixing them. It is as though you have got every type of music from classical to punk and stuck it in a blender and it has come out as a brown gunk – and that is what all music is sounding like these days. Another analogy I have used is plasticine. When you were a kid you would get new plasticine with strips of bright colours and after playing with them for six months you would be left with one big brown ball – and that is what indie rock has become for me. There isn't a pursuit of new genre.[6]

Balfe's frustration at a lack of innovation in contemporary pop music is shared by many of those interested in music who remember the Liverpool scene of the 1980s and were spoilt by the variety of inventive music emanating from the city. Balfe also reminisces about a time when young people demonstrated their rebellion against the older generation via their choice of music. This was a time when no self-respecting teenager who was interested in music would countenance the notion of buying a record, or going to a concert, by an artist who had won a talent competition on television.

In terms of youth culture in Liverpool in the 1980s, the idea of copying other bands was never an option. Listening to music that your parents enjoyed was uncomfortable. In a post-punk era, young people wanted their own music that reflected their energy and thoughts. In Liverpool in the late 1970s, the Probe Records shop, Eric's club, local radio and local record labels provided that option. Balfe comments:

> One of the things that has happened on a social scale is that indie rock was listened to by the naughty kids in class who should have

gone to college and didn't. Now indie rock is listened to and created by the nice kids. The naughty kids are off making music which to me sounds like dinosaurs mating – I like the concept of music sounding like that but I couldn't sit in a club and listen to a whole set of it. I wish my kids were into it – but they're not! My son is listening to Talking Heads and Radiohead. You could argue that musically he has been brought up incorrectly because he should have rejected all of that. It would have been like me growing up and listening to 'Danny Boy'. Whilst I have a soft spot for 'Danny Boy', I would not have dreamt of making music that sounded like it.[7]

One might consider Balfe's semi-retirement from the music industry premature, given that talent he has nurtured over the years has had such influence on British popular music, and wonder what more he might have achieved. In Chapter 2, Balfe commented that bands in Liverpool during the 1980s were different because they did not want to appear to be replicating trends that had been set by other bands – something that would have been regarded as "pathetic". Balfe deplores the reluctance of many contemporary bands to develop innovative styles and bemoans the mundane state of British pop music:

> Britpop seems like yesterday but actually it was twenty years ago. I said at a talk I gave to music students in Liverpool at LIPA,[8] "What new musical genres have you come up with over the past twenty years?" When we started making music it was all about innovation.[9]

Probe Plus

Geoff Davies buys a leopard-print shirt with a black collar from Pete Burns. If you can keep a straight face, then you're laughing. Angry customers attack employee-of-the-month Pete Burns in the Probe Records shop. Gary Dwyer is too nice to be a bouncer. Geoff Davies spends ten bob wisely!

The Probe Plus label emerged from Geoff Davies's record shop on Button Street in Liverpool city centre. For many record buyers in the late 1970s and early '80s, the Probe Records shop was indeed a special place: a hub for musicians and various youth trends. The shop itself was atmospheric, but its customers and staff made it even more important in the development of musical culture in the city. It was an unconventional shopping experience. It had the damp smell of an old building masked with joss sticks and patchouli oil. You might even receive some "friendly advice" about your selection of vinyl from Pete Burns, who worked in the shop alongside Paul Rutherford and Gary Dwyer. There would be different groups of youths such as punks, rockabillies,

Rastafarians and skinheads all huddled in different parts of the small shop. However, Geoff Davies had not always been a music retailer or label manager and Probe was not even his first music venture, as he explains:

> My first occupation was advising companies on high-quality carpets. It was a really posh shop above Marks & Spencer – velvet curtains and everything! However, I had been doing acid since 1969. It was the best ten bobs' worth you could have spent. It gave me a different perspective and I realized that I could not live in these two worlds of responsible weekday job and weekend hippie. Behaving myself during the week was a case of "if you can keep a straight face then you're laughin'", so I decided to get out of the normal nine-to-five and open a record shop in Clarence Street. It sold a wide range of music and was used mainly by students. I later had another shop called Silly Billy's which tended to specialize in reggae music. Eventually, when I got the shop in Button Street it became very popular very quickly.[10]

Figure 20: Geoff Davies, Probe Records Shop, Liverpool, 1986.
Photograph courtesy of Geoff Davies, digitalised by Dave Williams

As the shop grew in popularity, it attracted many of the same clientele that frequented Eric's club. Saturdays became "daytime Probe, night-time Eric's". It became the place to be seen for up-and-coming bands and unconventional dressers, and a meeting place for those wishing to appear alternative. Julian Cope, Ian McCulloch and Pete Wylie allegedly met in Probe to discuss forming their band the Crucial Three. The shop became so popular that Saturday afternoons became dangerously overcrowded, as Geoff explains:

> It was a peculiar mix of punks, rockabillies, Rasta lads and skinheads. Occasionally, the mix of different groups got a bit scary. I employed a variety of local people in the shop. I knew Pete Burns as a customer at Silly Billy's and he also had a clothes shop which sold the weirdest items of clothing – I've still got a shirt which I bought from him. It was a leopard-skin print with a black collar. Anyway, he worked in the shop with me along with others like Paul Rutherford. One Saturday there was a fight in the shop. One of the customers tried to beat up Pete Burns. The staff had to jump in and stop it getting out of hand. It got so crowded on Saturdays that I had to employ Gary Dwyer as a bouncer. He wasn't much good as a bouncer; he was too nice so I ended up having to move some of the kids out of the shop myself.[11]

The shop became successful enough to allow Geoff to set up his own record label. At first it was called Probe Records, but later renamed Probe Plus so as not to be confused with the shop. Geoff claims that there was no master plan for any of the shops. The label idea was also something that happened by chance and reflected the opportunities that existed at the time to develop an independent label. Schwartze (1987: 155) claims that Geoff sees himself as a fan more than a label manager. He admits to being a terrible businessman who has nearly brought the whole label to ruin several times. However, despite issues of competence and solvency, Geoff carried on:

> In the early '80s I was asked to join the Cartel independent distributors. Probe was their best customer. The Cartel would get independent records in shops all over Britain. I was a bit reluctant to do this as I'm not some great businessman, but eventually I was persuaded to do it. There were 92 shops selling indie records in the north-west. Independent records were selling like mad in those days. You had the main charts, and right next to them the indie chart. If you made it into the indie charts, then you were selling a lot of records.
>
> You could be played on Radio 1 in those days by John Peel, Janice Long, Kid Jensen and Andy Kershaw. With having the shop you get to know bands, and so John Allott from the shop told me of a

band called Ex Post Facto and he really liked them. I thought that having access to the distribution cartel that I would dip my toe in the water and put a record out with them. I didn't have any Probe Plus logo so we just used the band's artwork. The record did OK so I thought about doing other records with other bands.[12]

Encouraged by the first single, Geoff decided to release some more. He had established some essential contacts in terms of distribution and airplay and had also tapped into the increasingly popular independent-record-buying public who were hungry for alternative-sounding music. However, despite having set up a workable infrastructure, the label began to experience the difficulties that came with the economic recession of the 1980s. Geoff explains his thinking as he turned his attention away from the mechanics of the industry and focused more on the music and the production:

Unfortunately, by 1984 I had to give up the Cartel because shops would not pay me for their records and I was owed thousands of pounds. I couldn't go on sustaining those kinds of losses so started to think more about the label and the recording of the bands. I began to produce bands that reflected more of my tastes. I didn't know whether they would be successful or not. It was just what appealed to me. What we did have in our favour as a label was that there was more access to national radio and press. You could bring out a record and it would get played. There were also four big music papers which would review your releases. You could get a column in the new releases. It was free advertising for the label. You might also get a review of the band.[13]

So Geoff continued with his Probe Plus record label, looking to achieve success in the national independent charts. Freedom from the distraction of running the north-west section of the Cartel gave Geoff the opportunity to invest more time in the bands on his label. In 1984, when he received a demo tape from Birkenhead band Half Man Half Biscuit, he had discovered his biggest-selling artist. By then, Geoff had developed strong links with John Peel at Radio 1, who was always keen a keen supporter of the Merseyside area and his enthusiasm for the band is well documented. Geoff describes Peel's initial reaction on first hearing Half Man Half Biscuit:

With Half Man Half Biscuit I sent a test pressing to John Peel. It didn't even have a label on it. I said this is from some Tranmere Rovers supporters. Peel phoned me up the next day and said, "What's this you have sent me? It's marvellous!" He had only played the first side. He then phoned me back twenty minutes later and said, "I've listened to the other side and that's even better. Have they got any more material?" Well, I knew what he was after. He wanted some new material for one of his sessions. I knew they did *not* have any more material but I lied to him and said, "Oh yes." So I asked Nigel if he had anything he could record and he said he had a couple of ideas. The next thing was, we had a Peel session and after that the record started to take off.[14]

The success of Half Man Half Biscuit was remarkable in many ways. They were reluctant to promote themselves and conducted business on their own terms. This is a difficult situation for most labels to manage. However, the partnership between this band and label boss has become one of the most enduring relationships in independent music. Half Man Half Biscuit had a clear potential to be exploited for far greater commercial success but they largely shunned publicity and only selected the TV, radio or music press that they thought worthwhile. In fact, the band has a long-running humorous relationship with the press. Nigel Blackwell has teased the local press mercilessly with bogus letters to the editor under the pseudonym of "Nick Drake of Moreton", which slipped though the fingers of the editorial staff of the *Wirral Globe* much to the amusement of Half Man Half Biscuit fans. Letters published have included rants about men taking horses into public houses (Plough Inn) and upsetting the pony so much that it could no longer face contact with small children (Von Pip 2012).

This recalcitrant approach has afforded Nigel Blackwell anonymity while permitting him to make a living and control his own life without being reliant on media campaigns to promote his next album. During an interview with Peter Ross, Nigel openly admits to not being comfortable on stage but knows that music allows him to enjoy a lifestyle that may not otherwise be possible:

> I don't like playing live. I get nervous, and I don't think we're that good and only put up with having to do it so I can buy food and pay bills. I much prefer to simply write songs and put them out but there's not enough money in just doing that for me these days so I have to psyche myself up and walk onto a stage to perform. It's not a good state of affairs for me, to be honest, but I'm stuck with it as I don't have the skills to do anything else. I'm not qualified in anything and I am shite around the house. I do not possess any tools whatsoever and sandpaper sets my teeth on edge. I buy one scratchcard a week and fill out a fixed-odds coupon at William Hill's every Saturday morning in the vain hope of landing the big one so that I can be in a situation where I don't have to arrange concerts . . . I always just want to get it all over with and go home as soon as possible. I do, however, endeavour to do the best I can whilst on stage because people have paid hard-earned money for a ticket and I wholly appreciate that (Ross 2016).

Despite knowing all the aisles at B&Q, one could not imagine Half Man Half Biscuit cutting the ribbon to open a new DIY store in Birkenhead or being the guest speaker at Heswall Round Table. It is indeed a rare achievement that a musician's life is not organized by the industry and that he can pick and choose when to play and when to record. This arrangement could only be viable on the unique record label that is Probe Plus.

Geoff Davies simply released records that he personally considered to be of some worth. The Probe Plus label continues to release music today and has remained Half Man Half Biscuit's label since day one, the band's regular albums and EPs continuing to project the label into the album charts. Each band on the label has a select audience of fanatical followers, and the originality and diversity of the label continue to provide an alternative perspective in today's music world. Artists on the label include Mr Amir, Mike Badger, St Vitus Dance and Calvin Party. Jim Keoghan described the Probe Plus label as follows:

> As an indie label it might not be up there with Stiff, Factory or Creation, but for the last 30 years Probe Plus has championed a succession of innovative and unusual bands, including the Dead Poppies, Marlowe and Half Man Half Biscuit (HMHB), and walked along that seldom travelled path that puts greater emphasis on what's good rather than what just sells.[15]

Skeleton Records

Skeleton Records' shop is more successful at uniting couples than most dating websites.
There was no label sound or master plan. None whatsoever!
A trip to the dentist is scary and potentially painful.

Skeleton Records was a Merseyside record label based in Birkenhead. The shop and label were projects developed by Birkenhead businessman and authority on music, John Weaver. Although Skeleton Records was releasing singles and albums before Probe Plus, the label never got the same recognition as a musical fulcrum. The first shop in Argyle Street, Birkenhead had all the same traits as Probe: it was an old building masking the smell of age and damp with joss sticks and offering the unusual atmosphere that only vinyl record shops have. Specialist items were sold, such as live bootleg albums, deleted records, imports and new rock releases. In the early 1970s, the shop attracted the more rock-oriented and heavy-metal groups but towards the end of the decade Skeleton moved further down Argyle Street to a bigger shop with two levels: its capacity for a huge variety of records meant that, when punk and New Wave arrived, it became a hub for a more mixed clientele. Some of the interesting characters who frequented the shop were also in bands of their own and it became a focal point for the various youth trends and musicians in Birkenhead. Local bands would pass demo tapes to John Weaver as he was considered somewhat of an expert on music. John describes what he was looking for in the demos:

> I was really just looking for something that I liked. Something a bit different and something I could work upon. It is probably shown in the compilation album, *A Trip to the Dentist*. Every track on that album is different and there is a different reason as to why I particularly like each track. There was no label sound or master plan. None whatsoever! Bands were just coming up with different styles of music and were trying to do their own thing. I just wanted to get involved with some of the bands who were making new music.[16]

Figure 21: John Weaver (left) Skeleton Records, Birkenhead, 1984.
Photograph courtesy of Skeleton Facebook site

The rise of successful independent releases in the late 1970s and the emergence of new talent in the area encouraged John to start his own label in 1978. There were very few independent labels locally and John had spotted a gap in the market. John describes his reasoning:

> I had always been interested in starting a label since the mid-'70s. I wanted to explore the whole idea of putting out a record myself. The first release I put out was the Marseille 12" called 'Do It the French Way', with two other tracks, 'Not Tonight Josephine' and

'She Gives Me Hell'. The idea was to put the single out, do a tour and get a deal for the band. We pressed up 1,500 and it sold out, getting Single of the Week in *Sounds*. RCA were interested and had the band lined up as a New Wave version of the Sweet, who were coming to the end of their contract with RCA. Unfortunately, the UK arm of RCA at the time couldn't afford to sign them as their budget from America had already been spent.[17]

By the late 1970s the independent label phenomenon had established itself as a driver of innovation in British popular music (Hesmondhalgh 1997). John had decided to follow up his first release from Marseille with a single by another local band, the Stop Outs, and a continual stream of releases of local material ensued. Skeleton was several years ahead of the other local labels and set a precedent, demonstrating to others that releasing a record could be done on a limited budget with relative success. John's philosophy was:

> If I could do it – then I would do it. It was a way of me giving something back to music which had been my living for many years. I wasn't necessarily looking for huge commercial success – of course that would have been nice – but releasing records was just something that I wanted to do.[18]

The early releases on Skeleton Records featured some iconic names, such as Attempted Moustache, Afraid of Mice, Wayne Hussey, the Relations and the Geisha Girls. However, there were a couple of bands who were to become household names but slipped through John's fingers: most notably OMD and Half Man Half Biscuit. John explains:

> It would have been great if something had happened in a major way with one of the bands . . . I should have had the first OMD single. I could see OMD were going to do well. I saw their first performance at Eric's I thought, "Wow, this is good and it is different." I had a meeting with OMD the night before I went on holiday to America, and I thought things looked hopeful. They seemed quite happy to put something out with me but when I came back the Factory deal had happened with them. I also had the first Half Man Half Biscuit recording but just was not in a position to put anything out at the time.[19]

John's career as a label manager continued as he renamed the label Half Man Half Biscuit, confusingly sharing a name with the Birkenhead band. John also released singles and albums on his Pengwan label, most notably This Final Frame who made the top 20 on the local Radio City chart with their single 'The Mask Falls Away'. John says his involvement with the labels was hard work but enjoyable. The legacy of Skeleton is the unique bands and musicians that appeared on it during its existence. There are some who have fond memories of the Skeleton shops for other reasons, as John comments:

> The Argyle Street shop became a regular meeting place for people interested in music. Sometimes people come into the new shop and tell me about their recollections of the Argyle Street shop. There are couples who met in that shop and got married and are still married. That is success alone just for staying married for that long. We were also distinctly Birkenhead. We never used any connections with Liverpool in our publicity for the releases. We described ourselves as a Birkenhead shop and a Merseyside label.[20]

Inevitable Records

Factory/Inevitable, Inevitable/Factory. The egos of two label bosses meant that they could not agree on anything. Grammy award-winning producer Gil Norton arrives at Amazon studios on a Youth Opportunities Scheme.

Figure 22: Jeremy Lewis pictured in 2018. Photograph courtesy of Jeremy Lewis, JJL Guitars

Inevitable Records was the result of a collaboration between Pete Fulwell and Jeremy Lewis, two visionary characters on the Liverpool music scene. Fulwell was a great supporter and promoter of local musicians and managed successful artists such as Pete Wylie, It's Immaterial, the Christians, Holly Johnson and Pete Burns. He was closely connected with the characters that frequented

Eric's and nurtured the emerging talent from the Liverpool scene. He was particularly interested in local bands who were developing a unique sound. Jeremy Lewis was founder of Amazon Recording Studios and at the time was recording many of the emerging talents from the Merseyside area in their early careers. Lewis, too, was zealous in his desire to develop music in the city, as he explains:

> I felt that Liverpool in the late '70s was a musical wasteland. One of the reasons that I started a studio was that I had a mission to bring credible music back to Liverpool. Just as Ken Testi wanted to develop a live venue, I wanted to develop the recording side.[21]

The mixture of the two personalities and their skills seemed a perfect combination for developing a record label, as Jeremy explains:

> Pete Fulwell came up to see me at the studio because all the local bands like Nightmares in Wax and Wah! Heat were using us to record their demos. Pete asked if I would be interested in doing a label. I agreed and said that I would do all the recordings and pressings and he would do all the promotions and the nuts and bolts of the label. Then we thought about what bands to sign and Pete suggested some of the bands which were emerging from Eric's.[22]

Jeremy Lewis believed that there was a feeling nationally that a creative local music scene was emerging on Merseyside, stimulated by Eric's and its policy of giving various local artists the opportunity to perform. Jeremy had the ideal opportunity to hear local bands before anyone else as they passed through his studio, which gave Inevitable Records an advantage over rival labels and national record companies. This did not go unnoticed by other musical entrepreneurs, as Jeremy explains:

> Even before we set up Inevitable, we got a call from Tony Wilson in Manchester for a meeting at a hotel in Manchester. Roger Eagle was also invited to attend. Basically, Tony Wilson had an idea to set up his own label at the same time as we were considering setting up Inevitable. Tony suggested that we all join forces and create a mega northern label as an answer to the majors based in London. We had our acts: Dead or Alive, Wah! and It's Immaterial, and he had Joy Division, A Certain Ratio and a few others. He also had a producer, Martin Hannett. Roger also thought that unsigned bands that had played Eric's from outside Liverpool, such as the Stranglers, U2 and XTC could be offered deals too. Looking back, it was an amazing time because, if it had worked, we would have had a label probably as big and diverse as Virgin. The problem was that we had all these

egos in the room. Tony wanted to call it Factory and we wanted to call it Inevitable. There were suggestions about Inevitable/Factory or Factory/Inevitable and the conversation went round and round for three hours in the hotel. After the three hours we left the hotel murmuring things under our breath. Due to the egos involved, we just could not agree anything concrete. We couldn't even agree on a name for it and so we didn't do it. Tony went off and did Factory and we decided to do Inevitable.[23]

A similar attempt from Factory Records to join forces with a Liverpool label – David Balfe and Zoo – has been described earlier in this chapter. In hindsight, the thought of either Zoo or Inevitable in tandem with Factory would have been a mouth-watering prospect. However, the people behind the labels were mavericks and they had started their own projects because they did not want to compromise. The skill sets were strong and the ability to spot unique talent had been proven by the relative success of their early releases. The label managers even acknowledged the fact that each other's labels had some great bands. Nevertheless, strong egos seemed to be the factor preventing the formation of a Liverpool/Manchester label. The prospect of some permutation of the cast of Bill Drummond, Dave Balfe, Tony Wilson, Pete Fulwell and Jeremy Lewis sitting around a table to discuss the release of a Joy Division, OMD, Echo and the Bunnymen, Teardrop Explodes or Dead or Alive album would have been interesting.

The Inevitable story is similar to that of the other labels that emerged from Liverpool. There was no attempt to develop a label sound or identity. There was no real marketing plan or determination to appeal to a particular audience. It was just a gut reaction to what Jeremy and Pete considered good, different and interesting, as Jeremy explains:

> We did not have any particular business aims for the label: it just seemed to be the right thing to do at the time. We never thought of whether the bands were a risk. We just heard the songs and thought, "That sounds good, we'll release it." We didn't give it a second thought . . . It was like 'Seven Minutes to Midnight' by Wah! Heat. We heard it, we liked it and we released it. There were no agonizing meetings about what we should be doing. It was a case of spending a small amount of money pressing up the vinyl and getting it down to Rough Trade in a box. We couldn't even afford proper covers. The cover for 'Seven Minutes to Midnight' was a folded bit of paper inside a plastic cover. I remember sitting there doing boxes and boxes of records. We basically just did our own thing. We gave people a chance of getting something on vinyl and getting heard and appreciated for what they did. That is all they really wanted initially.[24]

The music industry was a fast-moving entity at the time of Inevitable's early releases and bands were keen to capitalize on interest in their music before another musical trend overtook them. From the viewpoint of the independent labels, it was an exciting time: potentially lucrative but extremely precarious. The Inevitable label was initially developed on an ad hoc basis, which suited the cash-strapped label and the ambitions and fleeting loyalties of the bands, as Jeremy continues:

> Nobody was talking about money and advances. It was a loose arrangement. We didn't have contracts. There were no formal arrangements. We were not putting huge amounts of money into it, so we did not have loads to lose. That is what the indie movement was about.[25]

Jeremy hoped to develop the bands on the Inevitable label and release records through a licensing arrangement with a major company. This would allow the label to continue to retain the artistic element of the music production, while using the mechanics, finances and promotional methods of the industry to project the bands onto a national stage. However, many major labels preferred to allow the independent labels to discover the bands and then poach them with big-money offers. Jeremy comments:

> The problem we had was that, unlike other labels, we had difficulty keeping hold of our bands because the majors would come sniffing around. It was initially Wah! that had stimulated interest, but by this time I had Dead or Alive and China Crisis on the books and was about to release 'African and White' [by China Crisis]. We were an indie label and we were getting attention. John Peel started to play Wah! and Pete Wylie did some sessions for him. The press got hold of us and we became flavour of the month for a couple of years on the front pages of the music press and in the indie charts. We would release records and if they sold out we would re-press singles and distribute through Rough Trade.[26]

Inevitable became a recognized and successful independent label. The bands on the label were receiving excellent reviews in the national music press and excitement about the emergent Liverpool scene was enhanced. The recordings produced at Amazon were attracting attention and being played alongside established artists on local and national radio. *Melody Maker* quoted Pete Fulwell:

> We are only just beginning to see Liverpool's real strengths. The strongest is yet to come and I don't just mean the new Wah! album. It's a whole new set of bands coming up – and it's like a permanent

wave more than anything else. I don't know why there is so much talent there – it must be something they put in the water.[27]

Prospects were looking bright for Inevitable as the major labels began to circle. *Melody Maker* reported that "Inevitable is currently negotiating with Warners for one of the most significant deals ever pulled off by an independent set-up."[28]

Paradoxically, the pressures from major labels to sign the bands on Inevitable and absorb the small independent project into the major music industry created its own problems. Jeremy Lewis and Pete Fulwell did not agree on some of the fundamental aspects of the deals being offered. Jeremy, through his studio role, wanted to retain some artistic control of the label. Pete was interested in developing the commercial potential of the bands while they were generating interest from the major labels. This led to the split between Lewis and Fulwell, as Jeremy comments:

> Pete then saw the big bucks and he dropped the Inevitable hat and put on the manager's hat. He waltzed off to Warner Brothers taking Wah! with him. He also created his own label called Eternal. I was left with Dead or Alive and China Crisis and we went to Virgin. That was the end of our indie period. It was difficult to hang on to your acts. They wanted advances and decent recordings and to get off the dole. So you can't blame them for that.[29]

Jeremy's Amazon Studios continued to record local bands after the split and the recordings began to gain international recognition. Echo and the Bunnymen's *Ocean Rain* album was considered groundbreaking at the time. Parke Puterbaugh described the album as follows: "Suspended somewhere 'twixt heaven and hell, Echo and the Bunnymen take an oddly visceral pleasure in their spiritual limbo, evoking a vast, white, arctic expanse that's silent, unbroken and pure."[30]

The Waterboys hit single 'Whole of the Moon' was recorded at Amazon in 1985 and received the Ivor Novello award for the best song in 1991 following its re-release. The airwaves were full of distinctive bands and distinctive sounds that had come from this creative hub in Kirkby. It was a magnet for many who wanted to make a living out of music, among them future Grammy award-winning producers Gil Norton and Ken Nelson. Jeremy explains:

> Gil Norton came to me at the age of 16 on a YOP[31] scheme and pestered the life out of me to give him a job. I let him sit in as a tape op. He was a nice guy and got on with people, He went from tape op to engineer simply because Echo and the Bunnymen liked him. He worked with bands on the Inevitable label at the time such as This Final Frame, the Light, Freeze Frame and the

Builders. He struggled at first, but then managed to cope really well and he worked on the Bunnymen's album *Ocean Rain*. He was very ambitious and went on to win Grammy awards with the Foo Fighters. Then there was Ken Nelson. Initially, I liked his band but that did not go anywhere, so he asked me if he could do some studio work at Amazon. When we moved to Parr Street, he asked if he could work for me again and I said OK. The next thing was he won two Mercury music prizes in succession and went on to work with Coldplay and the studios won a Grammy for that as well.[32]

Amazon relocated to Parr Street in Liverpool city centre and continued to record a string of local and international artists (Brocken 2016). The Inevitable Records label no longer exists, but it enjoyed considerable success thanks to the combination of Fulwell's knowledge of the bands around town and the technical know-how of Lewis in the studio. Bands in the city with a determination to do something new and different but which were not yet palatable enough to attract the mainstream found a spiritual home at the label where they could establish the style and substance of their music and retain artistic control. The bands knew that they were on a record label that made them the envy of other local bands.

Local radio's response to Scouse Pop innovation

Tony Snell threatens to quit Radio City over Kylie Minogue.
Billy Butler discovers musical innovation at the car boot sale.
Liverpool's local treasure Roger Hill explains why Pete Burns was a teddy bear.

Liverpool is fortunate in having some of the most informed DJs and radio presenters in the UK. Janice Long and Paul Jordan were recruited by national radio on account of their impressive ability to engage radio audiences and both eventually made their way onto *Top of the Pops* during the 1980s. Other presenters such as Roger Hill, Tony Snell, Billy Butler and Spencer Leigh stayed in Liverpool and continue to broadcast on local BBC radio to this day. Roger Hill hosts the longest-running local music radio show, *The Popular Music Show* ("PMS"), which has spanned four decades. Tony Snell has been the anchorman on the Radio Merseyside breakfast show since 1997. Billy Butler was a musician during the Merseybeat era and has been a DJ and radio presenter for Radio Merseyside and Radio City for over 40 years. Spencer Leigh has also presented a long-running BBC Radio Merseyside programme, *On the Beat*, since 1985 and is an accomplished author on music. These DJs have an extensive knowledge of local music and have tirelessly championed Liverpool talent: they have been at the forefront of the promotion of regional music, and have taken calculated risks in playing some unconventional material. Their knowledge, independence of thought and capacity to understand their audiences accounts for their longevity in a fast-changing media world. Collectively, they represent a huge bank of knowledge about the city's music, and all understand its importance to the city's culture and identity: not national treasures, perhaps, but undeniably local treasures. Each deserves more extensive coverage than this chapter allows.

There were two main radio stations in Liverpool in the late 1970s and early '80s: BBC Radio Merseyside and Radio City. The commercial station, Radio City, occupied an office building in Stanley Street, while BBC Radio Merseyside resided at St Thomas Street before moving to purpose-built studios in Paradise Street. Radio City was more concerned with mainstream pop music, but also had a specialist rock show called *The Easton Express* which began in 1975. Independent local radio had a managed playlist, although far less rigid than today's tightly controlled mandates.

Radio Merseyside, being a public broadcaster, had an obligation to cater for different musical genres. Although audiences for minority tastes would be small, off-peak evening slots were found for music from new aspiring bands. Phil Ross started such a show in 1976, called *Rockaround*, which featured demo tapes and sessions from local bands and gave information about band members, gigs and single releases. Later presenters such as Jane Buchanan, Janice Long and Con McConville fronted a Sunday night show called *Streetlife* which became a "must listen" for aspiring bands and featured all things local and alternative.

Tony Snell

As New Wave developed in the late 1970s and early '80s, Radio City decided to reduce their evening-show heavy-rock focus to run their own local alternative music show fronted by Tony Newman and Tony Snell. This later evolved into a nightly show called *The Noise*. Snell was a graduate of the Ariel Trust scheme which aimed to help local people into broadcasting and capitalize on their local knowledge. After his training, he began his radio career in the 1980s, a turbulent period for the city. He remembers the social context of the time:

> It was five years into Margaret Thatcher's reign. It was awful. Liverpool was a dirty city; it was an empty city. It was as though there was a wall around Liverpool. It was like a siege. It was a siege mentality. The feeling was that everybody hates us, so we didn't want to know about anyone else so we are just going to do our own thing. It was a "Who are you looking at?" attitude. This was Liverpool! But there was always a pride in this city and an ability to do something unique.[33]

The historical and political context as described in Chapter 1 spawned an attitude in which the ethos the bands created was often introverted or angry. Tony comments:

> Some of the bands hit back at the assumed unfairness of the situation which Liverpool found itself in. Others were more about escape. There were so many good bands about that I was spoilt for choice. I had plenty to choose from to play on *The Noise*. I think that there was so much competition between the bands that they kept coming up with something different to better each other. The music was clever and pushed the boundaries at the time. It was very different from the music played during the daytime on Radio City. However, there were quite a few bands that could make a crossover into daytime radio and when they did they stood out from the crowd because the attitudes and the sounds were not mainstream but were something to get listeners thinking.[34]

Tony suggests that the bands drew on frustration, sardonic humour, false confidence and an alternative viewpoint not shared by those who experienced life outside the city. The wave of bands emerging were competing against each other and the high standard set by successful forerunners such as the Teardrop Explodes, Echo and the Bunnymen and OMD.

It was through DJs such as Tony Snell that local bands could gain some exposure on independent local radio:

> The Bunnymen, Teardrops and OMD seemed to kick-start the New Wave bands' becoming successful in the 1980s. They had a different attitude to their music than a lot of the pop bands played on daytime Radio City at the time. Liverpool bands all sounded different and seemed to want to compete with each other to succeed but still kept their originality. We were different to the rest of the country and it was an exciting time to be around these new bands.[35]

Snell's appointment to Radio City in the 1980s enabled him to engage with the local bands that were now producing different styles of music and were also being signed by record companies. At first he was the "lad" around town and acted as co-presenter with Tony Newman, who was also a Radio City DJ and championed local bands, allowing the local independent radio station to sound local rather than derivative of other independent local radio stations who shared similar playlists. When Tony Newman became head of music at Radio City, he promoted local bands from the evening slots onto the mainstream playlist and had local artists such as the Real Thing presenting shows on the station.

Tony Snell eventually took over the early-evening *The Noise* slot in the mid-1980s. He recollects a time when the interest of the music world was focusing on Liverpool. It was because of the success of the Teardrop Explodes, Echo and the Bunnymen and OMD that the independent Radio City actually allowed him the freedom to play whatever he liked:

> I would get sent cassette tapes, reel-to-reels and vinyl records from the bands and I was allowed to play them. There was no playlist meeting for me to analyse whether that was the right sound for the station. I was just this lad from Anfield who didn't really sound like a DJ playing this wide variety of music. That worked for me in a way . . . and I developed a niche audience for the show. Some of the people running the station at the time didn't really understand local bands and local music. It wasn't daytime material so they left me to my own devices. I could play what I wanted to play and say what I wanted to say. I long for those days – not just for me but for radio.[36]

The refreshing aspect of Snell's testimony is that he played the music because he felt it was worthy of exposure, not because he wanted to discover Liverpool's next big band. In fact, Tony received the first demo tapes of songs that later sold millions worldwide, such as the Icicle Works' 'Love is a Wonderful Colour' and Black's 'Wonderful Life', and played them on his show along with other songs from local bands. He played the first demo tape of Frankie Goes to Hollywood's 'Relax' before it was released on vinyl and subsequently banned. No tsunami of complaints poured in to the station as a result of this airing: the show was so diverse that it simply fitted in as another different-sounding track from a local band. Scrutinizing the music to ensure it was palatable for all listeners was not high on Tony's agenda. He freely admits that he did not know whether the records would be successful or not and did not really care: his task was to give local bands exposure on a radio station that was supposed to support the city. He explains:

> In the '60s there was a Merseybeat sound. Some bands sounded like the Beatles or the Tuxedos or the Pacemakers. They all sounded jangly guitars – boy loves girl music. BUT in the 1980s it was so diverse. I could have tapes sent in with a rock band with a double bass followed by a band with a single synth. So I had no idea what was going to happen next. I remember a band called Box of Toys who sent in a track called 'Precious is the Pearl'. It was a fantastic song and so different. I had never heard anything like it. It had an amazing vocal, synths and an oboe! It was the sheer diversity in the music that was coming in to the station at that made the job so exciting.[37]

Snell points to another factor that he believes drove innovation: record companies were more patient and nurtured their artists. Most bands at the time were signed up for a minimum two singles and an album deal with options on a further album. By modern standards this seems generous, in view of the alternative nature of the music. However, Tony sees the wisdom in this: providing longer-term security in a fast-moving business to allow fledgling artists to develop. In addition, it was easier to gain access to the city's radio stations and the record shops, which stocked a diverse selection of music: DIY releases, mentioned earlier in this chapter, were popular at the time. Some of these independent releases became direct routes to success through airplay. Snell explains:

> In those days, if you were signed up to a record company you were given more than one chance. They would stay with an artist and nurture them. I think that '80s period was more innovative in Liverpool. It was less manufactured. It always sounded a bit more of a "street sound". I liked the fact that you could have an independent record out and you could deliver it to the radio stations yourself or to the local record shops. The local radio stations would play it. They backed a lot of the local bands then. They saw it as a local thing and something to be proud of. Today, all local stations are governed by one playlist. That would never have worked in this city at the time. It has never worked on Merseyside and should never work. I remember having a stand-up row with one of the bosses of Radio City who thought it would be a good idea to bring some mainstream daytime music into the evening slot. I told him "If I have to play Kylie Minogue then I'm leaving!"[38]

Snell now fronts the prime-time breakfast news show on BBC Radio Merseyside but remembers his early radio career with great fondness. The time, the place and the music still feature in his recollections and anecdotes on his daily show.

Billy Butler

Music produced by the new wave of aspiring Liverpool bands of the 1980s was not only heard on the city's night-time radio. In the early 1980s, one mainstream daytime DJ started playing bands who had previously been aired only on the "indie music" evening shows: that DJ was Radio Merseyside's Billy Butler. Billy was a former dockworker and later a member of 1960s rock 'n' roll band the Tuxedos. He also became a Cavern DJ and was a friend of the Beatles – a well-known character on the '60s music scene (Butler 2010).

On his peak-time morning show of the 1980s, Billy managed to make the transition from one genre of music to another sound natural. He made some brave choices without compromising the loyalty of the show's core audience: some local bands pushed the boundaries of what was deemed daytime-radio material. This considerable feat was achieved through instinct and confidence, attributable to his depth of music knowledge, an understanding of his audience, and an ability to recognize quality, originality and accessibility. Billy explains his endeavours to promote local bands and where he sourced his material:

> I would look for cassettes at car boot sales, as the cassettes are rarer than the vinyl. A lot of local bands put cassettes out as it did not make financial sense to put a vinyl out unless you had a deal. I loved the names of the bands; the names were great but it was the people that were real characters. People like the singer from Dead or Alive, Pete Burns.
>
> Because the bands were thought of as alternative did not mean they were not commercial. Most of the music I did play had to be suitable, and most of it was commercial. I thought these bands were local and a good listen. I think all the bands at that time were not trying to follow anyone. They were doing what they thought was different. If you are creative then you have got to do that.[39]

Billy Butler has stood the test of time, with his radio broadcasts spanning the decades. His relentless promotion of local talent has not only encouraged local bands but legitimized their right to mainstream play. Music that might have been considered inaccessible was presented in such a way that his audiences remained comfortable with it. Being a BBC daytime presenter, one might have assumed he would be under pressure to play mainstream material in order to maintain audience figures. Billy explains the mood of the time and whether he felt under pressure to conform:

> No. Not then! The BBC trusted the presenters. The BBC these days think that they know more than the presenters. All the bands you talk about were the ones who made it – China Crisis, Black, the Christians and the Teardrop Explodes – but it was bands like This Final Frame and the Wild Swans who didn't make it as big who I still played because I thought they fitted in . . . Maybe 'Electricity' by OMD was a bit strange at first but everything they did after that you could remember the melody after hearing it twice.[40]

Billy also recollects some of his favourite bands from the Scouse Pop era. Some of the music he played he also took into the clubs where he was still working as a live DJ in the 1980s:

I liked OMD because you have got to have melody and they wrote some great tunes. Flock of Seagulls I think were brilliant. I still worked at the discos until 1984 and I was amazed at the number of people who used to ask for China Crisis's 'African and White' because I never thought it was a record you could dance to. But the audiences really loved it.[41]

BBC presenter Tony Snell is appreciative of his colleague's approach:

Billy Butler has always been a maverick with regards to his playlists both as a radio DJ and a venue DJ. His choice of tracks is unusual at times but all are filtered through his own innate sense of quality. This instinctive approach has worked very well for decades as Billy continues in his own sweet way.[42]

Billy continues to play new local talent on BBC Radio Merseyside daytime radio – a rare phenomenon these days. Rigid prescriptive playlists are not compatible with Billy's musical principles, and his determined stance to play his own choice of music has led to conflict with previous employers. Following a stint at local independent radio station Radio City, Billy was suspended in 1996 for playing a non-playlist track. The *Birmingham Post and Mail* reported:

Billy Butler and his partner Wally Scott were sent home 30 minutes from the end of their breakfast slot on the Merseyside station Magic 1548 on Friday after playing 'Can't Keep This Feeling' ... Paul Jordan, programme director of Magic 1548 and sister station Radio City 96.7, said: "Mr Butler disobeyed my order and he and Mr Scott have been suspended."[43]

Butler returned to BBC Radio Merseyside where he continues to broadcast local talent on his afternoon show with a more flexible remit. He comments: "Luckily, our boss now is pretty good and if you listen to my show now you will realize there is loads of new music on it too."[44]

In 2013 Billy won a Lifetime Achievement Award at the Liverpool Music Awards.

Roger Hill

Fanzines, Fuzzy Ants, Goth Teddy Bears and Punk Snow.
Nigel Blackwell is a towering figure in a non-towering way.

Roger Hill is widely regarded on Merseyside as an authority on local and world music. Roger was instrumental in the development and promotion of local bands through radio broadcasting and writing. Roger was described by singer, club owner and fashion entrepreneur Jayne Casey as "Liverpool's John Peel" in a Radio 4 documentary about his life entitled *Man with the Mohican* (BBC 2015).

Figure 23: Roger Hill pictured in 2016. Photograph courtesy of Roger Hill

Roger Hill arrived in Liverpool in 1978 on the back of a motorbike. He was expecting a job as part of a theatre company. Unfortunately, within a week of arriving, the theatre company folded and he found himself unemployed in strange new surroundings. He fastidiously kept a diary about this period, which in recent years was translated into the acclaimed short film *Punk Snow*.[45] After a brief stint with the "Return and Learn" scheme, Roger began work at the Everyman Youth Theatre in late 1979 (Stewart 2013).

While settling in to his new surroundings, Roger became an Eric's regular and began writing for the fanzine *Merseysound* which was run by local music fan and entrepreneur Ronnie Flood. *Merseysound* ran for 26 issues and was considered by Roger the most credible account of what was happening in the music scene in Liverpool:

> My involvement with *Merseysound* was to try and get it as close to the music scene in Liverpool as possible. We know that *Merseysound* did encourage the scene. When bands have a media record of their music then it inspires musicians to do more.[46]

The fact that *Merseysound* chalked up 26 issues is a feat in itself for a fanzine. There was some initial start-up help from music historian Dick Witts, who was the music officer for Merseyside Arts, and this helped finance the first three issues. A few issues in, Roger's viewpoint began to diverge from that of proprietor Ronnie Flood. According to Roger, Ronnie was more interested in interviewing bands from Liverpool and celebrity bands. If "local" and "celebrity" combined, then all the better. However, Roger had a wider agenda which did not make the popularity of the band a priority. As he explains:

> I think as a fanzine we wanted to feature gig guides and interesting bands which came to play in Liverpool. We also wanted to raise issues like the cost of records in the shops, and items like trying to compile a discography of all the local bands releasing records. We were out there to do something and comment from a wider position, such as: What has the last year in music been like? What were the best venues? Is the local scene alive or dead? We also were asserting and examining values.[47]

Other local media outlets picked up on his grass-roots promotion of the local music scene with *Merseysound*. On Radio Merseyside's show *Rockaround*, presenter Phil Ross shifted the focus away from prog rock after the music scene's rapid changed in 1976, in favour of New Wave. Because of Roger's connections both at the Everyman Theatre and *Merseysound* fanzine, he was frequently interviewed for *Rockaround*, and this eventually led to his own slot on the station.

Roger took to the task with energy and enthusiasm, presenting a diverse and high-quality show. The fact that he is still presenting an alternative radio show four decades later is testament to his aptitude. The longest-running music show on local BBC radio (Stewart 2013), Roger's present-day BBC Radio Merseyside Sunday-night show features a wide variety of music both local and from around the world. He draws on his in-depth knowledge of music in his shows and retains a fondness for local, alternative artists of the early 1980s:

> I liked Alvin the Aardvark and the Fuzzy Ants. They were deliberately enigmatic and weird. I liked early Wah! because the energy was authentic. I liked Teardrop Explodes . . . and Jayne Casey always came up with something new.
>
> I am fond of the residual punk bands such as Instant Agony and the Ponderosa Glee Boys because they would not get swept up in other things. The Ponderosa Glee Boys epitomized real local anarchy. They were short-lived and always on the brink of falling to bits. That's really the punk ethic. The only thing a punk band should do . . . is to split up. But Instant Agony has soldiered on through the decades and that is the only part of the punk ethic they never lived up to. The more melodic post-punk bands were predominantly young men displaying a sensitivity which was not something associated with youth culture in a tough city. Even Pete Burns may have worn his blacked-out contact lenses but there was

never any thought that he was anything other than a big teddy bear. He was a great precursor of the gothic music movement. In fact, he was a fuller, better version of something that got genericized into something called goth.[48]

Roger also has a unique overview of what constitutes Liverpool's musical identity: a view informed by his insider knowledge of the city but also by his position as a non-native – he considers himself an outsider: "Being by a river is a conduit for trade and history. There are elements in the music from some local artists that was resolute and heartfelt. There are features in the music which are uniquely Liverpudlian."[49]

Roger's identifies three Liverpool artists whom he believes have made outstanding musical contributions to the city's musical development and exemplify the uniquely Liverpudlian features discussed in this book. Each is an innovator but all in different genres:

> There are three main characters from that early 1980s period who, for me, stand out as seminal. The first is Alan Gill from Teardrop Explodes and Dalek I. He later went on to write the soundtrack to the film *Letter to Brezhnev* and, more recently, *Punk Snow*. His creative genius has always impressed me.
>
> The second is Nigel Blackwell of Half Man Half Biscuit, who is a towering figure in a non-towering way. He is the type of person who will not go on the internet and won't answer his phone.
>
> The third is Paul Simpson of the Wild Swans. I recognize a poetic sensibility with an image depth and metaphorical reach. The enduring musical sensibilities of the time for me were people who had a sense of structure but a more refined version of the sensitive boys establishing their credentials. It was in fact reaching into the heart of something – and the heart it reaches into is a heart that Merseyside sometimes will not admit it has.
>
> Each one has captured a part of the Merseyside landscape in the best pieces which they have produced.[50]

Roger reflects on how the scene changed once several local bands had risen to national prominence: "I think as the 1980s progressed, the city began to realize that music was an industry and not just a playground for these fascinating characters."[51]

Photographing the characters with Francesco Mellina

Francesco Mellina becomes part of the furniture at Eric's.
For some reason, handsome young Italian men are popular in Liverpool.

Figure 24: Francesco Mellina pictured in 2016. Photograph courtesy of Francesco Mellina

One of the individuals in Liverpool responsible for capturing the faces, mood and atmosphere in the city was photographer Francesco Mellina, supplying the national press with depictions of life in musical venues and clubs around town.

While studying photography in Liverpool, Mellina was attracted to the local music scene with its abundance of fascinating characters. In the late 1970s and early '80s he captured youth culture, creativity and social history, as seen in his 2014 book *Revealed*, with its classic black-and-white photographs. His style is influenced by photojournalist Don McCullin, best known for his images of war and urban strife (while venues such as Eric's, The System and Plato's Ballroom were lively locations, they were not exactly war zones, even on Friday and Saturday nights). According to rock journalist Paul Du Noyer, Francesco's photographs are "A real slice of social history. Whether it's the music the fashions, the locations or personal memories, these photographs will stir something in everyone" (Du Noyer in Mellina 2014: 6).

Francesco's photographs were used by *NME*, *Sounds* and *Melody Maker* in the 1970s and '80s. Black-and-white was the medium of the day, and his portraits of prominent bands, both local and national, became classics. Most of Francesco's work was naturalistic observation and stands as an accurate record of a special time in the history of pop music in Britain. There are photographs of local bands such as the Teardrop Explodes, Echo and the Bunnymen, Wah! and Dead or Alive that capture the bands in their infancy, striving to be noticed and experimenting with looks and sounds. We are also fortunate that he was able to photograph some of the bands that visited Eric's and later found international success, among them the Ramones, U2 and Simply Red (Mellina 2014). In Francesco's words:

> My way of doing things is like photojournalism in the tradition of Don McCullin. So for me it was all about capturing moments, documenting things – and that was my passion. If I saw something that captured me, then I went for it. Most of the time the people in the photos were not aware of it – I was like a piece of the furniture at Eric's. People accepted me. They knew what I was doing so they ignored me. I always said that the audience were just as important as the bands I photographed because without the audience you wouldn't have the bands. I was naturally fascinated because I like to engage with people. I was fascinated by the way they looked. I was in the right place at the right time to capture it.[52]

He was limited by the processing costs, so only took shots of those bands that impressed him. But he had a good ear and heard promise where others remained undecided. He explains how he ingratiated himself with the locals at Eric's:

> I really felt that there was something special happening in Liverpool at the time. Going down to Eric's and seeing the likes of Pete Burns was fascinating. With being Italian . . . people reacted differently to me because most of the people at Eric's were from Liverpool. Because I was taking photos I became a bit of a curiosity.
> The beauty of the bands at that time was that they were all doing something different and that is what made them successful. The rivalry amongst the bands pushed them to do something unusual. The other bands might have watched them and said, "They're shit" but they were just saying that because they knew how good the songs were. The bands in Liverpool were great; you cannot deny it. Everyone from that period found their own niche. It was no coincidence that they all became successful to a lesser or greater degree.[53]

Francesco became more deeply involved in the music scene with a brief spell as manager of Dead or Alive:

> Pete Burns was a fascinating character and I made it my mission to photograph him. He was so amiable and said yes straight away.

I didn't know anything about him. He was fantastic with me and I started to take photos of the band. I never had a problem with him at all. It was only when I became manager of his band that we had the inevitable differences of opinion – and that was only business, never personal.[54]

A notable feature of his photography is a capacity to capture the attitude, mood and energy of the bands. This requires an instinctive eye for their distinguishing characteristics:

Bands like Wah! were brilliant. I remember their single 'Better Scream'. They were fresh and new and dramatic. Pete Wylie carried with him huge amounts of energy which I tried to capture at the time.[55]

During the mid-1980s, as the Liverpool scene became recognized as a unique hub of innovation and local bands were making themselves known in the charts, Francesco became established in the national press as a photographer with an eye on the local musical talent. He explains:

My aim was to get my photographs in the music press, and as the bands became more famous the press began to take my photos. I had already photographed the bands and so was ahead of the game. Paul Du Noyer started doing articles about the bands. I was at the right place at the right time and my photos were used. That is what established me and I got commissioned by *Melody Maker*, *NME* and *The Face*.[56]

Francesco's work portrays the energy of the city's youth in the early 1980s being manifested in creativity, innovation and fun. As such, his photographs provided a counterbalance to the negative image of Liverpool that the national media were pushing at the time, as well as a face to the sound of Liverpool. The work is an archive of truth about 1980s Liverpool and a vital reference point for a younger generation developing their own sense of belonging and for new musicians developing their own style. Francesco explains:

The photographs selected for my book all tell stories. It is about the music, the audience and the fashion side of youth culture. Younger people looking at the book are fascinated by their clothes and want to find out more about the people and the time.[57]

Hambi Haralambous and "The Pink" studio

Ex-hippie mystic starts studio in Liverpool and recycles Mike Oldfield's mixing desk.
Hambi goes away for a weekend as Vearncombe and Dix stump up £200 to record a demo.

Figure 25: A publicity shot of Hambi Haralambous from 1982. Photograph by Gary Lornie

There are several recording studios in Liverpool that feature in this story: Open Eye, Amazon and Alchemy were all frequented by aspiring musicians, as was "The Pink" studio. The Pink was located in a large Victorian villa in Ullet Road near Princes Park, and its owner was Hambi Haralambous, also a singer-songwriter with his own band Tontrix. Although parts of the building were used as rehearsal rooms for Tontrix, he also let other bands, such as Dead or Alive and Frankie Goes to Hollywood, use other rooms in the building.

When Tontrix split up, Hambi formed the exciting and accomplished Hambi and the Dance with Wayne Hussey on guitar and Steve Power on keyboards. They made recordings and played some local gigs, attracting good reviews, such as that of John D. Hodgkinson: "Hambi and the Dance played slick bright pop to support Hambi's fine voice."[58] Richard Branson of Virgin was also impressed, and signed the band in 1981. With the advance money, Hambi converted the rehearsal rooms into a four-track studio and live room, thereby combining writing and playing with his own band with the development of a commercial studio.

Despite good songs and performances, the band failed to break the charts, and Hambi focused his attention on the recording studio, inviting Steve

Power to take up an apprenticeship as an engineer and producer. Mike Score, who had been involved with Tontrix, brought in his new band called A Flock of Seagulls to record there. Another notable individual who used the studio was Chris Hughes, who played with Tears for Fears and Adam and the Ants.[59]

Hambi's life as a musician and studio owner was not one he had anticipated: he had stumbled into an occupation in music rather than making a conscious career decision:

> When I returned from India in the 1970s I lived in a commune in Liverpool. We used to meditate and write songs . . . and then punk happened! So Steve Lovell and I joined forces with Mike Score and Ian Johnson and formed Tontrix. We played gigs and were popular. We did the *Street to Street* album and released singles but didn't quite do enough to make a bigger impact. So we eventually split up. We used the time after splitting up to build a studio. We even bought Mike Oldfield's mixing desk – which he used for *Tubular Bells*.[60]

Hambi carried on recording his own material as well as that of the many local bands that frequented The Pink. Hambi remembers the 1980s as a period of intense creativity:

> There was such variation in the bands that came in to the studio. You did not know what would be coming in or what they would sound like. You needed to be flexible in your approach and use the right techniques to suit the bands without relying too much on standard studio clichés – because then the bands would just sound like others and we did not want that to happen.[61]

Hambi recounts one of the most famous songs to be recorded at The Pink: 'Wonderful Life' by Black. Despite the song's huge international success and longevity, the original recording was inexpensive to make:

> We were on Virgin Records at the time and Colin did some support gigs for us. After the Virgin deal . . . I went to Italy for the weekend with Francesco Mellina to sign another record deal with an Italian company. Colin said to me, "Look, I've got 200 quid – can I book some studio time?" When we got back on the Monday, Colin and Dave Dix played us the two songs. One was 'Wonderful Life' and the other was 'Sweetest Smile'. At the time, Colin had been dropped by his record company. The guy from the Italian record company heard the songs and wanted to sign him, but Colin opted to have a friend release 'Wonderful Life' on an independent label. It sold several thousand records when the radio picked up on it and A&M

signed them. The recording they did at The Pink remained the recording that eventually was tweaked and sold millions of records . . . So good on Colin and good on The Pink.[62]

Many successful recordings came out of The Pink in Ullet Road. It later relocated to become The Pink Museum in Lark Lane and further success followed with the La's, Oasis and OMD. Hambi later pursued a career in video production and worked closely with OMD on backdrops for OMD's *Energy Suite* and a live performance of Echo and the Bunnymen at LIPA (Liverpool Institute of Performing Arts).

Eric's and Ken Testi

The kids from the art school and loitering teenagers from Aunt Twacky's are dragged in as clientele for a new nightclub. Dave Palmer feels at home with the freaks in Mathew Street. Mike Badger finds a club where the misfits fit in. Colin Vearncombe comments on rock legends getting their balls out. Henry Priestman tries to change the world.

Figure 26: Ken Testi pictured in 2018. Photograph courtesy of Ken Testi

Ken Testi became involved in music in the late 1960s when he took his band Ibex to London. There he met Freddie Bulsara who would front the band for a short time in 1969. Bulsara changed the band's name to Wreckage and his own to Freddie Mercury. He left to begin a collaboration with Brian May in 1970 which would become Queen. The following year Testi was continuing to encourage Freddie's new band by arranging gigs and trying to attract the attention of record companies.

Ken returned to Liverpool in 1972 and by 1974 had met the members of Deaf School. He was so impressed that he became their manager and was successful in arranging tours and record deals (Du Noyer 2013). While managing Deaf School, Ken became friends with music fan and DJ Roger Eagle, an association that would eventually lead to the opening of a music venue in Liverpool city centre called Eric's.

Much has already been written about the influence of the legendary Eric's club in Mathew Street: for example, Jaki Florek and Paul Whelan's (2009) *Liverpool Eric's: All the Best Clubs are Downstairs. Everyone Knows That.* This section does not aim to repeat previous studies, but will concentrate on an interview with co-founder Ken Testi and hear opinions about the importance of the club from musicians who frequented it. It will also examine the influence the club had on the development of new ways of thinking in the city.

Eric's was opened by Roger Eagle and Ken Testi in the autumn of 1976. It is widely regarded as being the catalyst for the emergence of a new wave of bands that would eventually enjoy mainstream success throughout the 1980s. Together, the two decided to create a venue in Liverpool that would feature a variety of credible bands from around the UK and beyond. The club would also provide exposure for local bands writing and performing original material.

The venue in Mathew Street had previously existed as The Revolution club. The building itself was less than salubrious, but it was a good size, in the city centre and stood opposite the most famous club venue site in the city, The Cavern, which at the time was a car park. Ken had installed the Deaf School PA into the venue and had contacts with agents around the UK who could send new bands to play at the club.

Ken and Roger had a dream for the Eric's project and it was not built on a desire for commercial success. Ken recognized the stagnation in Liverpool post-Beatles and wanted to spark a renaissance. The way to do this was to provide the city with as many diverse influences as possible via a city-centre club – Liverpool, being a port, had always been influenced by musical trends beyond Britain's shores as evidenced in the Merseybeat rock 'n' roll era of the 1960s.

However, the venture did not make sense financially: there was no profit to be made in promoting bands that were not popular and commercial. Ken comments:

> Roger and I always knew that Eric's would not be a club which would return a huge profit. That was never the aim of the club. We knew that what we were doing had a limited shelf life and would eventually fail. The bands in Liverpool at the time were not inspiring. There was a lack of originality. There were also cover bands, but what we needed at Eric's was the widest selection of acts possible to get the music scene in Liverpool thinking. Our aim was

to keep it going as long as possible and bring in as many different types of bands to Liverpool before the project crashed.[63]

The bands selected to play were chosen on the completely subjective criterion of whether Roger or Ken found them interesting. Many of the first to perform were products of the punk revolution such as the Sex Pistols, the Clash and the Stranglers, but products of the post-punk renaissance later began to appear, such as the Cure, the Police and U2. The issues for Testi and Eagle were to: get a big enough audience to justify the fee for these up-and-coming out-of-town bands; and to organize support acts. Ken explains:

> We had two problems to face when we opened Eric's. Firstly, where would we locate an audience for this type of music? And, secondly, where did we get our support acts from? In terms of the support acts, I said to Roger, "I know what we'll do! We'll grow our own! So we'd decided even before we'd opened that would be the way forward.
>
> My first thought was that we had contacts in the art schools who would be interested in this style of music club and, secondly, there was a local arcade called Aunt Twacky's. The centre of attention there was a crazy-looking bald girl with a butterfly tattoo on her scalp. It was Jayne Casey – and all the more colourful people in town would congregate around her stall. People like Pete Burns, Holly Johnson and so on . . . So I said to Roger, "Here's the mission. You go into the arcade turn right and you will see Jayne Casey. We need her and we need her acolytes. I will go to the Art College because I know my way around there."
>
> So I went to the Art College and immediately walked into Henry Priestman and John Campbell. Roger spoke to Jayne and over the years formed a strong bond with her. The people we met that day were amongst the first customers to come to Eric's.[64]

What happened in the wake of the Eric's experiment was that the bands were encouraged as Ken Testi describes to "have a go". They did this without fear, without worrying whether they were complying with a national trend or whether they were fitting in with the marketing strategy of a record label.

Dave "Yorkie" Palmer of the Balcony, Space and latterly Moongoose was an Eric's regular who remembers the characters who frequented the club and how the atmosphere of Eric's inspired him to engage in a musical career. Ken and Roger's vision was now having a direct influence on youth culture in Liverpool. Dave's recollections are typical of the sentiments shared by many who frequented the club and joined bands themselves:

When punk happened, a little light on the musical front came on. When you went into Mathew Street everything appeared in technicolour. It was amazing! Characters like Holly Johnson and Pete Burns were around. Pete Burns was completely startling. Everything about his appearance was overly exaggerated and Pete and his wife looked fantastic – there was a feeling that they owned that part of town. Elsewhere they may have been looked upon as freaks, but in Mathew Street it was a complete reversal. Eric's had a great atmosphere. It felt like home and people treated each other with respect even though everyone looked completely different. If you belonged there and thought of it as home you appreciated that it was a safe haven for minority music and I wanted to be involved in the music scene.[65]

Mike Badger of the La's and the Onset also remembers Eric's as a club that provided the city with a diversity of bands and helped formulate a variety of styles among the city's home-grown talent. Mike considers Liverpool fortunate to have had Eric's as a focal point showcasing such a variety of styles. Aged only sixteen, Mike succeeded in appearing a little older in order to persuade the door staff to let him in to see some of his favourite rockabilly acts. He recollects:

It was a fantastic scene centred around Eric's. There was never any trouble there even though you could feel scared of the look of the people going in to the club. I always thought it was where the misfits fitted in. It wasn't just a punk club: it catered for all styles of music. There were jazz artists, blues, rockabilly as well as punk and New Wave. You had all these different styles and influences brought together in one place.[66]

For Hambi, who also frequented Eric's and performed there, it was a venue where difference and artistic experimentation were encouraged: "What the local bands at Eric's appeared to be striving for was difference. The bands were young, enthusiastic and were seeking out new ways to be creative; they looked for inspiration to fashion something new."[67]

Ken Testi's "have a go" ethos permeated the mind-set of the local musicians. As Colin Vearncombe of Black pointed out:

With regards to music in Liverpool in the 1980s, you had to define yourselves as to what you were. Many of the bands which played Eric's tried to do this. That is where the ontology comes in to it. We believed that we were authentic. Quite a few bands in Liverpool at the time were talking about being original but were skipping from one style of the moment to the next, grabbing the coat-tails of the power pop thing or the New Romantic thing . . . I just stubbornly believed that I had something different to contribute that was worth paying attention to . . . AND I had nothing at all with which to back that up!

Nowadays the bands know too much. When I look back at the Who, the Stones and the Beatles – they didn't know what they were doing. They were trying to claim a life that was different from the grim post-war existence. No matter what they pretended to do on stage they were fighting for their lives – to be believed . . . and they stood there – on stage – balls out, daring you to step on them. Nowadays, the new bands are plotting a course: "We will do this with that producer and package it to that demographic." It was not like this in the early days of Eric's. It was exciting because the bands were so different and nobody knew where they were going with it.[68]

Henry Priestman, the "lad" Ken Testi sought out at the Art College, also fondly remembers the early days at Eric's. His recognition of the punk ethos is captured in his wry composition 'Did I Fight in the Punk Wars for This?' Henry recollects the influence of the club on himself and others and how the club played a part in changing the musical landscape of the city and beyond: "We used to rehearse at Eric's. They were fabulous days and so exciting. We thought we were going to change the world . . . That didn't quite happen – but we changed music. Certainly after the New Wave scene music was different."[69]

5 The Audience Response

The concluding chapter of *Scouse Pop* consists of the responses of the fans of Liverpool music to the city's innovative bands. The impact they have had appears to take a variety of forms, which include a raw emotional response, a sense of space and time, aspiration, hope, excitement, rebellion, angst and love.

The contributors to this chapter come from all walks of life. Some were part of the Liverpool scene of the 1980s; others live thousands of miles away but were mesmerized by the music nonetheless. Fans from outside the city often fail to realize that so many of the bands they love hailed from one place, an understandable misapprehension when one band sounds quite different from the next. Notwithstanding this, the bands on their own merits have made their mark on all sections of society in many cultures around the globe: the global spread of testimonies in this chapter pays tribute to the endearing qualities of these Liverpool bands and their ability to touch the hearts and souls of music fans everywhere.

The Lotus Eaters

Michael Sutton, journalist and proprietor of Manila Radio Station WXB 102

They sang of the sun and the windswept beauty of young romance, but they were not afraid of enveloping themselves in the bleak embrace of despair. As a teenager attending high school in the Philippines during the mid-1980s, the Lotus Eaters captured the highs and lows of adolescence, from the dreamy innocence of 'The First Picture of You' to the crushed hopes of 'It Hurts'.

Out of all the New Wave and post-punk acts that emanated from Liverpool, England in the 1980s, the Lotus Eaters were perhaps the most emotional. Echo and the Bunnymen may have had the leather-clad swagger and reptilian angst for global conquest, but it was the Lotus Eaters whose songs seemed more personal, anchored in the alternately anguished or sweetly loving vocals of Peter Coyle and the bittersweet shimmer and sprightly jangle of guitarist Jeremy Kelly.

"You take hold of the flame in my heart," Coyle cries on 'It Hurts', his voice aching like a spirit breaking in half. "Makes me mad, makes me burn the stars / Makes you cruel, makes you push me outside / Do you know how hard I've cried?" Kelly's bleak riff sounds like a knife slicing flesh; it is howling in pain, an orchestra of melancholy only comparable to Johnny Marr's transcendent solo on the Smiths' 'How Soon Is Now?'

Woefully underappreciated outside of a loyal following in the Philippines and Japan, the Lotus Eaters speak to my feelings as powerfully at the age of forty-nine as they did when I was seventeen. From the buoyant ringing guitars and jumpy synthesizers of 1984's *No Sense of Sin* to the mood-spinning electronics and ominous cinematic textures of 2002's *Silentspace*, they will always occupy a special place in my heart, where both joy and loneliness reside as uneasy roommates.

Yachts
Les Glover, songwriter and musician

Figure 27: Yachts in 1977: (left to right) Bob Bellis, Henry Priestman, Martin Dempsey and Martin Watson. Photograph courtesy of Henry Priestman

I was weaned on Liverpool bands in the 1960s such as the Beatles, Gerry and the Pacemakers, the Big Three, to name just a few. My love affair with Liverpool music was rekindled by Deaf School in the mid-1970s. So when my own band was formed we looked at our local contemporaries such as the

Teardrop Explodes, Echo and the Bunnymen, the Icicle Works and Afraid of Mice for inspiration, often with more than a little envy.

One band emerged from Liverpool that became my favourite. Originally fronted by a cool, foppish Mancunian [John Campbell], later to be streamlined down to the four-piece power-pop powerhouse known as Yachts, I first saw them play at Eric's in Liverpool and over the following couple of years notched up half a dozen or so shows. Yachts were not part of the "cool brigade"; they were inclusive and smiled way too much to be cool. But you got the feeling that every show was a party and everyone there was invited. Their lyrics were clever, often hilarious, and their hook lines were as contagious as the common cold. Their first album was in retrospect maybe a little over-produced, but what it did do was capture the frantic energy of the band, and the songwriting talents of Henry Priestman.

A string of excellent singles [from 1977 to 1981] and a fairly strong follow-up album did nothing to secure their legendary status, but it did leave a body of work that shows that the cult position they achieved was well deserved. After all these years, I still get a buzz when Mr Priestman and I cover one of his early Yachts songs and I still cannot believe that I have run away with a yachting type.

The Pale Fountains
Chris Currie, DJ and presenter, Wirral Radio

Post-punk Liverpool was energized and inspired by the "just get up and play" attitude of the punk explosion. This saw a melting pot of musicians coagulate and evolve a distinctive Liverpool sound that comprised of jangly guitars, pianos and catchy hook lines. These were often sprinkled with trumpet or similar, with bands like the Teardrop Explodes, Care, This Final Frame, the Bunnymen and the Pale Fountains.

As a DJ playing alternative music, I was always happy to receive promotional records through the post. I remember receiving a 12" disc of 'Thank You' by the Pale Fountains in its cream sleeve with a flurry of scrolls emblazoned around the wording "The Pale Fountains" and "Thank You" in humble simplicity.

There is always something special about hearing a great tune for the first time and 'Thank You' was one of those tunes. From the airy piano introduction to the stirring orchestral lift, followed by Andy Diagram's sublime trumpet and the subtle hook line from the oboe . . . that was it! Caught hook, line and sinker before the first verse. That is how it is done! It was a perfect pop song. The melody was totally uplifting and beautiful. The 12" included two more tracks, 'Meadow of Love' with strings and a melody reminiscent of the movies, accompanied by 'There's Always Something on My Mind' with more of Andy Diagram's haunting trumpet lines.

That was my very first introduction to Michael Head, a Liverpool legend who was once described by the *NME* as "a lost genius and among the most gifted British songwriters of his generation". Michael Head and I have continued our musical journey together over the years, through the Pale Fountains to Shack, and the Strands, and his latest incarnation, Michael Head and the Red Elastic Band. Michael has written songs that capture the imagination and stir emotions every time you hear them.

God bless you, Michael, and THANK YOU!

China Crisis
aLfie vera mella, Journalist

The notion that New Wave and other closely related genres of pop/rock music which emerged in the early '80s entirely descended from punk has become a widespread belief among many music aficionados.

Many others were concocting something much more intricate, something that incorporated the orchestral characteristics of classical and baroque of the previous centuries and the artful indulgences of art rock and psychedelic rock of the 1960s. Many of these bands emerged in the same era and in the same area, but their music evolved in similar dimensions yet separate spheres of influences. Even if they have been fairly regarded as New Wave, they have also been inaccurately lumped with other proper post-punk bands. These bands with more arty, more intricate and more pop-oriented music include the likes of China Crisis, the Lotus Eaters, the Pale Fountains, and This Final Frame, all of which were associated with Liverpool, England, the so-regarded home of what became known eventually as Scouse Pop.

Among the lot, China Crisis now top my list, primarily because of the group's longevity and productivity as well as their penchant to use instruments that are not commonly used by many of their more rock-oriented peers.

Led by vocalist and keyboardist Gary Daly and guitarist Eddie Lundon, China Crisis may be best characterized by the smoothness and fluidity of New Wave and synth-pop music with strong pop sensibilities, a hint of the breeziness of basic jazz, and the instrumental intricacy of baroque pop. China Crisis achieved this kind of sound with the use of string and woodwind instruments on top of acoustic guitars, keyboards, synthesizers and percussion and with the marked absence of heavily distorted guitars.

Generally speaking, China Crisis may be regarded as one of the finest gems of Scouse Pop because of the high quality of their music; the meticulousness and sense of detail employed in the songwriting process is indubitable. Personally, though, I hold China Crisis in high esteem especially because I discovered the beauty of their music early on, in the early '80s, during the band's nascent phase and during my own early teenage years when music could be a powerful ally in establishing one's personal identity and niche in the world. Amid the guitar-oriented peers and contemporaries of this group that reigned supreme in that era, I found greater comfort in the music of such non-punk New Wave bands as China Crisis. But, in fairness, what continues to move me with the music of bands like China Crisis is not only the nostalgia that I feel in them but more so the intricate musicality that has stood the test of time and that can still stand tall amid the works of many contemporary bands classifiable under the same styles.

The Onset: late '80s Scouse roots-rock pioneers

Tim Peacock, journalist, writer and reviewer at Whisperin' *and* Hollerin'

Figure 28: The Onset in Berlin in 1990: (left to right) Simon Cousins, Tony Russell, Paul Hemmings, Mike Badger and Danny Dean. Photograph courtesy of Mike Badger

These days, he is recognized either as co-founder of the La's or else as an ITV-endorsed tin sculptor extraordinaire, but it was Mike Badger's post-La's outfit the Onset who turned my head back in the late 1980s.

The Onset immediately stood out back then. Instead of the usual Scouse head-feeders such as Pink Floyd and Arthur Lee's Love, their boat was floated by country-folk outlaws, especially the trail-blazing Hank Williams and rockabilly pioneers Marvin Rainwater and Charlie Feathers. Their first demo quickly attracted the attention of Geoff Davies, who released their gritty, roots-flavoured debut LP *The Pool of Life* on his legendary Probe Plus imprint in 1988, in effect launching the home-grown Americana revolution three years before Londoners the Rockingbirds made the cover of the *NME*.

Always a smokin' live proposition, the Onset also featured mercurial lead guitarist Danny Dean, fellow ex-La Paul Hemmings and rock-solid rhythm section Simon Cousins and Tony Russell. Several of their shows (the 1989 Sefton Park Earthbeat Festival, a late '89 Hardman House gig I reviewed for *Sounds*) remain seared into my brain; and a posthumous 2005 collection, *The Onset*, released on the Generator imprint, brought them a little much-overdue critical acclaim. Not before time.

The Icicle Works
John D. Hodgkinson, music journalist

I always knew the Icicle Works were special, although it was not immediately apparent. I was sent by local fanzine *Merseysound* to Brady's club in Liverpool to review their first gig. It was also my first ever live review. They were good, but my review was rather prosaic. I was, at first, taken with the melodies and the sci-fi fixation they exhibited. Song titles such as 'All in the Gleam of a Scientist's Eye' and 'Lunar Holiday' illustrated this. My copy of their demo came via the postman – Radio Merseyside's Phil Ross received his from a spaceman!

It was on a July night in 1981 at The Masonic pub in Berry Street, Liverpool, when I realized we were dealing with something a little out of the ordinary. That night they played with a rare intensity. Ian McNabb's voice soared, swooped and darted, Chris Sharrock's drumming was both manic and controlled, with Chris Layhe's bass an anchor that prevented the whole thing flying off into the Liverpool darkness.

From that night my proselytizing on their behalf knew no bounds. Many just shrugged and sneered, but I knew I was right . . . and so did the sizeable following they began to attract. Ian and I became friends. He would arrive by bicycle to my doorstep, cassette recorder in his bag to tape the Byrds and Neil Young. He still cites my influence as leading to his love of the Rickenbacker guitar, so songs like 'Hollow Horse' were my fault!

The Icicle Works released 'Love Is a Wonderful Colour' in 1983. It got to number 15 in the charts and they appeared on *Top of the Pops*.

I allowed myself a smug smile that night.

The Teardrop Explodes

From the diary notes of Colin Howe, fanzine writer and editor

Figure 29: Julian Cope during his days with the Teardrop Explodes, at the System Club in Liverpool in 1980. Photograph by Colin Howe, digitalised by Dave Williams

It was the cover of inky weekly *Sounds* magazine which caught my eye, the 25 August '79 edition, to be precise. "It's Alright Ma – Teardrop Explodes and the Zoo Connection". The cover showed two ordinary lads and a middle-aged housewife – not the usual image purveyed by the weekly rock rag. Turns out they were local. So began a national revival in interest in Merseyside music unseen since the heady days of the Fab Four (if we skip the likes of the Real Thing, Liverpool Express and Our Kid).

15/11/80, I am at Liverpool University's Mountford Hall, with Alison, a friend's sister who I meet each week on the bus home from night school. The hall is packed. A four-piece band called Thompson Twins (later to become a Talking Heads-like seven-piece, then an internationally charting three-piece) are playing their scratchy post-punk support slot.

The Teardrops take the stage and the pogoing crowd goes wild. It's hot. The lad in front of me rips both of the sleeves off his T-shirt. I lose Alison in the crush. Tunes . . . We are all Bouncing Babies. I rediscover Alison when it's all over. "I ended up over there!" she says. "Wasn't it brilliant?"

Summer '81, Liverpool Empire. We have seats in the rear stalls, but we are standing, of course. The stage is swathed in drapes, to make its vast expanse more manageable and intimate. Julian was a *Top of the Pops* pro by now. Horns aplenty, and with knee-bending Alfie Agius on bass the band parade their best album tracks and all the hits to an expanded audience. It does not get much better or bigger than this.

December '81 ... deep snow! My friend Huw arrives in naval sea boots. Liverpool's Pyramid Club is a warren of small rooms with a main disco floor, which lights up so you feel you are on *TOTP*. There is also a small stage area. Tonight it has a new name: "Club Zoo". The Teardrops, the Bunnymen *et al.* have arranged a series of residencies. We are here on a Teardrops night.

Support are: Virginia Astley (whose dad wrote *The Saint* theme tune and many more), Kate St John (later Dream Academy, 'Life In a Northern Town') and Nicky Holland (later Fun Boy Three/Tears for Fears collaborator), collectively known as the Ravishing Beauties. In their light-brown shift dresses, it seems the word "charming" was invented especially for them.

Then the main attraction arrives. Julian and Gary with new bassist Ronnie Francois and Dave Balfe, augmented by Troy Tate on guitar, who would later launch his own pop career and produce some songs for the Smiths. The venue is intimate, "up close and personal". The band are unique and thrilling. Julian sings a song with a red-and-white scarf over his face. I do not know what the significance of this was. The band was brilliant.

Thanks, Teardrops, for some utterly memorable moments.

The La's ticket
Mark Campbell, fan

Figure 30: The La's in the early days (1985) with Mike Badger on vocals, Lee Mavers on guitar and Bernie Nolan on bass. Photograph courtesy of Mike Badger

> I'll never forget when I bought the last ticket
> To see the La's, upstairs at the Picket
> Advertised in the *Echo* a few weeks before
> I thought at the time, "I'll just pay on the door."

But with flyers and posters all over the place
For once, Boxhead and Kevin had worked at a pace.
It soon became clear that I needed to act
So I went down the Courtyard: the Courtyard was packed!
"What's goin' on?" I heard someone shout.
"Look," said the doorman, "that gig is sold out!"
So with two weeks to go and my ear to the ground
I tried to secure the hottest ticket around.
No joy with my mates: they were in the same boat.
Geoff at Probe just thought I was acting the goat.
So if I was to see this Huytonian band
I needed to take matters in hand.
Now, I half-knew the gaffer from our old Eric's days;
It was time to badger one Philip Hayes!
I gave a high five, as if he was my bezzie.
"Alright Phil?" I said, "any chance of the gezzie?"
He looked at me, laughed, and said, "The last place has just gone."
I looked at the list: "Fuckin' Wylie plus one?!"
I even tried Townshend, but I knew what he'd say:
He just told me straight, "F-f-f-fade away!"
Yoko was no go, and Macca was too.
Pete Gabriel was amiable, but couldn't pull thru.
Neil Finn was not in. And nor was McNabb.
Enrico had just hailed a black taxi cab.
Noel was out, with a toothless Shaun.
And those lovely little Wombats, they weren't even born.
Prowse was waiting on a Merseyside train,
The "Nothing Special" Special
Driven by Casey J-J-J-Jayne.
No joy from Costello, Bill Bragg or Paul Weller.
So my thoughts started to drift, to the alternative sellers.
I Can't Sleep, in the Doledrums, Feelin', Way Out.
I need the dubious services of a ticket tout.
Now, I hate these bastards – they just take the mick.
But I needed a ticket – and I needed it quick!
So, on the night of the show, I took a little trip
Down to Hardman Street, town, on the Liberty Ship.
"Alright fellah? Got any spares?" said a spotty little kid
In a kaftan and flares.
"I need one meself" and I showed him my cash.
The ticket was out as quick as a flash!
"Twenty quid, kidda. This is the last one left."
Now, you know and I know that that is just theft.
But the balance of Power . . . and Mavers *et al.*

Lay firmly in the hands of this little scal.
I was over the barrel of this Son of a Gun.
So I reluctantly gave him a fifth of a ton.
Well, I strode in the Picket – the gig was just class:
'Timeless Melody', 'IOU', 'Looking Glass'.
I knew I'd been done, and I'd paid thru the nose.
But I had the last laugh, when they sang 'There She Goes'!

Echo and the Bunnymen
Andrea Bertolio, Italian DJ and indie label owner

Many Liverpool bands such as the Pale Fountains, Michael Head, the Mighty Wah!, OMD, Shack, the Wild Swans, the Teardrop Explodes soundtracked my life with their stunning releases. However, for me Echo and the Bunnymen were different. Ian McCulloch, Will Sergeant, Les Pattinson and a drum machine called Echo were a strange combination of mechanical beats, busy bass lines and unusual guitar sounds, topped with a heartfelt mature vocal. Although they are often compared with the Doors, there was nothing really like them in the music world. They were unique. But before they recorded their first album they replaced the drum machine with a truly great drummer, Pete De Freitas.

In the late 1970s and early '80s, I was into post-punk music. Many bands were really good and groundbreaking in an era of brilliant lyrics and compositions. Manchester blew me away by the immense Joy Division/New Order developments, but Liverpool for me meant Echo and the Bunnymen.

Their music encapsulated some of the great feelings which Liverpool music conveyed from the Beatles late '60s psychedelic era and even a transatlantic feeling with a crooner approach by the frontman.

Albums like *Heaven Up Here, Ocean Rain, Crocodiles* and *Porcupine* have great resonance with my youth in the 1980s, and I still remember the days when I went to buy these releases in my local record shops in Italy.

Echo and the Bunnymen had the talent to drive youths like me out of the post-punk anxieties by their sheer romanticism and positive musical attitude. My favourite song is 'The Killing Moon'. It is a real gem and has became an iconic song – a real masterpiece. As time goes by and the more I listen to it, the song just gets better with age. It takes me somewhere else to exciting times when music was fresh, original and different, when new ideas were everywhere and when I would wait excitedly for their next release to find out what they were going to do next.

Space
Lottie Holmes, fan

If you asked me to talk about Space, I would never stop.

As soon as I heard 'Neighbourhood' on TV, I knew this band were something special. The amazing thing about Space is that their songs are so original and diverse. No two songs on *Tin Planet* are the same! Compare and contrast the epic techno of 'Fran in Japan' with Tommy Scott going full-on Sinatra in 'The Unluckiest Man in the World' or the heart-warming Nilsson homage 'Bad Days' with the sheer kitsch craziness of 'A Liddle Biddy Help From Elvis'.

I could talk about how they were an influence on me as both a musician and a person. They made me realize it was OK to be different; and, with 'Avenging Angels', written in tribute to his dead father, Tommy managed to sum up exactly how I felt about my own father's death. How they got me through high school, university and difficult times with my work and family in recent years, how honoured I was to sing 'The Ballad of Tom Jones' with them at LIMF [Liverpool International Music Festival] in 2015, and what lovely, down-to-earth lads they are.

No band has ever touched me like Space. Tommy Scott, so often written off as a lame novelty act, is not only great at coming up with memorable tunes, but has a wicked dark sense of humour. Franny Griffiths, the man who inspired me to experiment with sonic textures and samples, is the secret ingredient that holds Space together; without his keyboard wizardry, Space would be the auditory equivalent of a bland meal. Allan Jones and Phil Hartley are the tightest rhythm section ever. Andy Parle, Yorkie, Ryan Clarke, Leon Caffrey and Jamie Murphy have each contributed something special and ensured no two Space albums are alike. They deserve major respect as a magnificent band in Liverpool's musical history.

Space
Lindsay Barnes, fan

It was my birthday and Tommy Scott jumped down from the stage and thanked me for the cake that I had baked for them and wished me happy birthday! He gave me a big cuddle. For that to happen after 20 years of loving the band was certainly special. The last 20 years has seen me, along with my best friend Nic, travel hundreds of miles across the country to watch them. During this last tour, we attended 12 gigs. During every gig Tommy and the lads put in 100%!

The fans feel appreciated. There is always an acknowledgement in some way: a stare, a laugh, a point, a smile. Tommy's way with the fans is second to none, and I am sure all fans feel this way. Not only are they brilliant musicians but they have a unique talent for making you feel very special!

The romantic lines in the songs are so distinctive. You only have to hear 'The Unluckiest Man in the World'. I relate to these words: "You brought a bright summer's day to my grey stormy heart / What do you think about love? / It is such a great place to start. / I just know that there's more though inside. / Feels like an orchestra swell / and now I know as well / You finally made me like myself."

These words mean a lot to me, especially dealing with the grief of my brother's passing. Space have changed my life – all for the good – both on and off stage. Backstage they make you feel like the celebrity, too. We love these guys.

The Wild Swans
Denise Hodgkinson, proofreader and music aficionado

Figure 31: The Wild Swans in 1981: (left to right) Phil Lucking, Alan Wills, Jeremy Kelly, Paul Simpson and Ged Quinn. Photograph by Gary Lornie

In 1980, I went to see Orange Juice at Plato's Ballroom, which was a club night at Pickwick's in Liverpool, run by Nathan McGough. I didn't know until I arrived who the support bands would be. They turned out to be the Wild Swans and the Pale Fountains, both of whom were playing their first gigs. As my favourite from the Teardrop Explodes had been Paul Simpson, I was understandably rather pleased to say the least. It was a memorable night and I have been reliably informed that the Swans won the battle of the haircuts that night. Image was always important for Paul, who at one time singed the collars and cuffs of vintage shirts so that he would look like he had just emerged from a plane wreck! The music was just as good as the styling, with a unique appeal, and Paul a very striking frontman.

What I didn't know that night was that my future husband was also in the audience, reviewing said gig for a local magazine. It was our shared interest in the work of the Wild Swans and Paul Simpson that conspired to bring us together some thirty years later. When I first joined Facebook in 2010,

I posted the cover of a copy of Liverpool fanzine *Merseysound* from 1981 which had a photo of the Wild Swans taken by Gary Lornie. Jeremy (Jem) Kelly, former guitarist with the Wild Swans, sent me a message asking if I had the article that went with the photo because he didn't have a copy of it himself. I duly scanned and shared the article, which was written by one John D. Hodgkinson. John then contacted me to point out that he had written the article and that he was pleased to see it, as his copies of *Merseysound* had gone missing. Soon after this, John bumped into Paul in Bold Street in Liverpool and Paul gave him a couple of copies of the Wild Swans' new single 'Liquid Mercury', one of which he sent to me. I was bowled over!

When we told Paul about all this, he immediately replied by saying that he hates that photo because his hair looks rubbish on it! Thankfully, the music is just as important and as impeccable as the image. Their classic single from 1982, 'The Revolutionary Spirit', is, in my opinion, one of the best songs to come out of Liverpool, although just a small part of a wonderful catalogue of material which never seems to date.

I did not manage to see all of the Wild Swans' gigs in Liverpool (regrettably, I missed the legendary Static Gallery gigs), but I am happy with the symmetry that I saw their first and last gigs. One of my all-time favourite artists, and now a friend, I continue to follow what Paul is doing with interest. He has taken a step back from performing and is now concentrating on writing with an eagerly anticipated play as one of his main projects.

Orchestral Manoeuvres in the Dark
Steve Meadows, singer-songwriter, Transitions Nouveaux

Orchestral Manoeuvres in the Dark originally formed with the sole purpose of playing a one-off gig at the now legendary Eric's club on Mathew Street in Liverpool. Their initial stage presence of just two guys and a tape machine was met with a mixed response. However, the dawn of electronic music was beginning to rise . . .

My first encounter with their music was hearing 'Messages' playing over the airwaves of my local radio station. It was 1980, and as soon as I heard the opening sequence I knew this was music for my generation. Their songs were not the usual pop song derivatives, but electronic music with extremely catchy melodies – melodies, that, as mad as it sounds, you could sing along to. Subsequent singles, such as 'Enola Gay' and the lush, dreamy melodic 'Souvenir', would become regulars on my turntable. To this day, I remember a friend and I being told off by our teacher for duel-drumming 'Maid of Orleans' in class.

Another old schoolfriend and I had a chance meeting with Andy and Paul one afternoon in February 1982. We were invited into The Gramophone Suite and given a first-hand exclusive on the workings of a recording studio. The sight of the control room, with its mixing desk, tape machines and an array of other equipment, was one that would shape my life forever. No more would I be wondering what I would be doing once I left school: it was going to be music or nothing. At that point, my friend and I started my first band.

OMD's influence would play a huge part in sculpting our sound, as the melody would be the most important part of any song I wrote. As I continued to craft my trade, I would often call on Andy for advice. I could always count on him for honest opinions and constructive criticism. I knew if he was not into a track on the tape we were listening to, as he would only focus on the ones he liked. When computer technology had begun to take its hold on the way music was written, he would be there again, helping me get to grips with those early programs.

In 1994, I received a phone call that would become one of the happiest moments in my life. OMD were performing at the RSH Gold Awards in Germany. Musician Phil Coxon was not available to make the trip and I was asked if I was able to travel across in his place. It was an opportunity I was not going to refuse. Well, why would you?

I was picked up in the early hours of Friday morning by Stuart Kershaw and travelled to Manchester Airport where we had arranged to meet up with Nigel Ipinson. When we arrived in Hamburg, Andy was already there to greet us and show us to our cars which would take us to our hotel. There was very little time for us to catch our breath, as no sooner had we reached our hotel rooms we were whisked off to the venue in Kiel for a rehearsal.

Saturday morning comes and a full dress rehearsal for that night's show is called. There is a lot of waiting around during such events. Stuart, Nigel and I sat in the auditorium watching the other acts go through their routines. The other performers on the bill were the Three Degrees, Slade, Paul Young and Chris Rea. It is not every day someone like me can get to sit and watch these artists for free. What an amazing experience and, as for OMD, what an amazing band. They are innovators and synth pioneers.

While that may have been a once-in-a-lifetime opportunity, Andy would continue to offer up words of advice and encouragement. I will always be grateful to both Andy and Paul for their words of wisdom throughout the years. I have always said: if it was not for that chance meeting way back in February 1982, I probably would never have become a musician.

Wah! Heat
Ian Banks, IT consultant and music fan

Mr John Robert Parker Ravenscroft was my hero, a man that I shared more than a birthday and a love of Liverpool Football Club with; I spent every night with him between 10 pm and midnight. The Peel show was my portal into a world of musical delights that living in Warrington had never offered me.

However, there was another man in my life that brought me even closer to this exciting world: Radio Merseyside's Phil Ross hosted *Rockaround* on a Friday evening and I was an avid listener.

It was in the autumn of 1979 when a tune from an unnamed Liverpool band came pulsing out of my transistor radio: Phil played a song called 'Come on Down to My Boat' and I loved it. It was then that Phil suggested that as the band needed a name, listeners should write in with suggestions. A week later Phil picked my suggested A Tentative Prod as his favourite name, but the band had already chosen a name: Wah! Heat.

A Tentative Prod or Wah! Heat, it didn't matter: I loved the sound of these lads and I wanted to know more. I gathered information on the enigmatic Pete Wylie from my visits to Probe, Penny Lane Records and the Armadillo Tea Rooms. In late November 1979, I thumbed a lift into Liverpool for the inaugural Wah! Heat gig at the Everyman Bistro. Wylie was the epitome of cool, looking moody and resplendent in an RAF greatcoat. His Sinatra-esque golden tones caressed my ears, leaving me hooked on Wah! The next day I was back in Liverpool and, if it was possible to buy cool, then I found it on the rails of the Army & Navy Stores on Ranelagh Street.

I waited patiently for the release of their first single, 'Better Scream', in February 1980. It was beautifully crafted with Wylie crooning over ringing guitars, the driving beat of the snare drum and an infectious bass line; I played it endlessly until the vinyl resembled a flexi-disc.

The first Peel Session followed on 10 June 1980. The four tracks really captured their live sound. Washington had replaced Pete Younger on bass. This was to be the nucleus of the band, although additions to the trio were made for live gigs and recordings.

The most memorable gig was with Pink Military at Manchester Poly on 31 May 1980, Wah! Heat as main support, and opening that night was a young band from Dublin. Whatever happened to U2? The Wah! Heat set was cut short following a PA failure but Wylie treated the audience to a rendition of 'Everybody's Talkin'', followed closely by Frankie Laine's 'Mule Train' with an audience member banging a metal tray on his head and knee to emulate the crack of a whip. Following this shambolic but memorable gig, my love of everything Wah! was now complete.

September 1980 saw the release of the second and final Wah! Heat single, 'Seven Minutes to Midnight', with Wylie's vocals cutting through and soaring above the magnificent wall of sound generated by the boys. Wah! Heat may have changed their name on numerous occasions but they never lost their ability to thrill me to the core. Thank you, Wylie, Washington and Rob: you will live long in my memory.

It's Immaterial
Paul Den Heyer, DJ and musician

From the moment I heard 'Let's Murder the Moonshine' on John Peel's radio show in 1983, I loved It's Immaterial. I've always been a sucker for a well-crafted pop song and this one was perfect: a special three-and-a-half minutes of great melodies over choppy jagged guitars and quirkiness.

By the time I got to see the band live for the first time, they were reduced to playing as a duo with a four-track reel-to-reel tape machine, but I wasn't disappointed. I left that gig with their songs floating around my head, melodies once caught, forever etched into memory.

Great songs such as 'Lullaby', 'Several Brothers', 'The Better Idea' and the wonderful 'Space' were exciting and innovative. It is rare to leave a gig humming tunes you had just heard for the first time, but I was singing the words to myself on the train home. "Space is what we need. Room to breathe. Call your own."

A couple of weeks later, I was rushing back from Probe Records with a copy of the *Fish Waltz* EP clutched under my arm, and as soon as I got home and the needle hit the groove I was taken back to that gig. Beatbox, bass and piano coming from the tape machine with guitar and vocals performed live over the top. Simple, haunting and melodic.

Thanks to Con McConville at BBC Radio Merseyside, my band were invited to play with It's Immaterial and the Icicle Works at The Albert pub in Lark Lane as part of a live recording for Streetlife. It was a bit daunting being sandwiched in between two more established and successful local bands, but everyone was charming and friendly. The Icicle Works would blow everyone away that night but "Itsy" treated us to their EP and a couple of tracks they would later record for their debut album *Life's Hard and Then You Die*: 'Rope', 'Festival Time' and 'Ed's Funky Diner', among others. Great songs! Great memories!

'Driving Away from Home' was released the following year and the rest, as they say, is history.

Black
Neil Duffin, TV producer and actor

The summer of 1987, in retrospect, was a pivotal point in my life. I was fifteen in 1987. It was the summer of a harsh and brutal end of my innocence. I had developed a knack of getting myself into trouble, both inside and outside of school. Not that I was actually in school that much. Even when I was not there, I was getting into trouble. The friends I had were not really the friends I should be hanging around with. The camaraderie I had assumed existed between these friends was just an illusion.

Feeling lonely and disenchanted, I was grappling – and failing – with growing up. "Was this it? Is this what it's going to be like as an adult? Pass! There must be more than this? Is there? What is it?" The future was something I was not so sure about.

Being totally lazy, I was sitting in front of the TV one Saturday morning, watching and recording *The Chart Show*, which was ITV's pop video compilation and their attempt to challenge BBC's *Top of the Pops*. Suddenly, I jumped up. A beautiful monochrome video appeared and was sung by an artist simply known as Black. The video assembled striking black-and-white images on a beach and at a fairground which looked familiar to me. A song with the sweetest of melodies, the breeziest of touches and yet full of melancholy and irony. It seemed to speak to me directly, intimately, echoing my experience from the inside out. Who was this guy?

I cobbled together my paper-round money and skipped to Woolworths. I grabbed the album by Black on vinyl and recorded it onto a cassette tape to listen to on my paper round. The album became my favourite. I played it so much that the cassette moulded itself to the Walkman. *Wonderful Life* was the anthem of my summer.

As the album played, the wondrous, enthralling, emotional narrative drive of the music seeped into my soul. 'Everything's Coming Up Roses' with its zestful rhythmic beat, 'Sometimes for the Asking', with its stony voice and electro vibe layered with angelic female harmonies, and 'Sweetest Smile' with its uncomplicated moody percussion of spiralling elegance.

Many other songs soon spirited their way into the heart: 'Finder', 'Paradise', 'I Just Grew Tired' and 'I'm Not Afraid', featuring irresistible melodies and rhythms created with enterprise and imagination which seduced the senses. The album was something of a mainstay. Other people heard me playing it and I heard a lot of other people playing it too. I realized, actually, I was not alone. Maybe it was me that actually needed to grow up. Life is not always great: it can be full of sadness and, at times, it can be profound. However, it is also contrasted with truly wonderful, beautiful, unique never-to-be-repeated moments. Maybe I was taking everything around me for granted.

In retrospect now, nearly thirty years later, the album *Wonderful Life* is just as evocative, if not more so, than it was in 1987.

Paul Simpson: the Care and Skyray period
Dave Wood, engineer

From the implosion of the first short-lived incarnation (and not the last) of the Wild Swans emerged their frontman and wordsmith Paul Simpson. He became the mainstay of a series of diverse local groups and musical genres, the first being Care, alongside Ian Broudie.

I could wax lyrical on the "Three Graces" that Care committed to vinyl [their three EPs]. I loved the songs and made some well-received fan videos on YouTube. The videos proved very popular in the Philippines. There were also a number of great songs which appeared on *Diamonds and Emeralds*, a Care compilation which was hastily released without fanfare over a decade after the group's demise, possibly in order to cash in on Ian Broudie's success with the Lightning Seeds. Care's classic tracks 'Chandeliers', 'Cymophane' and 'Such Is Life' are some of my favourite melody-driven pop songs. So whatever possessed Paul and Ian to put a misericorde into Care? Only they know. Let's just say 'All the Songs that Won't be Sung' is everybody's loss.

Paul moved into the '90s with a number of projects that produced further notable songs, including 'Astral Girl', 'Apollo Tomorrow', 'I'm Gone' and 'Beautiful French Degenerate'. Indeed, when I introduced my then eight-year-old daughter (now nineteen) to these tracks, she loved them. She learnt and still remembers all the lyrics at a time when she was immersed in *High School Musical*, so you could not say that the music was inaccessible to young ears and deserved a much bigger audience.

The latter two songs morphed into tracks on Skyray's stunning opus *Mind Lagoons* released the same year as Moby's *Play*. Unfortunately, where *Play* sold by the truckload, *Mind Lagoons* appears to have been relatively ignored, which is disappointing as I find it far more appealing in a "Pacific Northwest Coast" kind of way.

Paul may have consciously chosen not to be commercial or possibly it was bad luck? Either way, there probably will not be a ticker-tape parade through Mathew Street for him or a statue proclaiming "To 1 lad who shook L2 and other neighbouring postcodes", but his music still resonates with me as much now as it did then.

Fashioned in heaven? Forged in the stars?

Perhaps.

A Flock of Seagulls
Ged Ryan, mechanic

I remember seeing A Flock of Seagulls by accident back in the early 1980s. I had gone along to see a local band called This Final Frame who had a great single out at the time called 'The Diary', which had been played on local radio and Radio 1. A Flock of Seagulls were supporting them at a venue just off Mathew Street called Lincoln's Inn. There were only about thirty people there to see them as more people came later to see This Final Frame.

The Seagulls took to the stage and belted out a deafening set of heavy-rock songs. Some had the silly haircuts and did not look like rockers but were dressed in more trendy 1980s-style clothes. There was little in the way of tunes and there were no keyboards. Their line-up included a heavy-metal guitarist called Willy Woo. The sound seemed a bit dated compared with the more original-sounding bands that were playing around the city at that time. They did not appeal to my musical tastes at all.

I never really thought too much about them until about a year later when I was listening to Radio 1 and Peter Powell played a song which just jumped out of the radio speakers. It was power pop at its best with a great chorus and distinctive guitar sounds. I was amazed when Peter Powell announced that it was A Flock of Seagulls. A few days later, I bought the single 'I Ran' from Rox Records in Moreton. Their style had undergone a major transformation. The next thing was they were on *Top of the Pops*. 'I Ran' charted and they soon became the band of the moment and were touring America.

I bought their album of the same name and really enjoyed it. It was great music to drive along to. My friends used to make fun of me listening to it all the time in my car cassette player. They said that if I kept my window open long enough then I would get a hairstyle like Mike Score.

I wanted to go and see them play live again when they were next in the area but their gigs had sold out. They had left the area by then. I remember saying to my friend Gill, "Their shows might be sold out now, but I can remember them at Lincoln's Inn when they were crap."

The Seagulls have become the butt of a few jokes over the years but I really loved the big guitar sounds and excitement of their driving music. I have listened out for them whenever they have been on the radio and TV and even laughed when the characters of the comedy *Friends* relived their high-school years wearing hairstyles like A Flock of Seagulls.

Half Man Half Biscuit
Dave Croucher, schoolteacher

There is no greater pleasure than introducing another person to the songs of Half Man Half Biscuit. The usual response when you ask if someone has heard of HMHB is, "Oh yeah, I remember them from the '80s. Are they still going?" Moreover, the delight in meeting another fan is joyous. You know that they are going to be a decent person. The chance of sharing a lyric with a friend is a fine bond. Singing silly songs at the top of your voice with a room full of people at a concert, as the band rattle through their classics at pace, is a fine way to spend a few hours.

To be a Biscuits fan is to be a member of an exclusive club. With no intention of marketing their own wares, a person has to stumble across them, as did I. I knew nothing of *Four Lads Who Shook the Wirral*, even though I had lived on the Wirral for many years. I was living in Cheltenham and was feeling particularly homesick when I chanced upon the John Peel show while doing the dishes on a dark, damp Tuesday evening. 'Twenty-Four Hour Garage People' came on and I was hooked. The next day, I flew into

HMV and parted with cash to buy their back catalogue. Within months, I was back home and working in Birkenhead, virtually next door to Tranmere Rovers Football Club. I had heard about Nigel being a Rovers fan too, and was pleased to see him take his seat in the Kop along with a few thousand other perennially disappointed customers.

Despite being fleetingly "famous" in the '80s, I believe their best work was written in the 1990s and 2000s. They provide a superb soundtrack to any car journey, and they are a fine accompaniment to many menial, middle-aged jobs around the house, which is often HMHB's general topic of choice.

Yes, Half Man Half Biscuit are still going strong, and I fully recommend an evening away from the telly to catch up with them at a venue near you, sometime soon.

Appendix 1: List of interviews

The following people were interviewed for the Scouse Pop project:

- Mike Badger, 2014 and 2015 (*Scouse Pop* Bay TV show)
- David Balfe, 2015
- Noel Burke, 2014 and 2015 (*Scouse Pop* Bay TV show)
- Billy Butler, 2014
- Chris Currie, 2016 (*Scouse Pop* Bay TV show)
- Gary Daly, 2012 and 2016 (*Scouse Pop* Bay TV show)
- Geoff Davies, 2013 and 2015 (*Scouse Pop* Bay TV show)
- Les Glover, 2015 and 2016 (*Scouse Pop* Bay TV show)
- Hambi Haralambous, 2016 and (telephone) 2017
- Paul Hemmings, 2014 and 2015 (*Scouse Pop* Bay TV show)
- Carl Henry, 2015
- Roger Hill, 2014, 2015 and 2016 (*Scouse Pop* Bay TV show)
- Jeremy Kelly, 2012 (email) and 2013 (Skype)
- Spencer Leigh, 2014
- Jeremy Lewis, 2014 and 2015 (*Scouse Pop* Bay TV show)
- Eddie Lundon, 2012 and 2016 (*Scouse Pop* Bay TV show)
- Frank Maudsley, 2016 (*Scouse Pop* Bay TV show)
- Andy McCluskey, 2012 (interview by John Gorman)
- Ian McNabb, 2014
- Francesco Mellina, 2015 (*Scouse Pop* Bay TV show)
- Joe Musker, 2014 (email)
- Brian Nash, 2014 and 2015 (*Scouse Pop* Bay TV show)
- Gil Norton, 1982 (conversation at Amazon Studios)
- Dave Palmer, 2014 and 2015 (*Scouse Pop* Bay TV show)
- Henry Priestman, 2012, 2013 and 2015 (*Scouse Pop* Bay TV show)
- Ali Score, 2013 (Skype)
- Tommy Scott, 2016 (*Scouse Pop* Bay TV show)
- Paul Simpson, 2013
- Tony Snell, 2014
- Mike Sutton, 2014 (email)
- Ken Testi, 2014
- Colin Vearncombe, 2012 and 2015 (*Scouse Pop* Bay TV show)
- John Weaver, 2013

Appendix 2: *Scouse Pop* TV

Episode 1: Henry Priestman, Les Glover. https://www.youtube.com/watch?v=RUeiIeMBmNk

Episode 2: Geoff Davies, Jeremy Lewis. https://www.youtube.com/watch?v=XJJhhlXF5oM

Episode 3: Colin Vearncombe. https://www.youtube.com/watch?v=fldLBOHFNSA

Episode 4: Francesco Mellina, Dave Palmer. https://www.youtube.com/watch?v=n2AO0GrmqYU

Episode 5: Noel Burke. https://www.youtube.com/watch?v=GIYfIMzqfTc

Episode 6: Mike Badger, Paul Hemmings. https://www.youtube.com/watch?v=KIbRg1f7H68

Episode 7: Brian Nash. https://www.youtube.com/watch?v=TcUMXsHKgXI

Episode 8: Frank Maudsley. https://www.youtube.com/watch?v=hCDLp5PLWPs

Episode 9: Tommy Scott. https://www.youtube.com/watch?v=UpcE4qdi7Sg

Episode 10: Liverpool University archive show. https://www.youtube.com/watch?v=0IB3FnJ1LRA

Episode 11: Gary Daly, Eddie Lundon. https://www.youtube.com/watch?v=inciPw70BME

Notes

Chapter 1: A Sense of Place

1. https://www.youtube.com/watch?v=ypVdRv3dIpA
2. https://www.youtube.com/watch?v=oXDiHx477nM
3. Angie's lines in the "Shop Thy Neighbour" episode, broadcast 24 October 1982 on BBC 1. http://www.bbc.co.uk/programmes/b00v9glr
4. Interview for *Scouse Pop*, 2015. Much of the quoted material in this book is from interviews conducted specifically for the Scouse Pop project by the author. Some interviews have already appeared on videotape as part of the two Scouse Pop television series for Bay TV, but the remainder were conducted in person or by email; excerpts from the latter are published here for the first time. See Appendix 1 for a full list. Links to the TV programmes can be found in Appendix 2.
5. *NME*, 30 July 1977.
6. See the film *Punk Snow* (2015). https://www.youtube.com/watch?v=0NyTg4NjsgE
7. Interview for *Scouse Pop*, 2014.
8. Interview for *Scouse Pop*, 2012.
9. Ibid.
10. Ibid.
11. Interview for *Scouse Pop*, 2014.

Chapter 2: To Be Somebody: Ambition and the Desire to Be Different

1. Quoted in *The Guardian*, 24 April 2011
2. Interview for *Scouse Pop*, 2015.
3. Ibid.
4. Ibid.
5. Ibid.
6. 24 September 2004.
7. Interview for *Scouse Pop*, 2015.
8. Interview for *Scouse Pop*, 2015.
9. *Boston North Eastern News*, 17 February 1997.
10. Interview for *Scouse Pop*, 2015.
11. 24 March 1979.

12. Hoylake Festival of Firsts interview with John Gorman, 4 July 2012.
13. Ibid.
14. Quoted by Andy McCluskey at Hoylake Festival of Firsts interview with John Gorman, 4 July 2012.
15. Hoylake Festival of Firsts interview with John Gorman, 4 July 2012.
16. Ibid.
17. OMD, 'Messages', on *Top of the Pops*. https://www.youtube.com/watch?v=N0paRzJF1kM
18. Interview for *Scouse Pop*, 2014.
19. *Liverpool Echo*, 8 December 1987.
20. Ibid.
21. Interview for *Scouse Pop*, 2013.
22. Ibid.
23. John Peel, Radio 1, 10 July 1997.
24. The song derives its surreal comedy by imagining the idealized world of the established and well-loved children's TV programme being beset with the same social problems as Merseyside and becoming politicized and angry (with presumable reference to Toxteth).
25. Half Man Half Biscuit, *Old Grey Whistle Test*, 6 May 1986. https://www.youtube.com/watch?v=uFJIiueDXnI
26. *Trouble Over Bridgwater* album (Probe Plus, 2000).
27. Interview for *Scouse Pop*, 2013.
28. Two of Half Man Half Biscuit's most famous songs are entitled 'All I Want for Christmas Is a Dukla Prague Away Kit' and 'Joy Division Oven Gloves'.
29. *Q* magazine, November 1996.
30. Interview for *Scouse Pop*, 2016.
31. Ibid.
32. See http://spacetheband.com/reviews/releases/1996-nme-spiders
33. Interview for *Scouse Pop*, 2016.
34. Ibid.
35. Ibid.
36. Ibid.
37. Interview for *Scouse Pop*, 2012.
38. *Merseysound* 24 (June 1982).
39. Interview for *Scouse Pop*, 2012.
40. Ibid.
41. China Crisis, *Top of the Pops*, 27 January 1983. https://www.youtube.com/watch?v=rBzQDWKOD-g
42. *NME*, 25 May 1985.
43. Interview for *Scouse Pop*, 2012.
44. *Merseysound* 24 (June 1982).
45. Interview for *Scouse Pop*, 2012.
46. *Melody Maker*, 6 April 1985.
47. *NME*, 29 November 1986,
48. Interview for *Scouse Pop*, 2012.
49. Interview for *Scouse Pop* TV, 2016.
50. Ibid.
51. Interview for *Scouse Pop*, 2015.
52. *NME*, 27 September 1980.
53. Interview for *Scouse Pop*, 2014.
54. *NME*, 3 November 1984.
55. *The Guardian*, 21 September 2014.
56. Interview for *Scouse Pop*, 2014.
57. *The Guardian*, 28 August 2014.

58. Interview for *Scouse Pop*, 2014.
59. Interview for *Scouse Pop*, 2014.
60. Ibid.
61. Ibid.
62. Ibid.
63. *Friends*, "Flashback Thanksgiving 1987". https://www.youtube.com/watch?v=ZFskf5fQYgI
64. Interview for *Scouse Pop*, 2013.
65. Interview for *Scouse Pop* TV, 2016.
66. Ibid.
67. Ibid.
68. Interview for *Scouse Pop*, 2013
69. Interview for *Scouse Pop* TV, 2016.
70. Interview for *Scouse Pop*, 2013.
71. Interview for *Scouse Pop* TV, 2016.
72. Interview for *Scouse Pop* TV, 2016.
73. Ibid.
74. *Record Collector*, July 1984.
75. *Melody Maker*, 18 October 1980.
76. *The Face*, August 1980.
77. Interview for *Scouse Pop*, 2014.
78. Echo and the Bunnymen, *Top of the Pops*, 1982. https://www.youtube.com/watch?v=c7jqdUBtWMc
79. *Downbeat* TV show, 1983. https://www.youtube.com/watch?v=NMSHRQSZ5Rk&index=2&list=RDxzWP1nkMDKs
80. Interview for *Scouse Pop*, 2014.
81. Ibid.
82. VH1 TV interview, 1994. https://www.youtube.com/watch?v=va14SpmfXfk
83. *Downbeat* TV show, 1983. https://www.youtube.com/watch?v=NMSHRQSZ5Rk&index=2&list=RDxzWP1nkMDKs
84. *Melody Maker*, 17 May 1986.
85. Interview for *Scouse Pop*, 2014.
86. Interview for *Scouse Pop*, 2014.
87. Ibid.
88. Conversation at Amazon Studios, 1982.
89. Interview for *Scouse Pop*, 2014.
90. Ibid.
91. Ibid.
92. Interview for *Scouse Pop*, 2013.
93. Cope is not a native Liverpudlian but moved there from his home in Tamworth to study aged 18.
94. Interview for *Scouse Pop*, 2013.
95. Ibid.
96. *NME*, 24 March 1979.
97. The Teardrop Explodes, *Top of the Pops*, 1981. https://youtu.be/G5KdGPCpf-8
98. Interview for *Scouse Pop*, 2015.
99. *The Sydney Morning Herald*, 12 March 1982.
100. MOJO Awards, 18 November 2010.
101. *Melody Maker*, 18 January 1986.
102. *Merseysound* 25 (1982).
103. *Sounds*, 7 March 1987.
104. Interview for *Scouse Pop*, 2014.
105. Ibid.

106. The Icicle Works, *Top of the Pops*, 1984. https://www.youtube.com/watch?v=3niDVY-DqiU
107. Interview for *Scouse Pop*, 2014.
108. Ibid.
109. Interview for *Scouse Pop*, 2015.
110. Ibid.
111. Ibid.
112. Interview for *Scouse Pop*, 2013.
113. Ibid.
114. *NME*, 24 October 1987.
115. *Spheres* magazine 9 (October 1987).
116. Interview for *Scouse Pop*, 2013.
117. See https://www.youtube.com/watch?v=fldLBOHFNSA
118. Interview for *Scouse Pop*, 2012.
119. Ibid.
120. Ibid.
121. Ibid.
122. Email interview with Terry Lennaine, 2013.
123. Interview for *Scouse Pop*, 2012.
124. Ibid.
125. Ibid.
126. Interview for *Scouse Pop*, 2012.
127. The Lotus Eaters, *Top of the Pops*, 1983. https://www.youtube.com/watch?v=A-6QPyZ49iA
128. *Melody Maker*, 2 June 1984.
129. Interview for *Scouse Pop* (Skype), 2013.
130. Interview for *Scouse Pop* (email), 2014.

Chapter 3: Rainy-Day Music: Art Pop and the Scouse Romantic

1. Interview for *Scouse Pop*, 2014.
2. Interview for *Scouse Pop*, 2012.
3. Peter Coyle website. http://www.petercoyle.com/bio
4. Interview for *Scouse Pop* (Skype), 2013.
5. Interview with Sarah Greene on BBC TV programme *Going Live*, c. 1989. https://www.youtube.com/watch?v=RhzpkVEeU6Q
6. *Scouse Pop*, Episode 7. https://www.youtube.com/watch?v=TcUMXsHKgXI
7. Interview for *Scouse Pop*, 2014.
8. Interview for *Scouse Pop* TV, September 2016.
9. Ibid.
10. Ibid.
11. Ibid.
12. Ibid.
13. Ibid.
14. Ibid.
15. *Scouse Pop*, Episode 9. https://www.youtube.com/watch?v=UpcE4qdi7Sg
16. Interview for *Scouse Pop* TV, September 2016.
17. Interview for *Scouse Pop*, 2015.
18. Interview for *Scouse Pop*, 2013.
19. Ibid.
20. Ibid.
21. The Wild Swans, 'Bible Dreams'. https://www.youtube.com/watch?v=zU_Hnc9ynpo

22. Interview for Scouse Pop, 2016.
23. A Flock of Seagulls, 'The More You Live, the More You Love'. https://www.youtube.com/watch?v=TROOtt-68F4&list=RDTROOtt-68F4
24. Interview for *Scouse Pop*, 2017.
25. *Sounds*, 26 June 1982.
26. Interview for *Scouse Pop*, 2017.
27. *Merseysound* 19 (November 1981).
28. *Merseysound* 20 (December 1981).
29. Hambi and the Dance, 'L'image Craqué'. https://www.youtube.com/watch?v=WWSkPl0qR2k
30. Interview for *Scouse Pop*, 2017.
31. Ibid.
32. Hoylake Festival of Firsts interview with John Gorman, 4 July 2012.
33. OMD documentary about 'Souvenir' filmed for www.OMD-dvd.com. Also available at https://www.youtube.com/watch?v=dhoooS0yr4I
34. Ibid.
35. Interview for *Scouse Pop*, 2012.
36. Ibid.
37. Ibid.

Chapter 4: Some Aspects of the Music Industry in Liverpool

1. *Sounds*, 23 March 1979.
2. Interview for *Scouse Pop*, 2014.
3. Ibid.
4. *NME*, 30 August 1979.
5. *Melody Maker*, 4 April 1981.
6. Interview for *Scouse Pop*, 2014.
7. Ibid.
8. Balfe gave a lecture at the Liverpool Institute of Performing Arts in 2014.
9. Interview for *Scouse Pop*, 2014.
10. Interview for *Scouse Pop*, 2013.
11. Ibid.
12. Ibid.
13. Ibid.
14. Ibid.
15. *The Quietus*, 15 April 2011.
16. Interview for *Scouse Pop*, 2014.
17. Ibid.
18. Ibid.
19. Ibid.
20. Ibid.
21. Interview for *Scouse Pop*, 2013.
22. Interview for *Scouse Pop*, 2014.
23. Ibid.
24. Ibid.
25. Ibid.
26. Ibid.
27. *Melody Maker*, 4 April 1981.
28. *Melody Maker*, 4 April 1981.
29. Interview for *Scouse Pop*, 2014.
30. *Rolling Stone*, 19 July 1984.

31. Government Youth Opportunities scheme.
32. Interview for *Scouse Pop*, 2014.
33. Interview for *Scouse Pop*, 2014.
34. Ibid.
35. Ibid.
36. Ibid.
37. Ibid.
38. Ibid.
39. Interview for *Scouse Pop*, 2014.
40. Ibid.
41. Ibid.
42. Interview for *Scouse Pop*, 2014.
43. *Birmingham Post & Mail*, "Loyal DJ in cliff-hanger", 8 October 1998.
44. Interview for *Scouse Pop*, 2014.
45. https://www.youtube.com/watch?v=0NyTg4NjsgE
46. Interview for *Scouse Pop*, 2014.
47. Ibid.
48. Ibid.
49. Ibid.
50. Ibid.
51. Ibid.
52. Interview for *Scouse Pop*, 2014.
53. Ibid.
54. Ibid.
55. Ibid.
56. Ibid.
57. Ibid.
58. *Merseysound*, 6 April 1980.
59. Paul Browne interview with Hambi Haralambous, 12 September 2008 (revised text, 26 January 2014). Official OMD website. http://www.omd.uk.com
60. Interview for *Scouse Pop*, 2016.
61. Ibid.
62. Interview for *Scouse Pop*, 2014.
63. Interview for *Scouse Pop*, 2014.
64. Ibid.
65. Interview for *Scouse Pop*, 2014.
66. Ibid.
67. Interview for *Scouse Pop*, 2016.
68. Interview for *Scouse Pop*, 2012.
69. Interview for *Scouse Pop*, 2013.

Bibliography

Alton, D. 1983. HC Deb vol 45 col 127 (4 July 1983). *Hansard*. http://hansard.millbank-systems.com/commons/1983/jul/04/liverpool-unemployment

Aughton, P. 2012. *Liverpool: A People's History*. Lancaster: Carnegie Publishing.

Avraham, E. 2004. "Media strategies for improving an unfavorable city image". *Cities* 21.6: 471–9.

Barton, L. 2012. "The Power of Love: A magical hit in which the secular and the spiritual entwine". *The Guardian* (15 November). https://www.theguardian.com/music/musicblog/2012/nov/15/power-of-love-magical-hit

BBC. 1982. "Music from the Mersey: The story of pop music in Liverpool. Dancing in the rubble". *BBC Radio 4*. http://www.bbc.co.uk/archive/mersey/5186.shtml

—— 2011. "Thatcher urged 'let Liverpool decline' after 1981 riots". http://www.bbc.co.uk/news/uk-16361170

—— 2015. "Man with the Mohican". *BBC Radio 4* (9 March). http://www.bbc.co.uk/programmes/b054pp6c

Beckett, A. 2012. "Thatcher, Murdoch, Hillsborough and beyond: What the 1980s did to Britain". *The Guardian* (27 October). https://www.theguardian.com/politics/2012/oct/27/1980s-britain-thatcherism-final-reckoning

Belchem, J. 2006a. *Merseypride: Essays in Liverpool Exceptionalism*. 2nd edn. Liverpool: Liverpool University Press.

—— ed. 2006b. *Liverpool 800: Culture, Character and History*. Liverpool: Liverpool University Press.

Boland, P. 2008. "The construction of images of people and place: Labelling Liverpool and stereotyping Scousers". *Cities* 25.6 (December): 355–69.

Bolton, P. 2012. Education: Historical statistics. UK Parliament House of Commons Library (November). http://dera.ioe.ac.uk/id/eprint/22771

Brocken, M. 2016. *Other Voices: Hidden Histories of Liverpool's Popular Music Scenes 1930s–1970s*. Oxford: Routledge.

Brown, P. 2008. An interview with Hambi Haralambous: *OMD*. http://www.omd-messages.co.uk/hambi-haralambous-interview-2008

Butler, W. 2010. *Billy Butler M.B.E.* Liverpool: Trinity Mirror Sport Media.

CLG (Communities and Local Government). 2010. *The English Indices of Deprivation 2010*. London: Department for Communities and Local Government.

Cohen, Sara. 1991. *Rock Culture in Liverpool: Popular Music in the Making*. Oxford: Clarendon/Oxford University Press.

Cohen, Stanley. 1973. *Folk Devils and Moral Panics*. St Albans: Paladin.

Comfort, N. 2013. *The Slow Death of British Industry: A 60-Year Suicide 1952–2012:* London: Biteback Publishing.

Connelly, C. 1983. "1982 in review: Who won, who lost". *Rolling Stone* (17 February). http://www.rollingstone.com/music/features/1982-in-review-who-won-who-lost-19830217

Cooper, A. 2015. Album Review: *Spiders* by Space. *50 Third and 3rd* (31 March). http://www.50thirdand3rd.com/album-review-spiders-by-space

Cooper, C., J. Flint-Taylor and M. Pearn. 2012. *Building Resilience for Success*: London: Palgrave Macmillan.

Cooper, K. 2015. "Interview: Eddie Amoo". *UK Music Reviews* (10 August). http://www.ukmusicreviews.co.uk/interviews/interview-eddie-amoo

Crick, M. 1986. *The March of Militant*. London: Faber & Faber.

Doran, J. 2008. Review of OMD, *Messages. The Quietus* (9 September). http://thequietus.com/articles/00464-omd

—— 2011. 30 Years On: OMD's *Architecture & Morality* Remembered. *The Quietus* (29 November). http://thequietus.com/articles/07491-orchestral-manoeuvres-in-the-dark-architecture-and-morality

Du Noyer, P. 2002. *Liverpool: Wondrous Place. Music from the Cavern to the Coral*. London: Virgin Books.

—— 2013. *Deaf School: The Non-stop Art Punk Rock Party*. Liverpool: Liverpool University Press.

Drummond, B. 2014. "The five lessons I learned from Ken Campbell". *The Guardian* (18 November). https://www.theguardian.com/stage/2014/nov/18/bill-drummond-five-lessons-i-learned-from-ken-campbell

Fay, S. 1985. "Militant versus the people". *The Spectator* (13 July). http://archive.spectator.co.uk/article/13th-july-1985/10/militant-versus-the-people

Florek, J., and P. Whelan. 2009. *Liverpool Eric's: All the Best Clubs are Downstairs, Everyone Knows That*. Liverpool: Feeedback Publishing.

Frost, D., and R. Phillips, eds. 2011. *Liverpool '81: Remembering the Toxteth Riots*. Liverpool: Liverpool University Press.

Frost, D., and P. North. 2013. *Liverpool: A City on the Edge*. Liverpool: Liverpool University Press.

Garcia, B. 2006. *Press Impact Analysis (1996, 2003, 2005): A Retrospective Study: UK National Press Coverage on Liverpool before, during and after Bidding for European Capital of Culture Status*. https://www.liverpool.ac.uk/media/livacuk/impacts08/papers/Impacts08(Dec06)Press_analysis-96-03-051.pdf

Gibson, D. 2008. "I think I like the Echo & The Bunnymen record without Ian". *Idolator* (15 July). https://www.idolator.com/398589/i-think-i-like-the-echo-the-bunnymen-record-without-ian

Goldstein, T. 1982. "A Flock of Seagulls". *Trouser Press* (15 October).

Grady, H. 2014. "The city that wanted to 'break away' from the UK. *BBC*. http://www.bbc.co.uk/news/magazine-29953611

Guy, P. 2013. "Deaf School: Liverpool International Music Festival, Sefton Park, Liverpool". *Getintothis* (10 October). http://www.getintothis.co.uk/2013/10/deaf_school_liverpool_internat

Hann, M. 2013. "Old music. The Mighty Wah! – Come back". *The Guardian* (24 January). https://www.theguardian.com/music/musicblog/2013/jan/24/old-music-mighty-wah-come-back

Heseltine, M. 2000. *Life in the Jungle*: London: Hodder & Stoughton.

Hesmondhalgh, D. 1996. "Flexibility, post-Fordism and the music industries". *Media, Culture and Society* (18 November): 461–88.

—— 1997. "Post-punk's attempt to democratise the music industry: The success and failure of Rough Trade". *Popular Music* 16.3 (October): 225–74.

Holland, R. 2006. "Kicking against the pricks! An interview with Half Man Half Biscuit. *Pop Matters*. https://archive.li/sfcg9#selection-1393.38-1397.1

Hoskyns, B. 1984. "Phenomenal: Frankie Goes to Hollywood". *New Statesman* (13 August).

Hughes, R. 2015. "Liverpool in the 1980s". *Ronnie Hughes: A Sense of Place*. https://asenseofplace.com/2015/01/26/liverpool-in-the-1980s

Jackson, N. 2011. "Developing Personal creativity through lifewide education". Education in a Changing Environment (ECE) 6th International Conference, Creativity and Engagement in Higher Education, 6–8 July 2011, University of Salford, Greater Manchester, UK.

Johnson, A. 1996. "Militant and the failure of acherontic Marxism in Liverpool". In *To Make Another World: Studies in Protest and Collective Action*, ed. C. Barker and P. Kennedy, pp. 139–73. Aldershot: Avery.

Jones, B. 2016. "Carla Lane's sitcom *Bread* and its legacy in Liverpool". *BBC*. http://www.bbc.co.uk/news/uk-england-merseyside-36425330

Jones, P., and S. Wilks-Heeg. 2004. "Capitalising culture: Liverpool 2008". *Local Economy* 19.4: 341–60.

Leonard, M. 2010. *The Beat Goes On: Liverpool, Popular Music and the Changing City*. Liverpool: Liverpool University Press.

Lester, P. 2014. "Frankie Goes to Hollywood: 'No one could touch us – people were scared'". *The Guardian* (28 August). https://www.theguardian.com/music/2014/aug/28/frankie-goes-to-hollywood-30-years-welcome-to-the-pleasuredome

Lewis, C. 2016. "'Gizza job! I can do that!' The unmaking of the British working class on Alan Bleasdale's *Boys from the Blackstuff*". In *Social Class on British and American Screens: Essays on Cinema and Television*, ed. N. Cloarec, pp. 31–36. Jefferson, NC: McFarland.

Lewis, T. 2011. "David Morrissey: 'I am not afraid to say the M word'". *The Guardian* (24 April). https://www.theguardian.com/stage/2011/apr/24/david-morrissey-macbeth-everyman-liverpool

Macefield, M. W. 2003. *In Search of the La's: A Secret Liverpool*. London: Helter Skelter Publishing.

Main, B., and M. Shelley. 1990. "The effectiveness of the Youth Training Scheme as a manpower policy". *Economica* 57.228 (November): 495–514.

Marks, P. 2015. "Albums revisited: Echo and the Bunnymen's *Reverberation* at 25". *Smells Like Infinite Sadness* (22 October). http://smellslikeinfinitesadness.com/albums-revisited-echo-and-the-bunnymens-reverberation-at-25

Mellina, F. 2014. *Revealed: The Photographs of Francesco Mellina*. March Design.

Merrick, J. 2012. "That's not wallowing. It's emotion, the Scouse way". *The Independent* (25 March). http://www.independent.co.uk/voices/commentators/jane-merrick-thats-not-wallowing-its-emotion-the-scouse-way-7584388.html

Muncie, J. 2000. "The Beatles and the spectacle of youth". In *The Beatles, Popular Music and Society*, ed. I. Inglis, pp. 35–52. London: Palgrave Macmillan.

Murden, J. 2006. "City of change and challenge: Liverpool since 1945". In *Liverpool 800: Culture, Character and History*, ed. J. Belchem, 393–485. Liverpool University Press.

Nash, B. 2012. *Nasher Says Relax*. Liverpool: Trinity Mirror Media.

Parkinson, M. 1985. *Liverpool on the Brink*. Oxford: Policy Journals Hermitage.

Paterson, B. 2013. "On second thought: *The Best of Liverpool Express* (2002)". *Something Else* (25 September). http://somethingelsereviews.com/2013/09/25/on-second-thought-liverpool-express-the-best-of-liverpool-express-2002

Pooley, C. 2006. "Living in Liverpool". In *Liverpool 800: Character, Culture and History*, ed. J. Belchem, pp. 171–255. Liverpool: Liverpool University Press.

Redhead, S. 1987. *Sing When You're Winning. The Last Football Book*. London: Pluto Press.

Rohrer, F. 2002. "My Scouse pain". *BBC News* (22 March). http://news.bbc.co.uk/1/hi/uk/1886355.stm

Rolling Stone. 2012. "Where are they now? 1982's biggest pop acts". *Rolling Stone* (8 August). http://www.rollingstone.com/music/pictures/ where-are-they-now-1982s-biggest-pop-acts-20120808/a-flock-of-seagulls-0758690

Ross, P. 2016. "A very British Odyssey". *The Big Issue* (6 June).

Russell, T. 2017. "A Flock of Seagulls: Remixes and rarities" (Cherry Red). *God Is in the TV* (14 March). http://www.godisinthetvzine. co.uk/2017/03/14/a-flock-of-seagulls-remixes-rarities-cherry-red

Schwartze, K. 1985. *The Scouse Phenomenon Part 1:* Birkenau: Druckerei und Verlag Bitsch.

—— 1987. *The Scouse Phenomenon Part 2:* Birkenau: Druckerei und Verlag Bitsch.

Scraton, P. 2007. *Power, Conflict and Criminalisation.* London: Routledge.

Shakespeare, N. 1986. "Little of a future". *The Times* (16 May): 15.

Shuker, R. 2015. *Understanding Popular Music Culture*: London: Routledge.

Sinclair, D. 2014. *Liverpool in the 1980s:* Liverpool: Amberley Publishing.

Stewart, M. 2013. "Roger Hill". *Bido Lito* 39 (November). https://www.bidolito.co.uk/ roger-hill

Sullivan, J. 2013. "15 songs you didn't know were about drugs". *Rolling Stone* (14 June). https://www.rollingstone.com/music/lists/10-songs-you-didnt-know-were-about-drugs-20130614/the-las-there-she-goes-19691231

Sykes, O. 2004. ' "Bringing it all back home': The making of place and planning practice in the age of globalisation". mimeo, Department of Civic Design. University of Liverpool.

Sykes, O., J. Brown, M. Cocks, D. Shaw and C. Couch. 2013. "A city profile of Liverpool". *Cities* 35 (December): 299–318. http://dx.doi.org/10.1016/j.cities.2013.03.013

Sykes, W. 2012. *Sit Down! Listen to This! The Roger Eagle Story*: Manchester: Empire Publications.

Turner, A. n.d. Review of *The Boys from the Blackstuff* by Keith Miles. *Trash Fiction.* http://www.trashfiction.co.uk/blackstuff.html

Universities UK. 2016. 'Higher Education in Facts and Figures 2016'. 25 August 2016. https://www.universitiesuk.ac.uk/facts-and-stats/data-and-analysis/Pages/facts-and-figures-2016.aspx

Von Pip, A. 2012. " 'Risk it for a biscuit?' Half Man Half Biscuit interview". *The VPME* (3 August). http://www.thevpme.com/2012/03/08/ risk-it-for-a-biscuit-half-man-half-biscuit-interview

Vulliamy, E. 2011. "Toxteth revisited, 30 years after the riots". *The Guardian* (3 July). https://www.theguardian.com/uk/2011/jul/03/toxteth-liverpool-riot-30-years

Wainwright, M. 2012. "Michael Heseltine is given the Freedom of Liverpool". *The Guardian* (13 March). https://www.theguardian.com/uk/the-northerner/2012/mar/13/ michael-heseltine-liverpool-freeman-margaret-thatcher

West, M. 1982. *Orchestral Manoeuvres in the Dark*: London: Omnibus Press.

Wilks-Heeg, S. 2003. "From world city to pariah city? Liverpool and the global economy, 1850–2000". In *Reinventing the City? Liverpool in Comparative Perspective*, ed. R. Munck, pp. 36–52. Liverpool: Liverpool University Press.

Index

Note: page numbers in *italics* refer to photographs.

A Flock of Seagulls 52 57–62, 103–4, 167–8

Alton, David 6–8

Amoo, Eddie 19

Badger, Mike 80–2, 148

Balfe, David 75, 112–7, *113*

Black 87–91, 108–10, 165–6

Blackwell, Nigel *38*

Bleasdale, Alan 13

Burke, Noel 64, 65

Butler, Billy 134–6

Byrne, Tony 10

China Crisis *25*, 25–8 33, *45*, 45–51, 153–4

Christians, the 82–5, *83*, 96–7

Cope, Julian *67, 72, 156*

Costello, Elvis 20

Crossley, Neil *38*

Daly, Gary *25*, 26, 27

Davies, Geoff 39, 117–22, *118*

Deaf School 20, 21

Eagle, Roger 22

Echo and the Bunnymen 52, 62–6, 159

Foot, Michael 10

Frankie Goes to Hollywood 52–6, 98–9

Fulwell, Pete 22, 23

Glover, Les 85, 151–2

Half Man Half Biscuit 32, *38*, 38–41, 168–9

Hambi and the Dance 104–6

Hamilton, John 8, 9

Haralambous, Hambi 104–6, 143–5, *143*

Hatton, Derek 8, 9,10, 11

Hemmings, Paul 81

Henry, Carl 41

Heseltine, Michael 5,8

Hill, Roger 30–1, 32, 33, 136–9, *137*

Hooton, Peter 8

Hoskyns, John 6

Howe, Geoffrey 5

Humphreys, Paul *33*

Icicle Works, the *76*, 76–8, 155

Inevitable Records 24, 27, 28, 63, 68, 125–30

It's Immaterial 165

Jenkin, Patrick 10

Jones, Trevor 5

Kelly, Jeremy (Jerry/Jem) 91–3

Kinnock, Neil 10

Kinsley, Billy 19, 20

La's, the *79*, 79–82, 157–9, *157*

Lane, Carla 13, 15, 16

Leigh, Spencer 130

Lennaine, Terry 89

Lewis, Jeremy 24, 27, 28, 63, 68, 125–30, *125*

Lotus Eaters, the 91–4, *92*, 97–8, 150–1

Lundon, Eddie *25*, 26, *45*

Maudsley, Frank   *57*, 58, 59, 60, 62
McCluskey, Andy   *33*, 34–7, *36*
McCulloch, Ian   *62*
McNabb, Ian   77, 78
Mellina, Francesco   140–2, *140*
Musker, Joe   68, 69

Nash, Brian   52–6, *53*
Norton, Gil   69

Onset, the   154–5, *154*
Orchestral Manoeuvres in the Dark   31,
   32, *33*, 33–7, 107–8, 162–3

Pale Fountains, the   152–3
Palmer, Dave   *70*, 70–2, 147–8
Priestman, Henry   96–7, 149
Probe Plus   39, 117–22

Schwartze, Klaus   23, 70
Score, Ali   58, 60
Scott, Tommy   *42*, 43–5, 99–101

Simpson, Paul   72–4, 166–7
Skeleton Records   122–5
Snell, Tony   131–4
Space   32, 41–5, 99–101, 160–1
Sutton, Mike   94, 150–1

Teardrop Explodes, the   72–6, 156–7,
   161–2
Tebbit, Norman   15
Testi, Ken   19, 22, 145–7, *145*
Thatcher, Margaret   6, 12

Vearncombe, Colin   85–7, *86*, 108–10,
   148–9

Wah!/Wah! Heat   *66*, 66–69, 163–4
Weaver, John   122–5, *123*
Wild Swans, the   101–3, 161–2 *161*

Yachts   151–2, *151*

Zoo Records   75, 112–117